RED LIGHT ZONES
The world's most unsavoury nightspots
HEADPRESS 26
Edited by David Kerekes

www.headpress.com   Critical Vision
An imprint of Headpress

Red Light Zones: Headpress 26
Published in February 2005
by Headpress

Headpress/Critical Vision
PO Box 26
Manchester
M26 1PQ, United Kingdom
[t] +44 (0)161 796 1935
[e] info.headpress@zen.co.uk
[w] www.headpress.com

Text/artwork copyright © respective contributors
This volume copyright © 2005 Headpress
Layout & design: David Kerekes & Walt Meaties
Front cover (& inset, detail): Borrowed from *Amateur Cine World* magazine, Feb 11, 1965
Back cover images courtesy: Marie Shrewsbury, Joe Scott Wilson, Rik Rawling, The Faceful, Gary Spencer Millidge, The Monks
World Rights Reserved

No part of this book may be reproduced or utilised in any form, by any means, including electronic, mechanical and photocopying, or in any information storage or retrieval system, without prior permission in writing from the publishers.

Views expressed in this publication are not necessarily those of the editor, and are for informational purposes only. Nothing may be reproduced without prior written permission from the editor. Brief passages of text, however, may be used for review purposes. We request a copy of any published review. Ideas, suggestions, contributions, reviews, artwork and letters are always welcome. All unsolicited materials ought to be accompanied by an sae. If it's valuable, send it registered. Sorry, although we won't consciously bin your valuables, headpress cannot be held responsible for unsolicited items going astray. "Where can I get...?" type enquiries will get no reply.

British Library Cataloguing in Publication Data
A catalogue record for this book is available from the British Library.

ISBN 1-900486-44-X
ISSN 1353-9760 | EAN 9781900486446

Red Light Zones Introduction

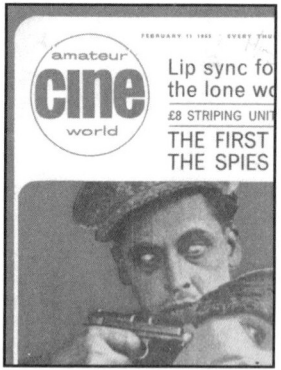

AS USUAL, THIS edition of Headpress arrives a little late. And in the tradition of late, the contents adhere to a rather more formal identity than that of earlier editions (red light zones, in this instance, as it says on the cover).
The reader will see that there are plenty of surprises and diversions on route.
If you have arrived at this book expecting a travel guide in the conventional sense then I feel you may be disappointed. The red light zones covered here are as much psychological as they are geographical, and are often deeply personal. Or a combination of both. In some cases the zones don't exist in a relative sense at all (see Village Life) and in other instances a liberty has been taken — I like The Case Of The Manacled Mormon, Nympho Nuns and Carry On Denmark and that's why there're here.
That's how Headpress behaves. I like the way it works and the way it hangs together.
The next edition has a serial killer theme. Where that will take us I won't really know until the whole sordid business is bagged and tagged.
Enjoy the ride.

—*David Kerekes*
Manchester
Jan 31, 2005

If you have something to say, drop us a line (to the address on the left). If you like what you see take out a subscription and buy stuff (see our website [w] www.headpress.com or the back of this book).

Grateful thanks to Miss Nailer, everyone who has submitted material, and to all those who sing our praises.

Red Light Contents

- **Introduction** 2

- **Death Takes A Back Seat** 4
Hanging around in Dubi with MARTIN JONES

- **The Russian Girls** 10
Ignoring the constant banging on doors and windows, JANE GRAHAM accepts drinks in a Finnish lap dancing club

- **1991** 16
JONNY TAIT leaves the party

- **The Case Of The Manacled Mormon** 26
A look back at the tabloid wet dream that was Joyce McKinney by DEAN JAMES

- **Nympho Nuns** 33
Transcript of a nun themed porno loop and a brief pictorial look at nun fuelled fantasy by DAVID KEREKES

- **"I Have Been Barred From Them All"** 41
Poetry doesn't have to be about flowers or war or being gay — as WILL YOUDS found out talking to socialist transvestite Chloe Poems

- **Amsterdamned** 44
The setting is Amsterdam, notorious pleasure zone of Northern Europe. RIK RAWLING is on a stag do

- **Carmilla Tamaki & All-Day Shifts At Ruby** 55
Carmilla Tamaki is not like the rest of Japan's SM practitioners. MILES WOOD finds out why

- **Extreme Modulation** 58
MARIE SHREWSBURY is in sync with the dark heart of New York City

- **Dead On The Inside** 72
JAN BRUUN visits the mütter museum — Philadelphia's still life freak show — and talks to its director, Gretchen Worden

- **A Short History Of Motorcycle Clubs In The Media** 80
TOM BRINKMANN unearths *Colors*, a motorcycle Bad Mag from the seventies

- **Pigalle Place, Paris** 88
JOE SCOTT WILSON goes to France and takes the Metro to the sex shops

- **Wild Weekend** 90
Three nights of non stop sixties garage music and go go dancing. DAVID KEREKES is on another planet

- **Subway Suicides** 106
MIKITA BROTTMAN is on the New York subway system, where suicide is a regular hazard, more common than in other major cities

- **l'abecedaire chimerique** 111
PROGEAS DIDIER makes it to V, W & Z

- **More Fun Than An Open Casket Funeral** 112
CARLO STRAPPA goes to the exhibition of funeral and cemetery articles

- **Carry On Denmark!** 114
JACK STEVENSON takes a look at Denmark's most popular sex-comedy double act

- **Village Life** 120
Strangehaven is a village from which there is no escape. DAVID KEREKES takes a one-way ticket to interview Gary Spencer Millidge, the creator, artist and publisher of this independent comics phenomenon

- **Culture Guide** 129
The latest round up of book, film & music reviews, including articles devoted to *Mad Artists* [p.129], *Psychic TV* live [p.143], *Kenneth Grant* [p.152] and *Alan Moore* [p. 155]

Death Takes a Back Seat

The trip had given birth to opposing missions for each of us: from the tomb to the womb we had so far scampered, the explorer Richard Burton's Arabian mausoleum in Mortlake, London our one and only shared beginning. After that, death and life — thanatos and eros — split and went their separate ways. I was picking a selective path around ossuaries and cemeteries, whilst Kirby — seemingly without prejudice — fucked his way through the prostitutes of Europe. Death and life in ancient, freezing transport, with only our stewing thoughts as accompaniment (the stereo and my jacket had been stolen in Paris...)

DRESDEN WAS THE BLEAK GATEWAY WE HAD TO PASS through to get out of Germany. A damp, stunted city devoid of life, it was seemingly populated only by solitary monuments, lit up with spotlights, the night sky their backdrop. Fitting images for a tiring journey south. Already Elvira — the 1965 split-screen VW camper propelling us — had broken down three times in three different countries, and more breakdowns from machine or human could be expected. The road from Berlin to Prague is not something to be knocked off in an evening (although by Christ we were trying), and, with conversation between myself and Kirby reduced to a few choice mumbles, the only entertainment was watching the frail windscreen wiper deal with the build up of squelched flies. Escape from Dresden is a narrow strip that takes you higher and higher, away from the illuminated concrete below, into a two-tone silhouette world of black trees against slightly less black sky. No signs of life beyond Elvira's fading globes, and virtually no other traffic in front or behind us. Kirby remarks that the road will probably

Hanging around in Dubi with Martin Jones

NEXT PAGE
Le château de Lacoste. Says Martin: "The place is private property, so we had to break in. Afterwards we retired to the Café de Sade (!), where we were served by a woman who looked like one of the storytellers straight out of *120 Days*..."

Death Takes a Back Seat

widen soon, seeing as it *is* the main route to Prague. But it doesn't open up, just trundles on, steeper and steeper, until I'm certain that Elvira, finally resolved to her fate, will simply breeze to a halt, and begin an unstoppable and final reverse run back down into Germany...

We were gunning into Bohemia, literally; and at some point of darkness the road began to descend, and to ease the lurch downwards reflective bollards suddenly appeared on the margins: big enough to allow only one vehicle to get past at a time. Unsurprisingly, the few cars we encounter are here, making Kirby step on the already numb brakes and myself dig nails into the dashboard. More ominously, I notice something else as I look through the passenger window: slices of the edge of the road are missing. I mention it to Kirby, but, like me, he is itching to sleep, to stop, to do anything to get sorted again.

Then vague shapes break the smudge of night. Houses, maybe a shop. Some kind of mill, silent and threatening, looming to one side. No lights, no humans. Ghost village. We pull over onto a dirt track for some food and coffee. Sitting in the back of the van, I peer through the glass — my face lit only by a few tea candles — and expect some bearded madman to materialise on the other side. Staring at my tired reflection, I am only half wrong, for not even the hiss of the kettle boiling can cover the sound of footsteps passing close by outside. Unable to see a figure, myself and Kirby exchange quizzical glances over ham and boiled egg sandwiches. The footsteps stop, then walk on. Soon after, a bus nearby lets off recognisable humans: one man pauses to look at our amusing vehicle, then lugubriously moves on.

"And this is the *main* road?" I comment.

The break on level ground over, Elvira soon gets back on the track, again in ascendance. The village is left behind, another bollard is dodged, and then, with no signs or warning lights to announce it, a gaping bite of a hole appears in the right of the road. We both swear at high volume. Instantly, Kirby swings Elvira to the left in order to avoid toppling into the blackness. Crawling past, we gaze into the depths of the pit: it had eaten half the road away, and was big enough to take a small bus. And the hazards don't end there. The road ahead becomes more and more precarious. No sooner had we recovered from the maw of death than a giant gnarly tree trunk appears as we round yet another blind corner.

Kirby observes, correctly, that this assault course must be due to the recent floods. Elvira growls down to a cautious crawl. Face glued to windscreen, I try to see beyond feeble illumination for more obstacles. Kirby leans over the big steering wheel like he's about to leap it. We pass

> As the image fades from my eyes, its skeletal white frame lingering, I suggest we get the hell out of here...

across scars of dirt road, past more tree trunks, more holes of smaller size. A few signs helpfully inform us that the area is liable to landslides... And at one tenser than tense point the paper-light tarmac disappears altogether, leaving just a curved track with deep trenches either side...

And then the road stops. A thick wooden gate and a universally understood 'No Entry' sign block our path. The only way out is a diversion to the right, across a

barely wide enough wooden bridge. After creeping over it, travel becomes noticeably easier, and eventually we leave the darkness behind to hit the bright lights of border control. Only to find it closed. The place is supermarket huge with not a vehicle in sight. I look around and spot two figures in the main building, watching us with disinterest.

Kirby moves to get out of the van, then gets back in as a humongous figure in uniform slowly approaches. I reach for the road map as the officer barks a greeting and leans on the door. Kirby visibly flinches as the man gets closer. His dead breath drifts into the cab. I notice thick ropes of hair lining his nostrils. Zombie border patrol. Speaking in broken German, he does his best to point out, using the map, that we have to follow another set of directions to get to another, smaller border control. Slightly bewildered but a bit more confident of where we're going, we thank him and take off. As Kirby turns Elvira around, I look down at the map: Where the guard had been pointing, there is now a fingerprint size wet brown stain of fuzzy origin. I feel sick.

All this just to get to Dubi.

Kirby had found the place weeks back, via the promiscuous internet. A small town barely inside the Czech border, Dubi is home for prostitutes brought in from surrounding countries. He enthusiastically related to me how the streets were lined with women ready to vault on your wallet. The deranged mountain roads were the footnote of this particular chapter. Into the Severocesky region of northwest Czech Republic we came, touching the Ore Mountains, driving along better roads but through tarantula black forests of deathly stillness. Places of engulfing nightmares. At one point I tell Kirby to stop, and reach into my bag for the camera. He goes the whole hog and turns the engine off. We say nothing as I wind the window down. Tar thick silence. We are trivial specimens trespassing in a world that has no use for us. Naïve tourists on another planet. I stick the camera out the window, touch the shutter release, and for a blinking instant twenty odd square feet of forest is lit up like Judgement Day, for our eyes only. White light and congealed shadows etching images of trees and scrub, rocks and earth, and whatever else further back we can't — or don't want to — see. As the image fades from my eyes, its skeletal white frame lingering, I suggest we get the hell out of here. Elvira starts first time (and, perhaps thankfully, the photo never developed).

Past midnight and the road down into Dubi is a tenebrous corkscrew. A night drive along this route is necessary; it averts the wary motorist from seeing any steep drops beyond the edge. And there, at the bottom of the mountains, is Dubi. Another ghost town, or so we thought. There's little traffic on a needle cold main street at one a.m. Then we spot it, ahead on the left: the first whorehouse. A café façade betrayed by neon signs either side of its display window. As Elvira crawls past, mine and Kirby's heads swivel to the right, watching the seemingly empty café suddenly become occupied with three or four women; straight to the glass they come, shapes and colours and hair merged into randomness, dancing provocatively at this mobile sign of life.

And then after that there is another, and another, and another, and another. The girls are sensible and stay in the warmth, sirens reserving their energies for human contact. You could *feel* the warmth, ready to melt the wax in your ears, ready to untie you from the mast. And yet as the enticing beauties were left behind and replaced by closed shops and unlit houses, I spot two girls — the only two we have seen outside so far — walking up towards the main drag. Each is plastered in a fashion magazine's approximation of make-up, wearing hip-high fur coats and short skirts. They can only be about eleven or twelve. So this is the 'downside' of Dubi, as mentioned on Kirby's found website: girls play acting for real cash in a grown up world.

We turn around and cruise back up the street. It gets the same reaction, a mirror image of our last five minutes: women in summer clothes moving elegantly but with speed to the windows. I clock the faces of a few of them. All have features you could fall for. Kirby finds a lonesome cash machine and we make a third and final journey downwards, pulling into a car park opposite a couple of cafés, the warm shapes within bathed in purple light. As soon as Elvira's wheels hit the tarmac, two girls come marching confidently out of one establishment. Big strides and arms hugging their bodies, as if to say: look at the warmth within us. One is petite and curvy, the other leggy and graceful. Both have luxurious dark hair of varying lengths. Both wear clothes designed to get a rise out of a client and then slip off easily. Both are smiling and waving at us like long lost girlfriends. We can only gawp in amazement at the ruthless efficiency. We have hit the rocks…

"HI!" They greet us in unison. Exempt as I was from this aspect of our trip, I sheepishly stay in the van — causing curious looks from the girls — while Kirby steps out to haggle. He is at their mercy. No sooner has he got round the front of the van than he receives a grateful hug off the pair of them. I wind my window down to listen. Kirby asks how much. The leggy girl states a baffling amount of Koruna. When he asks if they take euros they both nod eagerly. Kirby shows them thirty euros and asks what that will get. The petite girl says a fuck, and then mimes a blow job. Kirby grins and then — despite the girls looking back at me in bewilderment — is led off by them, arm in arm. (Later, Kirby tells me they asked him why I wasn't coming too. He told them I had a girlfriend, to which one of them replied, "Yes, me!")

Death Takes a Back Seat

I settle in for a good half hour of freezing wait. I lock the van doors and reach into the back for one of the few beers left. Cracking it open, I still see the occasional glimmer of a twelve year old walking by over on the main street. Splinters of unhappy reminders. A welded together car drives past and pulls into the car park of a 'motel' next door. Two paunchy men stagger out of it and wander across the road, bottles in hands; bloated on this freely available Oz. Then, from nowhere a woman crosses my line of vision and walks round to the passenger side. I wind down the window and say hello. She is older than Kirby's pair, arms folded inside a crisp leather jacket; thin legs in blue jeans. The second to last resort for many a border crosser. Deadpan, she asks me if I want to get a room. I smile and say no thanks. She then asks if I want a fuck. I shake my head and take a swig of German beer as a full stop to our conversation. But still she stands there, looking at me, through me, as if she knows that I will give into her 'charms' sooner or later. I wind the window back up as a final sign. She walks off fast, never glancing back.

And Dubi never sleeps, just catches five minutes here and there. We had arrived smack bang in the slumber hour. But even as I waited through it, the town was alive: a surface of normality broken soon enough at the first sniff of euros. Dubi is a point of concentrated industry, a dedicated sci-fi town of the future. A biological extension of the factories surrounding it. Whereas cities have their own zones for the procurement of sex, here was a whole community of soft, available flesh. The women of the town had arrived from nowhere and were determined to make something; determined to show the passing trade the best time, so that they'd come back again, and again, and again. As if to underline this ethic, I watch a black clad woman walk over to her car nearby. As she puts her key in the door lock she notices Elvira, then me within the darkness. I look away, so as not to encourage her, but even as she reverses her vehicle out of the car park, she keeps an eye on me, lest I suddenly change my mind.

About twenty minutes after he'd been abducted, Kirby returns, smirking like a schoolboy. He gets in the van shaking his head in wonderment.

Elvira's engine is turned over to warm her up and then he describes what happened: Once inside, he discovered that it actually *was* a restaurant, with even a family eating at a table. Kirby made a difficult decision and chose Monica, the petite girl, and she introduced him to the diners like he was her new boyfriend (their joy led him to think that they ran the place). Monica was from Latvia. She led him out to a neat, heated little room, and then proceeded to give Kirby the works.

"Great tits," he slurs, drunk on spent energies. "Great thighs, all the right noises *and* she let me grope her… and I got a French kiss!" A novelty to Kirby, so far used to fleeting, epicentral encounters and well-oiled butcher slabs…

Euphoric, Kirby punches Elvira's horn as we drive up past the café of his dreams. Monika and others wave happily from within, a signal decoded that says: *It's never over, it can always begin again*. We do one last cruise by, Kirby blissfully oblivious that he is speeding past on the wrong side of the road, whilst declaring it the best fuck he's ever had. Coming from a man who had already experienced the cold-eyed Hottentot of Paris, the pink neon *Penthouse* zoo of Amsterdam, and the guileful parks of Berlin, that was some compliment. For the last time on this trip, the life force wins. For now, death has taken a back seat.

But as we drive down a gloomy slip road to get back on the route to Prague, we pass a lit up, deserted service station. Ominous forecourt and empty shop. Standing on the grass verge up front is a girl fighting the two a.m. shivers. She can't be older than twelve or thirteen, sleeves of her dated leather blouson pulled over her hands, mutton legs bare beneath a miniskirt. She regards the van as we speed by, then turns her gaze elsewhere once it becomes clear we aren't going to stop. A barren goodbye to passing trade. Death and life shut up after that, silenced by this final, lone merging of misery and scant pleasure. ■

The Russian Girls

Ignoring the constant banging on doors and windows, **Jane Graham** accepts drinks in a Finnish lap dancing club

SO THIS GUY SAT LAUGHING TO HIMSELF buying me vodka colas, he keeps patting me on the head for some reason, anyway he goes and points to the woman with the hot ironed big blonde hair, and he says, "I like that one, don't you? Which one is your favourite?"

She looks like a doll, minus the innocence; her look is all together too deliberate. She has a lovely smile and wears a pretty yellow cotton sundress with a flower pattern on it, pulled tightly in provocative crisscrosses over her breasts.

The scene is a large room with a dancefloor in the middle rather than a raised stage in the corner, and this space lends itself to straight backed, ass wiggling promenades across its length. It's like a stage made up to look like a street corner, a theatrical set rather than a street itself, and through the night and through the week the show has swelled until it has reached its grand finale now, just gone eleven o'clock on a Saturday night. The chorus line is centre stage; on a chrome railing making a right angle between entrance and bar hang a quintet of female bodies leaning, lolling, waiting, their eyebrows arched into a, 'yes, sir?' They use their hotel room keys as indispensable stage props, swinging them hypnotically from rings on their fingers into the face of their chosen audience. The tableau here makes subtle changes; in synchronisation girls move position to the half moon bar, where they are adept at raising one eyebrow across to the other side.

It was all too much at first. Initially everything seemed to be about sex, and everything about sex seemed terrible and out of control, as if caught in a vortex steadily sucking me in. The staff or the girls coming and going with piles of white sheets, replacing the soiled ones with fresh ones; the men sat in the easy chairs at the entrance to the sauna, clothes thrown over the backs of their seat, sat laughing and wrapped only in white towels; the man who was always there with the girls, sat on a double bed with the door to the room wide open into the corridor, or buying them a cognac in the bar. His face looked bulbous and red, like it was afflicted with some skin complaint most likely brought on by alcohol. Was he part of the Russian Mafia I had heard tell of?

And the worst, the constant banging on the windows and the door. Leaving the blinds always half slatted so the faces didn't press up against the pane. Opening the door in the morning meant voices imploring with unintelligible words, holding out notes I wasn't prepared to accept, so after a day or two I never heeded the knocking. Sometimes my roommate might, but I turned my head the other way, squashed my pillow against my ears.

Yet after a while it all became perfectly natural, in this strange country. They say people can adapt to most things, and I adapted to my new environment. Just now, for instance, I find myself also in the pantomime walk, staring at the men across the bar with arched eyebrows and a mocking smile, part of a show which I find difficult to read as reality. I suppose I am a little fresh, a little merry, should we say, but then it's so easy to have my drinks bought here, men understand heavy drinking easier than they do the concept of tipping me, and when in Rome, you know? So this will be my cue to enter; approaching these men, their shy, drunken faces confused, beckoning them with one waggled ring finger — summoned, they slowly lurch upwards and forwards and walk over, leaning and breathing alcohol and touching me with their stumpy, solid, squat digits. I always make a note of a man's hands and all of the men here have tiny, fat fingers, hereditary traits to a forgotten race of bear like, peasant stock.

It was mainly curiosity which led me here, after I phoned my agent and asked her what contracts she had available and she said, well, the usual — Switzerland, Germany, Austria — oh, and

Art this chapter: Dogger

The Russian Girls

there's always Finland. A place I'd never been to. After I'd booked my flight, two days before my leaving date with little opportunity to back out she ventured to say over the phone, you do know about the Russian girls, don't you?

"…Mmm, yeah…?" I stammered, hoping for elaboration.

"—Oh, they go out with the men from the club. Don't worry, they'll do their thing and you yours," and with that she dismissed the subject as abruptly as she'd brought it up.

Kind of like a guest house, with a restaurant in the building where you can eat your evening meal for free, was how she described it. A brothel, would have been a more apt description, with the club at one end and the bedrooms leading off from it. As far as having a restaurant goes, the bar makes potatoes and meat balls most nights for those who want it.

After I have danced, only dressing as far as my g-string, I might catch a certain man with my eye and walk his way, topless, purposeful, predatory, hands on hips, swaying and refusing to lower my laughing eyes from him, reaching my target and placing my hands on his shoulders, adjusting my gaze to meet his. He appears half terrified, half ecstatic. But I am drunk and creating scenarios.

Sometimes I walk the floor a little less purposefully. I do the circuit, checking out the scene, putting a little rhythm into my step, bouncing my ass and holding my hands deliberately at my side in a jitterbug. Sometimes I don't make it all the way round before someone grabs me just above the elbow, hard and bear like, and I try to slide the grasping fist down towards my hand so it doesn't hurt and make it more of an invitation than a threat. In a few seconds I must diffuse this clamp into a mild flirtation. The alternative is being dragged by the arm around the dancefloor, as seconds turn into minutes in a terrifying, out-of-control whirl. Language is rarely the best form of communication in this place. Eyes, lips, hands, body. These are better to convey what you mean. I will allow myself, if freed, to accompany him on the dancefloor.

They're all Russian girls. That's how they're known and of course that means something more than just the literal meaning. Russian girls leave with men. Russian girls have streetwalked their way all over Europe; they come as a group, bring with them gangsters and trouble in the eyes of the West, and no matter how diplomatic I am I am always considered superior by way of being English, or — more to the point — not Russian.

Actually that is untrue, I discover later. None of them are actually Russian and don't appreciate being called that. Most are Estonian. Two or three are Latvian, one I think is Lithuanian, another from the Ukraine, and all are fiercely proud of their homelands. But to ignorant westerners like myself, they converge into a group known simply as 'Russian girls'.

There's the one I think of as Farrah Fawcett, because of the perhaps unintentional seventies style to her appearance; blonde hair sprayed scratchy stiff, older than the others, dressed always in pastel pedal pushers and suntop, big tits, no bra, nipples erect, blue eye shadow, always waiting by the railing. There's young and perky and then there's older and more classy, big tits and small tits and one girl who's all tits.

In the hotel corridor there's a girl doing a crossword in a magazine. I look over her shoulder at the squares filled in with cyrillic like hieroglyphics, to me bizarre symbols but to her everyday doodles holding no more meaning than a way of killing time. She's sitting by a table outside her door with the magazine in one hand and a burning cigarette in the

CZECH REPUBLIC | **FINLAND** | UK | NETHERLANDS | JAPAN | USA | FRANCE | SPAIN | UNDERGROUND | REVIEWS

> There's young and perky and then there's older and more classy, big tits and small tits and one girl who's all tits.

other, smiling at me like it was the most normal thing in the world, like we had just met at a bus stop or something, while from within the bedroom the sound of sex rises and falls, and she asks me: how is business. Okay, I shrug. We exchange small talk.

It's like there's different girls in the day here. I lose track of how many are working, trying to add up their faces and counting the same girls twice, seeing an outfit rather than a person. Gradually they're starting to break free from their group identity as I begin to put names to bodies, personalities and histories even.

I walk back in after going out for breakfast and one of the girls calls me over. She's sitting by the untended, unopened bar with two others. She tells me to sit down and asks me my name. As usual in the daytime and like most of the other girls, she's dressed sporty casual in an orange Adidas tracksuit jacket with a Nike baseball cap over her long, ash blonde hair. She tells me she speaks English because she studied in England when she was seventeen. In Tunbridge Wells. I tell her I've never been there. She introduces herself as Irina. She's studying to be a lawyer.

She asks if I'd like a drink and I'm made a fruit tea with honey, same as themselves. "No money, no honey," says one girl in a thick accent, taking a big spoonful and sucking it eagerly into her mouth, and everybody laughs. It's funny because it's a stock phrase they've learnt even though their English is very limited. Except for Irina. Her voice is deep and husky, as though she's been shouting and smoking continuously for days.

"This is my friend, Marina," Irina introduces the girl who I met in the corridor last night doing the crossword puzzle. She's older, dressed more maturely and less casually, with a pronounced, regal nose and a high forehead, black hair tied back from her face. "She arrived yesterday."

"Hello," I shake Marina's hand.

"Please," she says, passing me a box of chocolates. "From Latvia. My home. Take. Very good."

I take a chocolate and eat it. It's incredibly sweet. She says, please, take more.

"And this is Julia," Irina introduces me to the other girl, the one who was spooning out the honey. She's more slightly built, dressed in tight beige jeans and a smart matching top. I shake hands with her too.

"You like Finland?" Irina asks me.

I say, yes, I think, and she makes a face. "Jane, please, listen to me," she begins. "In Finland the mans have one word — rakas — it means my darling and it also means to fuck."

Everybody bursts out laughing. Irina pulls a romantic face, puts her hands over her heart and cries, "My darling," then, with the same degree of emotion she utters, "my fuck."

The girl whom my drinking buddy had described as his favourite wanders in to use some boiling water from the kettle, unmade up in her pink satin robe, smiling a weak but genuine smile.

In a few hours the pantomime will begin again. Around seven, half open bedroom doors will reveal girls vacuuming in black underwear. Each girl will make her entrance separately, surreptitiously, and take her place in the tableaux, standing or sitting, always holding a key and a packet of cigarettes.

Before work tonight, Irina and Marina suggest we take a sauna together. Every hotel, no matter how primitive, has a sauna in Finland. To own a sauna in one's home is not entirely for the rich; it is perhaps as common as, say, owning a dishwasher in England. One of the club's regulars is fond of telling me, "We have a saying here in Finland. If you cannot be happy with drink, cigarettes and sauna, then there is no hope for you."

Irina and Marina are very specific about how we should go about our sauna. Marina has taken a half full jar of honey and poured a great load of salt into it, and spent some ten minutes industriously mixing the two ingredients together with a spoon. First, we sit covered in the facepacks Marina has given us. Then, we wash them off and cover ourselves with the honey and salt mixture, which Marina assures me is very good for the skin. Marina helps me rub it into my back and around my shoulders and I do the same for her. And so we sit, naked and silent together, the heat building up until we can take no more. Then Marina says to me, "Come, now is enough."

Irina has a moisturising lotion, very expensive, Yves Saint Laurent, from duty free. She insists I try a little.

It sometimes seems as if I am establishing close friendships with all these girls in all these different countries, but in actual fact it boils down to little more than talking about make-up and clothes, maybe boyfriends too. As if fashion and appearance is our only point of reference, or maybe we're just playing safe. Don't try to bring the conversation onto another level. Perhaps I can never comprehend the enormity of the situation which drives girls to follow their cousins in their thousands over the world to hustle and fuck. I don't dare to discover just exactly who the man with the alcoholism blemish across his face is or what his relationship to Irina, Marina, Julia and the rest of them is. Nor do we talk about politics. I don't know if I really want to get too intensely involved in a conversation about politics; I just know I don't want to talk about perfume.

After the sauna Marina smokes a cigarette lounging in the soft chairs just outside and asks me how I feel now. "You feel good? Sauna is very good. But sauna in Estonia is better."

I nod. I do feel good. Relaxed. I touch the skin just below my neck. "It's so soft!" I exclaim.

"You have children?" Marina asks me out of the blue.

I shake my head, no. "You?" I ask.

"One daughter," answers Marina. "She is with my mother. I miss her very much. You want to see photos?"

I nod. "Come," says Marina.

I dress and follow her into her room at the end of the corridor, opposite the one I share with Victoria, the other dancer. It is similar to mine, only instead of two single beds there is one large double bed filling most of the space. There is also a plant and a bland landscape painting on the wall, a very small one, and, just as in my room, a television set standing in the corner. The room is very tidy and all the clothes have been hung neatly in the wardrobe.

Marina takes out a small photo album and sits down on the bed to the side. I sit down on a chair next to her and watch her open the album and show me the photos. A dark eyed, smiling girl, maybe three years old, her face full of wonder and curiosity, stares out at me, standing in a snow covered forest.

"She's beautiful," I say. "What is her name?"

"Katia," Marina answers. "She is four now. This was last year. Near my home, in Latvia. I miss her so much."

She turns the page, and shows me a photo of Katia when she was a baby. It looks like a family gathering: Marina is holding her, and an older woman, I suppose it is Marina's mother, stands next to her with her arm around them both.

"And all those trees," I say. "Are there many forests in Latvia? It looks wonderful,"

"Yes, Latvia is very beautiful country."

To think of all those other countries… I remember with a slight jolt that I'll be leaving in a couple of days. I've promised to keep in touch, exchanged addresses with Marina. She says I can visit her in Latvia sometime. I imagine her there, in the snow-covered woods, with her daughter. I know deep down it won't happen; friendships made in these kind of places, however tight, don't function well outside of the clubs. I promise too that I'll come back and work here again; of course I never do.

On my home, the Finn-Air plane is full of Finns drinking whisky, the cabin crew pouring it into their coffee from huge pitchers. I recollect a newcomer on my last night at the club, a very young girl with long, wavy blonde hair and a chubby teenage countenance. Like anyone was looking at her face; this girl had a pair of the hugest breasts I've ever seen.

"Why you must work here?" she asked me, smiling, and there was no hint of malice in her eyes, only a complete lack of comprehension. "You must buy new clothes?" ∎

> "In Finland the mans have one word — rakas — it means my darling and it also means to fuck"

1991

Maria Zaza and the Wisdom of the Snake

I WATCHED ON AS MARIA ZAZA LUGGED HER HAVERSACK into the fashionable Reds bar with her black hair in pigtails. A Gio-Goi woolly hat. Black leather gloves. And bizarre emerald green tortoise shell spectacles — with no glass in them. Her dead granma's, she explained. They made her feel close to her. And they would make a good disguise.

She was running away to London. To sort her head out, she said. Needed to get away for a bit. Hardcore dance music pounded, heavy bass lines vibrating through the stained pine floor boards. The early evening crowd were all faces on the local rave scene. Beautiful, blonde haired podium dancers, skin-headed vicious looking drug dealers, lads with pony tails; all decked out in designer clothes, drinking designer bottled lager.

It had been a strange day. I'd been on a fiddle job, painting the walls of a local garage with white masonry paint with my maverick cousin Rob, when the phone call came through. Maria needed to see me urgently. I'd taken off my paint-splattered overalls and jumped on the first bus. Now I sat at a table sipping at a glass of Bushmills Irish whiskey with a hollow, empty feeling of sadness. I knew I'd lost her.

It was like the feeling I'd had as a child when my grandmother passed away. My father and an uncle had tried to persuade me to see her laid out in state, a hangover from her old Irish catholic upbringing. But I was having none of it. I stood at the bottom of the bank that led up to the house on a council estate and cried. I had a nightmare vision burning in my mind of a skeleton sitting in a dusty room with dust rising in the shaft of light that penetrated the thick, drawn curtains. When you die, you're a skeleton. Of course. But I never voiced my fears and the family was baffled by my bizarre behaviour. It remains my earliest memory.

Maria had also suffered loss in her childhood.

In bed one night she told me how, years ago, her mother and father had taken her and her sister for a drive in the country. As she stood at a five bar gate, the others got in the car and drove

> The pattern was set for the next couple of years. Raving. Starting on Es, then progressing to mix with speed and LSD, magic mushrooms, smoking marijuana to take the edge off the come downs which eventually came with increasing levels of despondency… **Jonny Tait** leaves the party

away, her father telling her that they were leaving her for the gypsies. It was a joke. The car stopped within metres, but the shock had stayed with Maria all her life. Her parents had split up. Her father had been caught selling cigarettes for the Neapolitan Camorra as a child. He'd been sent to a school run by nuns as a punishment, but he and a friend had escaped. They had been on Italian TV, the two young fugitives. When eventually caught, her father was sent to live with relatives in Britain to keep him away from the Mafia. Her grandfather had been a high-ranking officer in Mussolini's fascist army, though this was never talked about.

I won't pretend that I can make any sense of the time we spent together. There was no sense. Maria would turn up unannounced and moody with me. Disappear for days on end. Cry after I'd slammed down the phone on her in frustration after prolonged silences. Sometimes — sometimes, if I saw her coming down the street I'd hide as I couldn't face holding down a conversation or commit myself to being that close to someone. We'd go to parties and she'd have to drag me home unconscious after I drank myself into a stupor. I drank so I could hide. Remove all responsibility for my actions. I'd walk along bridge parapets, drunk, and ask her if she'd die for me. She said no.

But Maria and I also shared some magical moments. Lying together in bed, hallucinating and giggling, we shared an amazing, almost religious feeling of cosmic consciousness at exactly the same time. For a flash, everything in the universe slotted neatly into place and the sudden, resounding truth was ours to savour. Ah, but of course.. how stupid I've been .. it's all so simple.. but as quick as the answer was revealed, it was snatched away. Maria felt it was like dying. Being shown a glimpse of heaven, where a white horse was waiting for her. Although a Catholic, Maria became increasingly drawn to Buddhism and wouldn't allow anyone to hurt any insects or animals. She became quite agitated about it. After the abortion, all life seemed so precious to Maria — except her own. I, meanwhile, had been raised a Presbyterian. No religious icons and ecstasy for the Billy Boys. Different cultural frames of reference. I couldn't understand religious guilt and confessions, the hell-fire damnations of the Vatican. My church had been built around the work ethic and a distaste of precious golden trinkets.

Maria and I had seen nirvana on LSD — a sacrament that, along with whiskey and vodka, would fuel our relationship.

We first met in high school, where we sat together in art lessons. Maria had skinny legs and was a tremendous athlete and runner. She had a manic, nervous laugh that constantly got us in trouble with the teacher. I wanted to be a footballer. Or a bricklayer. After watching Jimmy Nail kick a sink off the wall in the television series *Auf Wiedersien Pet*, I had decided — that's the game for me. My mates all shared similar dreams, the desire to leave school and earn money. Become men. Drink pints and get into fights. I would also have liked to become a painter and decorator like my dad, my favourite uncle and my Granda Paddy, who I never met as he died of cancer in the fifties. Even Rob had been my father's apprentice. The family trade. But the family was determined for me to do better and set me up on a YTS as a joiner. "You'll never be out of work," my dad had said. How wrong he was.

My Granda Jack was a miner and had taken voluntary retirement when his pit was shut down. I had watched aghast as pictures flashed on the television of lines and lines of black uniformed policemen laying into the striking miners.

"Your Granda's there today," my mother had said. I began to hate authority, equating it with the violence I had seen. My quiet, smiling Granda talked with hatred about scabs and it affected me. He told me to never cross a picket and his left-wing politics became a major influence on me.

But some of my older mates had taken Thatcher's advice and were enterprising businessmen, selling fake Rolex watches, perfume, duvets. I saw the way that the housewives and the men on the estates had respect for these likeable rogues. An older friend, Paul Morgan, a good looking dark haired lad, was regularly travelling into Newcastle city centre with a cut throat razor concealed in his boot. Paul was like a guru to me and my best friend Mickey. We all grew up together on the same estate, went to football matches together and watched mad kung fu films. Drinking ouzo brought back from Paul's family holidays. Paul was now running with a gang of Tyneside hooligans, the Gremlins.

Mickey and I were introduced to these older lads and were accepted almost immediately. We were sent on a job for the Gremlins. "Go and stand outside this shop," one of the top boys had said. "They'll get the message."

So Mickey, me and my younger cousin Phil had trooped up and stood outside the shop. After a few moments, one of the sales assistants had turned around, spotted us and with a look of pure terror on his face had jumped over the counter and was frantically phoning the police. Female assistants looked on at our trio with fearful looks. We cleared out and returned to the Monument in the City Centre where the top boy met us.

"What happened?" he asked. We explained.

> I wanted to be a footballer. Or a bricklayer. After watching Jimmy Nail kick a sink off the wall in the television series 'Auf Wiedersien Pet', I had decided — that's the game for me.

I, were set to block either end of the narrow street.

No one comes on, and no one goes off, we were told. It was a buzz.

The top boys went into the shop, dragged out the assistant, and gave him a beating, taking off his hand tooled leather cowboy boots and smashing them over his head before one of them topped off his indignation by urinating on his bloody, crumpled body. Terrified assistants looking on from the surrounding shops got the message and the Gremlins had a virtual free reign.

As the acid house scene kicked off, the Gremlins moved into drug dealing.

I had seen my more adventurous friends Paul and Mickey take a Super Smiley trip one night. I was afraid to try it, being brought up on posters of Zammo McGuire slouched against a wall smacked out. And my parents would kill me if they found out. No thanks, I said. But my friends didn't turn into ravaged junkies. In fact, despite their brains being on fire, they didn't look high at all. They didn't think they could fly. They didn't lose their minds. It was a one off experiment and although I felt like he'd missed out somehow, I wasn't that interested in drugs. I was working as a joiner on the building sites and drinking a few pints at the weekend, despite my father's weak complaints. I was grafting, learning a trade, my father figured. If I was a man through the week, I could be one at weekends. I went to a few warehouse parties with the Gremlins, and avoided the temptation put in front of me by getting through the night on lucozade and amyl nitrate.

On a Gremlins bus to a Middlesbrough rave in 1989, they held a raffle at £2 a ticket. First prize — a gloop of brown toffee like substance. A Havana punch. LSD, speed and ecstasy all rolled into one powerful hit.

"Good. He'll be shitting his pants now. Cheers, lads," he had said. Now we were faces. They're with the Gremlins, people said, wary. An immense feeling of power and untouchability.

The Gremlins were knocking over shops and selling the fashionable clothes at a third of the price. You could put in an order in the morning, and collect your clothes in the afternoon from a designated pub.

One shop assistant on High Bridge Street had stopped a Gremlin from stealing from his shop.

The Gremlins were mobbed up, around 200 wild lads, and set off to High Bridge. The younger associates, like Mickey and

Then I lost my job. The YTS came

to an end and the employer announced that he wasn't keeping me on. My cousin Phil replaced me. I entered a strange new world of job centres and interviews and rejection. Luckily, Rob was also out of work at the time and showed me the ropes. On one form, in the 'what I did to look for work this week' section, Rob wrote 'applied for manager's position at Newcastle United.' In the 'what I will do next' section he wrote, in his neat handwriting, 'consider their offer.' I realised it was all a joke. The DSS treat you like a number. Turn up, fill in the forms, that's all they care about.

Then one night, in a Newcastle club, Mickey said he was going to score. The madness around was too intense, flashing incessant strobe lights, spinning green lasers, and grinning, sweaty, hugging people with glazed eyes and wide smiles. He came back with three little white pills in his fist. £20 a pop. Ecstasy. Mickey, I and our friend Stevie stood in a dark corner and threw the pills down our necks nervously. We went onto the dance floor and waited for the MDMA to kick in.

As I danced to the throbbing tunes, my body started to spread with warmth. I felt totally loose. Started to grin. Felt the basslines like a low flying bomber. "I'm going for a walk," I said, tapping Mickey on the shoulder. He understood and smiled his approval. WHOOOOSH! YA FUCKA!! Mad rushes surged through my body as I wandered up a dark staircase. My head threatened to spin clean off. I slumped against a wall, my mind saying — I'm too high. If this gets any more intense, I pondered, I'm FUCKED. As I sat against the wall the initial rushes eventually began to ease off a little, leaving me blissfully, joyously high. A beautiful redhead girl came and sat beside me. She gave me a hug and it felt like the most wonderful feeling in the world. "Are you alright?" she said. I nodded, my eyes rolling, my tongue hanging out.

"Come on, you've got to dance," she said. "If you sit here now, you'll end up here all night."

She led me to the dancefloor and I felt at one with the music. The fucking coolest cat that ever walked. I grooved like a bad thing, swimming through the treacle like air. The girl scratched her fingernails down my neck and an amazing rush soared through my body. I repaid the compliment, running my fingers slowly through her hair pressing hard on her scalp. She groaned with pleasure. A man with white gloves and a builders' dust mask gave me a huge hug, cheering loudly in my face. I moved through the swaying crowd stomping to the beat. I lost the girl. Never even knew her name. Climbed on a dance platform and reached for the sky in bliss. My glasses steamed up with the heat. Stevie suddenly appeared pounding through the crowd and cheered in recognition, hugging tightly.

"Where's Mickey?" I said breathlessly. My body felt like it was constantly on the verge of coming. Whistles, air horns blasting out. Ecstasy!!! I closed my eyes and saw luminous green clock faces spinning and hurtling through the blackness. Mickey, stoned, had thought his first E was a dud and he bought another. Just as he swallowed it, the same crippling rushes that had floored me swept through him. OOPS, Mickey thought, as he told me later. I've dropped a bollock here. But he too was now pleasantly cabbaged, dancing in a conga line around the large balcony that overlooked the main dance floor, having also been saved by an angelic woman.

Everyone was high, and everyone was beautiful. The second Summer of Love. Really friendly — even the dealers cared if people were alright, stepping out of their shadowy groups to shake hands and laugh. Spinning blue and green neon lasers cutting through the thick dry ice hanging like a heavy indoor fog. Lying against massive stacks of speakers and feeling the music blasting through my body like a subsonic helicopter. The Shamanic pounding of the drums before the Rotterdam influence sent it rocketing to 180 bpm and warp factor speed. That was it. The pattern was set for the next couple of years for the lads. Raving. Starting on Es, then progressing to mix with speed and LSD, magic mushrooms, smoking marijuana to take the edge off the come downs which eventually came with increasing levels of despondency as the doses increased. Partying. Edinburgh, Newcastle, anywhere. Clubs, massive outdoor marquees, leisure centres. Dancing with the UVF. Smoking with big name gangsters. *Injected with a poison!!* The great white and gold-

Images used in this chapter are taken from the remarkable *Tragédies à la Une: La Belle Époque des assassins* by Alain Monestier (Éditions Albin Michel S.A., Paris, 1995).

en flash of the lights coming up, hands stretched for the sky in bliss. It was in all this madness that I met Maria again. She too was a raver. I could have sworn that I had seen her one night wearing an oxygen mask being helped by St. John's ambulance men, but it was someone else. Empathy made me stay with the strange girl though.

Then, later, I saw Maria going out with a lad I knew. Bastard, I thought. But when we met that night, I'd said: "Ti amo," and grinned. She'd replied with a ti amo too, her boyfriend too thick to understand what was going on under his nose.

We eventually bumped into each other on New Year's Eve outside a pub as the town square buzzed with drunk ravers.

She grabbed me, kissing me passionately. She was with her best friend Lucie Royal. I had a strange night with Lucie a couple of years previously. A girl had come up to me in a party and had cried out my name in excitement. "Don't you recognise me?" I wracked my brains, desperately trying to remember the girl, but had drawn a blank. I badly wanted to get her name right. I wanted a shag.

"I'm Lucie Royal! We went to school together and I loved you all the time we were there!"

"Why didn't you ask me out then?" "I was scared you'd say no."

Our lives are permeated by such incidents. We are all afraid of looking foolish and bear that guilt as we race towards the grave. Our souls are not so precious that they can't cope with a few bruises.

Fuck it, I thought. I'd better make up for lost time then. I grabbed her and we locked together. When she eventually broke free, she announced with a frown: "That's my boyfriend. I don't like him. I want you." She indicated a lad with a ponytail sitting at a table. He was clocking me with daggers in his eyes. Fucking marvellous. "I love you. I always have."

" Give me your number and I'll call you," I said. "But I'm going to America to be an au-pair in two days," she said mournfully. She promised to write and I promised to write back. I could have loved her.

Now, as we stood outside the pub, Lucie said: "Why did you never write back?"

"Eh? I sent you about a dozen letters, but you never wrote back. I thought you weren't interested." I had never received the letters. My paranoia moved up a couple of notches.

I had a laugh with Maria and Lucie, but didn't think much more of it. Several days later, Maria rang. She wanted to go out with me. She had rung every one of my surnames in the phone book to find my number. She didn't want to lose me again. And so it was done. I found strange

1991

number compatibility games with my name scrawled on under her bed. Two people drawn together through fate, coincidence and chance. Soulmates. Might as well spin a coin.

Her mother wouldn't let me stay at the house and always asked if we'd been drinking. So did her sister. We had sex in the kitchen with her mother sat in the living room next door. Sometimes I'd just lie in bed, my body flying with interior speed, incapacitated with drink and drugs, wondering with a morbid curiosity how we would die. I was convinced I was going to have a heart attack and I didn't care. After heavy weekends my chest would ache with sharp stabbing pains.

I'd wander up to her house tripping like mad and we'd spend a night in the woods or in a graveyard seeing crazy ancient shapes in the heavy dawn mist. I'd snort whiskey and speed and ask her what she thought she was doing with an idiot like me. The closer we got, the further I would push her away. I only felt safe in the darkness of a club with booming bass lines throbbing through my senses. I couldn't hold down a sensible conversation, I was avoiding people in the streets as I shuffled along with my head sunk into my chest. I was nasty drunk, nice high, and I didn't know who I was anymore. Maria said it was like seeing three men and she didn't know which one I was going to be from day to day. I felt the same way about her.

When she told me of an abortion she'd had before we were together, I wasn't bothered about the child, but instead the fact that she'd been that close to someone else. It was her most intimate secret; she loved me, she confided in me and it brought us closer together. Nobody else would ever find out — not the father, no one. It's a scar that we both have to carry. Sometimes she refused to have sex as she was scared of getting pregnant again and I had to ride it out. All our schoolday innocence gone. She called me 'Johnny Walker' after we spent a day on the stuff in Newcastle.

There's something wonderful about daytime drinking, leaving the dark sanctuary of a bar and blinking into the sunlight. But on sober days we could laugh and hug and joke and everything was fine. We talked about getting a flat together but it never happened.

3.27 a.m. Rob and I sit contentedly on our sofa deckchairs sunbathing in the glorious sunlight of the sitting room bulb.

Every now and then we break from our talk about roast beef and mustard sandwiches and bottles of Guinness to demand if people have tickets for this trip to the coast. Most people look bewildered; Laid-back grins at us in his laid-back way, so he is allowed on the bus.

> On a Gremlins bus to a Middlesbrough rave in 1989, they held a raffle at £2 a ticket. First prize – a gloop of brown toffee like substance

I can feel the soft sand squeezing through my stockinged feet on the carpet, and the sea rolls gently in from behind the TV. Seagulls arc and cry in the clear blue skies of the bare magnolia walls.

The desperate feeling of an out of season British coastal resort can be overwhelming. Dilapidated guest houses and boarded up amusement arcades, empty, dank pubs and tacky gift shops.

The golden glow of a fish and chip shop provides some respite, but the sea crashes hard on the harbour walls sending spray high into the colourless sky. Always the sad, dull roar of the sea.

Mickey and Big-chip are in the kitchen laughing at shiny tins of spam, breathing tablecloths and wallpaper that is slowly sliding off the walls. Big-chip is carrying an array of weird junk: an egg timer, a broken radio and a kitchen knife — he likes to talk about building and violence — and Mickey gets into this.

Gypsy girl and Maria are sitting cross-legged with huge, gleaming, black pupils in the corner of the beach giggling and smoking someone else's cigarettes. A golden packet of Bensons decimated. A crazy looking older woman with wild dark hair asks if she can have one, then starts screaming and shrieking obscenities as she realises they are hers. She storms out of the house and into the moonlit mist. Gypsy girl runs to see Mickey and Maria shrugs.

The wild woman returns later and places a sad, sagging bunch of fresh picked daffodils in a bowl on the living room table. People look at each other in disgust as she apologises. It's so false. A front. *Yeah, I can see behind the mask, can see those cogs spinning in your head like a cheap Tenerife fake Tag watch.*

As Maria and I leave the after rave party, cool fresh air strikes us as we blink into the pale blue light of dawn. Hunched up in a black leather coat like a crow with a buzzing head.

"I hate that bitch," says Maria. " I didn't know they were her fags."

The amazingly clear architecture of an ornate sandstone bank appears far too big and unreal as we walk arm in arm through the empty, silent streets. Birds sing. Thousands of birds. A solitary black London cab roars by. *There was no driver, I'm telling you — it was a ghost car!*

We crash into bed for uneasy, vivid dreams. A psychedelic, tie-dye, triplicate Hitler ranting in German. Maria's warm curves press against me like a VW bonnet.

The high ringing of the telephone rouses me.

"Who was that?" asks Maria, sitting on the bed with wet dark hair fresh from the shower, pulling on a green and white striped uniform for her work as a petrol station cashier.

"Bloody Rob. Wanted to know if I had a hammer, some screws and some wood glue in my toolkit. Someone smashed a table last night. Big-chip says he can fix it. Are they stockings you've got on?" I said, a wide grin crossing my face, laughing like Sid James. The woodsaws in my toolbag, and old grey RAF holdall that my Granda gave me, were beginning to rust from lack of use.

The waves fast receding from the shore with a dull hush.

With the heavy flashback over, Maria caught my eye, came over to my table in the Reds bar and smiled.

When she smiled, her face lit up like a prize paying one armed bandit. Sparkling deep brown eyes.

"Where are you going to stay?" I asked in desperation.

"At Lucie's," she said. "Didn't I tell you?" she spluttered, noticing the puzzlement on my face. I'd had horrible visions of her being raped and killed on the streets of London, grabbed by an immigrant gang and tortured. Exploited. No, she'd neglected to tell me she was staying at Lucie's. I didn't know Lucie was in London. I tried to change her mind, imploring her to stay. But she said no, stroking my long, wavy brown hair. Her mind was made up. She had to go, and was going to jump the train and hide in the toilet to avoid paying for a ticket. And she had to go now and catch her bus.

I picked up her heavy haversack and we made our way through the crowd of drinkers and into the cool air. Street lamps were just beginning to flicker into life and light the pavements with a weak orange glow.

"Quickly, in here," said Maria, as we walked past a busy working men's club.

I followed her in past the old flat-capped man with a craggy face on the door.

"Hey, you've got to sign the book!" he cried.

"It's alright," Maria said. "I'm just going to the toilet." He grunted and watched us disappear down the corridor.

Maria grabbed me and pulled me into the ladies toilets. No one was in. She held my hand and led me into a cubicle. We locked into a deep, passionate kiss, and I felt her warm, firm body through her clothes as she pulled against me tightly.

I slipped my hand down the front of her silky trousers, inside her cotton knickers, and felt the warm wetness slide up my fingers.

"No," she giggled, squirming. "Not here ... not now."

She reached into her jacket pocket and produced a wrap of white powder which she dabbed into and put on the cistern, indicating for me to do the same. I felt the sickly, chemical tang slip down my throat as I snorted the speed. My goodbye present.

We kissed once again before Maria broke free.

"I've got to go," she said forlornly.

We strode past the startled onlookers in the corridor, ignoring comments, and completely oblivious to their stares. We walked the short distance to the bus station where Maria's bus was revved up and waiting. I broke down in tears. They rolled down my face as I tugged at my hair. The amphetamine coursing through my veins sent waves of dull rushes around my body. I loved her.

I passed her the haversack as she kissed my cheek and told me not to worry. She would call sometime. As I looked down at my feet, embarrassed by my tears, Maria clambered onto the bus with her heavy bag.

As it pulled away she waved from the top deck, turning around and still waving as the bus drove her out of my life.

Or so I thought. Maria called a week later. She was back home, at her mothers. She'd jumped the wrong train and ended up in Edinburgh. But it was finished. She'd slept with a squaddie in the Scottish capital. She was high, she explained, it meant nothing.

Mickey's girlfriend Gypsy girl had tearfully told me that Maria had also slept with another bloke in town. Mickey made her tell. I became a tightly packed ball of smouldering violence. Completely paranoid. I heard people talking, and when I looked around the corner, there was no one there. I did a Ouija board with Mickey, and the light bulb in the room exploded. Mickey's mother was pushed down the stairs by an unseen force. Cups filled with water in the kitchen. At a party, the maverick Rob, a squat skinhead with a broken nose — and the life and soul with his quick one liners and sharp humour — fled from the house after being attacked by a neon man. Mickey heard jabbering voices, arguments. Demons told him that they were going to kill his little nieces. He got very spiritual after nearly dying of an amphetamine overdose, beautiful little colours dancing in the corner of the room as he clasped at his tightening chest. The party was over.

As Mickey and I drove down to Tilbury Docks to take a large Landrover for transporting to South Africa for a local businessman, we pulled in at a service station. Mickey returned with an apple, which he gave to me. "Dunno, thought you might want an apple," he shrugged at my puzzled look.

"Can you smell that?" said the businessman's son as Mickey got back in the car. We could. It smelt of roses. A departing spirit.

The Northumbrian poet John French Jackson, a small, hunched man with a face like a currant, a former army boxer, once stopped me at the top of some steps.

"Wheor ye gannin', son?" he asked. Jackie was also an alcoholic and a painter and decorator. He played the mouth organ and dipped it in his pint.

"Aa'm away to scheul, Jackie."

"Whey, ye divn't waant to dee that, man. Gerra way up on yon hill an' playuh wi the snayiks."

The wisdom evaded me at the time. Play with the snakes. Don't learn out of books, but experience.

I still think of Maria Zaza. Some nights she invades my dreams, and I, she says, hers. When the night is dark and the stars gleam like tiny headlights I might just hear the dull thump of drum and bass in a distant club and I smile when I remember her mad laugh. I have one photograph of her. I turn it over in my fingers and wonder what could have been. Sixteen years a soul mate. I hunch my shoulders deeper into the long leather jacket, head down to avoid the gritty wind, turn a corner and am gone.

Eyes on the road again. Watch out for them snakes. ■

The Case of the Manacled Mormon

WHEN YOU SPEND ANY LENGTH OF TIME CHAINED TO a bed in a remote country cottage, even if it's only a matter of a few days, you presumably have the chance to do a lot of thinking about things in general.

For trombone-playing Mormon missionary Kirk Anderson, whose religious zeal had brought him all the way from Utah to suburban Epsom, the experience must have been a good opportunity to look back over his relationship with former beauty contestant Joyce McKinney and wonder where it all went wrong.

Joyce hit the headlines in 1977, at the tail end of a newspaper silly season dominated by stories about the death of Elvis Presley. Journalists dubbed her the Sex-In-Chains Girl when it emerged that she had been arrested on suspicion of abducting Kirk and repeatedly raping him at a cottage in Okehampton in Devon. The story was greeted with a loud collective sigh of relief by the nation's tabloid editors. It was the year of the Queen's Silver Jubilee, and hard news had been thin on the ground for months. They badly needed a nice juicy scandal to restore their flagging spirits and the Case of the Manacled Mormon was just what the doctor ordered. A steamy tale of sex, intrigue and thwarted passion, it promised to be a sure fire circulation booster.

Joyce was the archetypal loony girlfriend. She and Kirk had been lovers back at Brigham Young University in Utah, but their relationship had proved short lived. Some things aren't meant to last. Kirk had led a sheltered life. An Elder in the Mormon Church's devout order of Melchizedek, he was ill-equipped to deal with the redoubtable Joyce. There's no way of pinpointing the exact moment when he finally decided he'd had a bellyful of her erratic behaviour. It may have been when she smashed his windows or slashed his tyres. Some men are funny about things like that. Or perhaps it was when she chased him at high speed in her Chevrolet Corvette and forced his car off the road. Either way, there inevitably came a point where he began to drop subtle hints that it was all over between them — little things like moving to another state without leaving a forwarding address, adopting a false name to throw her off the scent and finally fleeing all the way to England in a desper-

PREVIOUS PAGE
Joyce McKinney on the phone

A look back at the tabloid wet dream that was Joyce McKinny by **Dean James**

ate bid to place himself beyond her reach. Missionary work is a cornerstone of the Mormon faith, and a stint in darkest Surrey, taking the gospel to the heathens of suburbia, must have seemed the ideal opportunity to make himself scarce for a while. What he didn't count on was Joyce's extraordinary single mindedness and tenacity of purpose. She wasn't the type to take defeat lying down, and followed him to England with devoted acolyte Keith May in tow, determined to exact her due.

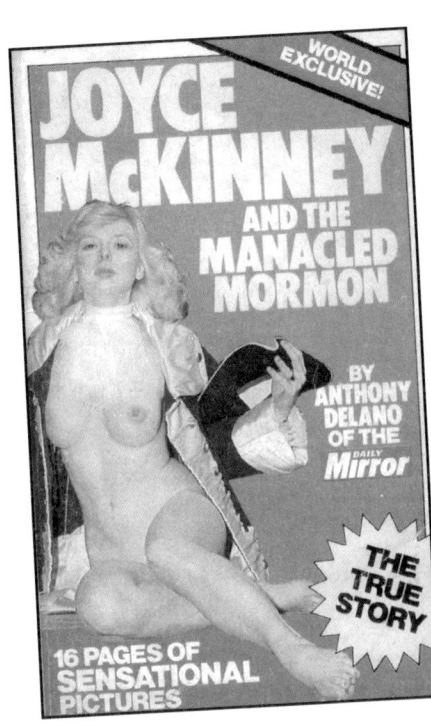

Keith May was a fresh faced trainee architect with blond hair and a wispy apology for a moustache. Three years Joyce's junior, he doesn't appear to have been overburdened with common sense and happily went along with her bizarre plan to kidnap Kirk, seemingly viewing it as "a rescue operation from [an] oppressive and tyrannical organisation" [i.e. The Mormon Church]. Applying for bail after he'd been arrested, defence solicitor Robert Marshall Andrews ascribed his involvement in the case to "mixed up emotions". It was, as *Daily Mirror* journalist Anthony Delano later remarked, a classic example of British understatement.

On balance it's difficult to see why Joyce was so infatuated with Kirk. A walking definition of the word 'gormless', he dressed conventionally and weighed as much as both his alleged kidnappers put together, tipping the scales at an impressive eighteen stone. There was certainly nothing conventionally attractive about him, but Joyce was obviously too besotted to care. She couldn't wait to renew their acquaintance. Her method of going about it was highly unusual but then, her method of going about most things was highly unusual. Arming herself with an imitation .38 revolver and dragooning Keith May into service as driver and strong arm man, she abducted Kirk and spirited him away to a cottage at Lower Holstock Farm on the northern edge of Dartmoor (having first taken the precaution of reinforcing the windows with bullet proof glass), where he was chained to a bed and raped repeatedly. "Joy told me [that] if there was to be a ransom, the ransom would be that I would have to give her a baby," he related afterwards. "She said she was going to get what she wanted whether I wanted to or not. She said she might keep me there for another month or so, until she missed her period."

In the event, Kirk was held captive for only four days before being released unharmed near Victoria Station. Filled with righteous indignation, he wasted no time in reporting his abductors to the police, who arrested them shortly afterwards at a roadblock on the A30 between Devon and London. Told she'd been accused of kidnap and rape, Joyce reacted indignantly. "I don't have to beg for boys' services," she spluttered at one point, "I am 38-24-36. I was Miss Wyoming in the USA pageant." It was a persuasive argument, but the Crown decided to prosecute anyway, charging her with abduction, false imprisonment and possession of an imitation firearm with intent to commit an offence.

Joyce's antics were a breath of fresh air for tabloid journalists tired of writing anodyne rubbish about the Queen's Silver Jubilee. Her first remand hearing was typical. Arriving at Epsom magistrate's court in a police van, she kept the assembled hacks entertained by sobbing histri-

Manacled Mormon Nympho Nuns

onically at the window and holding up a series of notes scrawled on pages torn from a Bible.

> PLEASE TELL THE TRUTH.
> MY REPUTATION IS AT STAKE

one hastily scribbled message implored.

> HE HAD SEX WITH ME FOR 4 DAYS

another declared.

> HE MADE IT LOOK LIKE A KIDNAPPING
> ASK CHRISTIANS TO PRAY FOR ME.

Denied bail on the grounds that she might abscond or attempt suicide, Joyce was sent to Holloway Prison in North London and left to ponder the error of her ways. It was presumably a salutary experience. Holloway is easily Britain's most notorious women's prison. Joyce was later moved to describe it as "a horrid English dungeon [full of] drug addicts, lesbians, prostitutes and murderers." The lesbian contingent, she added, just would *not* leave her alone. It isn't hard to see why. Itemised in no particular order, she had a tip-tilted nose, masses of elaborately lacquered blonde hair (allegedly sculpted to hide a scar on her jaw) and a smile like a segment cut out of a watermelon. Cantilevered breasts and a husky Southern drawl completed the picture. There was obviously a screw loose somewhere, but we all have our peculiarities. At least no one could have accused her of being dull company. Whatever faults she may have possessed, they didn't include being predictable.

An astute media manipulator, Joyce habitually spoke in overheated tabloid journalese. At subsequent remand hearings she made a point of asking for reporting restrictions to be lifted, giving journalists a heaven sent opportunity to regale their readers with tales of bondage and oral sex in the heart of rural Devon. Indignantly denying Kirk's allegations, she accused him of "lies and fabrications," adding unctuously: "He is the one who has to be tied up. I prefer to do things the *normal* way." Her finest hour came at a hearing on December 6, when she was finally allowed to address the court in person, rather than through her defence counsel Stuart Elgood. 1 loved Kirk so much," she famously told the assembled magistrates, "that I would have skied down Mount Everest in the nude with a carnation up my nose." It was a statement destined to go down in tabloid history. *The Sun*'s editorial staff were so delighted that they mocked up a composite photo showing Joyce's head superimposed onto the body of a girl on skis with a carnation protruding from the appropriate orifice (i.e. her nose, toilet brain). "We have to be honest, with apologies to Joyce, [and] confess that only the face is hers," they felt constrained to add in a rare moment of journalistic integrity.

Kirk, for his part, was anxious to disavow any suggestion that he might have enjoyed having sex with Joyce. "I did not want it to happen," he blubbed to the delight of countless newspaper readers; "I was very upset."

Kirk was particularly upset that Joyce had done irreparable damage to his 'garments' in her unseemly haste to undress him. "They are so sacred to me that any time they are desecrated in any way, the proper method to dispose of them is to burn them," he related soberly. 'Garments', for the benefit of the uninitiated, are an essential part of every self-respecting Mormon's wardrobe. Elaborate suits of underclothes resembling an old fashioned gent's bathing costume, they are embroidered with Masonic symbols intended to protect the wearer against sin and temptation. (At one time they were even credited with the power to deflect bullets.) Unfortunately for Kirk, no amount of fancy embroidery was enough to cool Joyce's ardour. There was no stopping her once she got going. He was lucky to have escaped with nothing more serious than sore wedding tackle. It could have been a lot worse, that's for sure.

Considerable hilarity was occasioned by Kirk's testimony. It had the assembled pressmen in stitches. Joyce herself was quick to point out some of the more obvious logical objections to his version of events. "A woman raping a man?" she said incredulously. "Him eighteen stone and me eight stone? Come on, who's kidding whom?" Then, warming to her theme, "If he was so unwilling, then why was he lying there grinning like a

Madam Ma

NUN ON THE RUN: The infamous LA hooker Joyce McKinney dressed in a habit in South Carolina and, left, in more typical attire

Southern states and I eventually filed my report back to Fleet Street. The photographer had sent his pictures.

The Daily Express took her story t face value and ran the story, with 1cKinney dressed ... n the front ... ound J...

that Joyce was, in truth, a distur^k hooker from Los Angeles who h peculiar obsession for bond Mormo... priests.

A ... ed he... d...

Manacled Mormon Nympho Nuns

monkey?" she wanted to know. 'Why was he moving his hips with me?"

Joyce had a natural flair for the dramatic and obviously enjoyed giving evidence. Her statement was full of intimate personal details. "Kirk was raised by a very dominant mother," she explained to the bemused magistrates. "He has a lot of guilt about sex because his mother has over protected him all his life. When we make love he has to have the lights out and wash up afterwards. He truly believes sex is dirty. Kirk has to be tied up to have an orgasm. I cooperated because I loved him and wanted to help him. Sexual bondage turns him on because he doesn't have to feel guilty. The thought of being powerless before a woman seems to excite him."

Joyce instantly became a national heroine. Her exploits endeared her to the public at large. There can't have been many men who didn't feel a pang of envy for Kirk. It was the stuff of fantasy. The general consensus was perhaps best summed up by Detective Chief Inspector Bill Hucklesby, the officer in charge of the initial investigation, who clearly found the entire case highly amusing. "I'll tell you what," he remarked wistfully to reporters shortly after Joyce had been taken into custody, "I've never been lucky enough to have anything like that happen to me."

Released on bail after three months in Holloway, Joyce was immediately besieged by pressmen eager to secure the rights to her story. Nothing material to the case could be published until after the trial, but every tabloid editor worth his salt was determined to get her signature on an exclusive contract. Competition was fierce, but the bidding war ended abruptly when she and Keith May fled to Ireland in the unlikely guise of deaf mutes, assuring all and sundry (by means of scribbled notes) that they were en route to perform with a mime troupe in Canada. *Daily Express* columnist Peter Tory later tracked them to the Hilton Hotel in Atlanta, GA, where they were masquerading as nuns* in a characteristically bizarre bid to avoid detection. Tory's visit was brief but eventful. At one point he was obliged to seize Joyce by the ankles to prevent her leaping from an eighth floor balcony in a fit of pique. "She had bitten her father after he arrived," he later wrote, "and was now howling like a vampire. I don't think I have ever been so frightened in my life. Come dawn, having leapt at the curtains and brought them down around her, Miss McKinney sprinted past the front desk of the hotel in her nightie and across a highway of thundering pantechnicons…"

Joyce's vanishing act came as a bitter blow to journalists, but it was by no means the end of the story. *Daily Mirror* photographer Kent Gavin, who fortuitously happened to be working in America at the time, began digging into her past and discovered that she had once supplemented her income by posing for top-shelf magazines with self-explanatory titles like *Knotty*, *Hog-Tie* and *Bound to Please*. He also tracked down a call girl known only as Laura who revealed that she and Joyce had previously worked together on the Los Angeles vice circuit, Laura, "a deeply relaxed woman of about twenty five," evidently had a colourful turn of phrase. "I was the one who got laid," she is quoted as saying in Anthony Delano's unashamedly self-serving paperback potboiler *Joyce McKinney and the Manacled Mormon*. "Joyce would, you know, orally copulate. And she was into heavy bondage. She would pull out her chains and stuff and tie the guy up… The lady was really into sexual things, you know. She would buy the raunchiest magazines, and she used to dig watching me. When I would be having a client, her eyes would be right down there…"

Gavin's revelations took everyone by surprise — not least Joyce herself. Published under the headline 'The Real McKinney', they demolished her carefully constructed façade of respectability and left her out on the proverbial limb. No longer able to claim the moral high ground, she faded from view like the Cheshire Cat, leaving behind only the memory of her expansive, all embracing smile, It was an appropriately bizarre conclusion to one of the strangest sagas in British tabloid history.

Seven years later, in June 1984, Kirk Anderson's worst nightmare returned to haunt him. *'Sex-in-Chains Joyce Is At It Again'* the headlines screamed. The accompanying story had a comforting air of familiarity. Joyce, along with the inevitable male accomplice, had been spotted lurking outside Kirk's office in Salt Lake City and arrested on suspicion of plotting a fresh kidnap attempt. It was almost like old times. Kirk, who had left his missionary days behind him and gone to work for an airline company in Utah, was understandably afraid that history might be about to repeat itself. He needn't have worried. The story soon fizzled out. Charged with disturbing the peace and giving false information to the police, Joyce entered a typically dotty plea of *"extremely not guilty"* and loudly protested her innocence to anyone prepared to listen. "She only wanted to see him for old times' sake," her lawyer explained implausibly. "She is writing a screenplay about her experiences and wanted to find out how the story ended." Magistrates eventually dismissed the case and Kirk was finally allowed to slip into the obscurity he so richly deserved.

Later still, in April 1994, Joyce was herself the victim of an alleged abduction. Snatched from her home by armed men and bundled into a waiting car, she managed to escape but was beaten up so badly that she ended up confined to a wheelchair. "I will be handicapped for the rest of my life," she claimed at the time. "We are talking serious felonies here. We are talking abduction, assault, violation of human rights."

Journalist Walter Ellis, who interviewed her shortly afterwards, evidently felt that something didn't quite ring true. "Why should, as she claims, a network of organisations and individuals have gone to such lengths to discredit and harm her?" he asked. "Because I am a myth," she told him with a kind of perverse pride. I am Joyce McKinney, who raped the Mormon. I am not a real person. It's a feather in their cap if they can destroy me."

Somehow, without wishing to seem uncharitable, it's difficult to take Joyce's claims entirely seriously. Always an inveterate attention seeker, she frequently lied and exaggerated when dealing with officialdom, distorting or selectively rewriting events to cast herself in the role of blameless victim. Her court testimony and press statements were so highly embroidered that it's impossible to be certain whether many alleged incidents actually took place. She may indeed have been subjected to some kind of assault, but there's no way of knowing what really happened. Public interest in the case has evaporated and Joyce herself has gone to earth, making it unlikely that the real truth will ever emerge.

They don't make 'em like Joyce McKinney any more. She was a real one off. *Mirror* journalist

Anthony Delano's *Joyce McKinney and the Manacled Mormon* is probably the nearest we'll ever get to a definitive biography. Published by Mirror Books in 1978 and now quite rare, it chronicles her fifteen minutes of fame in lurid detail and contains what a cover blurb describes as '16 pages of Sensational Pictures'. Apropos of nothing, it's fortunately neglects to reprint any of them. Rarely can an author have raised his readers' hopes only to dash them so cruelly. The last word is perhaps best left to the economically named Laura, who retained fond memories of working with Joyce. "The girl did not even use drugs," she told Kent Gavin (presumably in suitably awed tones), recall-

interesting to observe that in nude photos Joyce's areolae appear permanently engorged — two swollen conical mounds adorning breasts enhanced, according to ungallant hack Delano (boo-hiss!), by the plastic surgeon's art. Delano also refers tantalisingly to the existence of photos depicting Joyce in a variety of gynaecological poses, but un-

ing her old partner's erratic behaviour and weird flights of fantasy. "She was *naturally* insane. One of the wonders of nature."

*I'm charitably assuming that May shaved off his moustache to pose as a nun, but given the case's surreal overtones and general air of absurdity, it's by no means certain. ■

Nympho Nuns

CHURCH ORGAN MUSIC. LOBBY OF HOTEL WITH *manager (?) behind a desk. The title 'Nympho Nuns' appears (optically imposed on the actual film as opposed to it appearing on a plain white background — as is usually the case with seventies porn loops). Two nuns walk into the frame, dressed in habits and wearing large wooden crucifixes around their necks. Both appear to be in their early to mid twenties, and are attractive.*

MANAGER	Good evening.
NUNS	Good evening.
MANAGER	Can I help you?
NUN #1	A double-room please. Is a double okay with you?
NUN #2	Sure, Sister Agnes.*
MANAGER	[*holding up a key*] Harry!

A Bellboy walks into shot.

BELLBOY	Yeah. Coming.
MANAGER	Room 105.
BELLBOY	[*picking up suitcase*] Okay. Room 105 it is.
MANAGER	Goodnight.
NUNS	[*following BELLBOY*] Goodnight.

There are no exterior shots and, other than the final exchange, no indication of the time of day. It would appear that the two nuns have turned up without a reservation in the middle of the night.

Cut to corridor.

BELLBOY	[*opening the door to a room*]: Here you are.
NUNS	Thank you.

The nuns enter the room. Shot remains on Bellboy in the corridor.

NUN #1	[*offscreen*] What a nice room.
NUN #2	[*offscreen*] Yes, so clean.

NYMPHO NUNS
circa 1970s
dir: not known
Color Climax, Copenhagen

Transcript of a nun themed porno loop and a brief, pictorial look at nun fuelled fantasy by **David Kerekes**

THIS PAGE News headlines. *Daily Mail*, Saturday, May 24, 1997 (above). Georges Pichard interpretation of Denis Diderot's *La Religieuse* (Creation Art Press, France, no date) (right).

Next page *National News* No 11 (no date). The cover bears no relation to what's inside.

* No attempt has been made to transcribe all the giggles and sexual exasperations in *Nympho Nuns*. One exception is this curiously protracted laugh from the manager when he first sees the nuns on his CCTV monitor.

Cut to interior of the room. Bellboy brings in suitcase.

NUN #1   You can leave the suitcase there. Thank you.

Bellboy leaves.

NUN #2   At last we're alone together, Sister Mary.
NUN #1   At last.

Cut to Manager at his desk flicking through the channels on a Closed Circuit Television set. It shows the interiors of the guest rooms at the hotel (!).

MANAGER   [*on seeing nuns embracing on his CCTV monitor*] Hello!

Cut to nun's room. Nuns are standing, kissing, lifting one an-

other's habits up and bottom feeling. They wear stockings and suspenders but no underwear.

NUN #1   It was a good idea of yours — this hotel.
NUN #2   Let's make good use of it.
NUN #1   I've been looking forward to it for a long time.
NUN #2   Oh, if only I'd known before.

Cut to lobby and Manager watching CCTV.

MANAGER   Cor! God Almighty, lesbian nuns! It's too good to be true!

There are three 'creative' edits in this particular sequence: CCTV as viewed by the Manager; closeup of CCTV screen showing the nuns on the bed; medium-long shot of Manager.

MANAGER   Look at that!

Cut to nun's room. Nuns are on the bed performing cunnilingus.

NUN #2   Oh, Sister Mary! Put your tongue there!

Cut to image on CCTV screen.

NUN #2   Wonderful!
MANAGER   Ha ha ha ha ha ha!*

Dissolve to nun's room. (Only such optical effect in the whole film.) A dildo is brought into play.

NUN #2   This is a heavenly feeling!

Cut to lobby.

MANAGER   A-ha! So that's what they do at the con-vent! [Seems unable to pronounce 'convent' as one word]

Telephone rings.

MANAGER   Uh. Yes. Can I help you, madam?

Manager is surprised to discover that it is one of the nuns on the end of the line, despite the fact that he must have seen them reaching for the phone on his CCTV.

NUN #1   Could we have some cold drinks?

"Suffering is beautiful. I want to be beautiful"

—Agnes, *Agnes of God*

The image of nuns in a sexual context has been a popular one for many years, in literature, art, cinema and of course pornography. In 1728 the English bookseller and publisher Edmund Curll was convicted and fined for publishing an obscene book, *The Nun in her Smock*. The French encyclopaedist, philosopher and critic Denis Diderot wrote his 'scandalous' novel *La Religieuse* [*The Nun*] in 1760, which centred upon the plight of a girl kept against her will in a convent and forced to endure its sexually frustrated sisters. Diderot's novel was beloved of the Marquis de Sade, surrealists and other writers

Continued on p.37

MANAGER   Certainly. In a second.

Corridor. Manager walks into shot with a drinks tray and knocks on door.

NUNS   [*offscreen*] Come in.
MANAGER   Your drinks, Sister. I'll put them near the bed, okay?

Manager walks round to the nuns. First nun is standing, second is sitting on the edge of the bed. Both are still fully clothed.

MANAGER   [*to nun on bed*] Is that really necessary, Sister? I don't think so.
NUN #2   I don't know what he's talking about. Do you, Mary?
NUN #1   [*in a really poor Irish accent*] I really don't. [*The Irish accent is not utilised prior to or after this scene*]
MANAGER   [*lifting nun's habit*] Then what have you got tight up between your legs? [*Removes dildo from under habit*] You don't need that sort of a thing. [*Waving dildo*] What you need is a real prick!
NUN #1   Well, actually, it's better than nothing.
MANAGER   No wonder they sell bananas to the con-vent.

Manager unzips his fly and draws out his penis and testicles.

The nun in mainstream comics reinvented as a sexy gun tottin' battle heroine fighting on the side of law and order. Below are three variations on essentially the same theme courtesy of different authors and publishing houses. L–R *Bloody Mary: Lady Liberty 1* by Garth Ennis and Carlos Ezquerra (DC Comics 1997), *The Crimson Nun 1* by Brian Farrens and Bobby Diaz (Antartic Press, 1997) and *Sister Armageddon 1* by Mark S Zimmerman and Christopher Auman (Draculina, 1995).

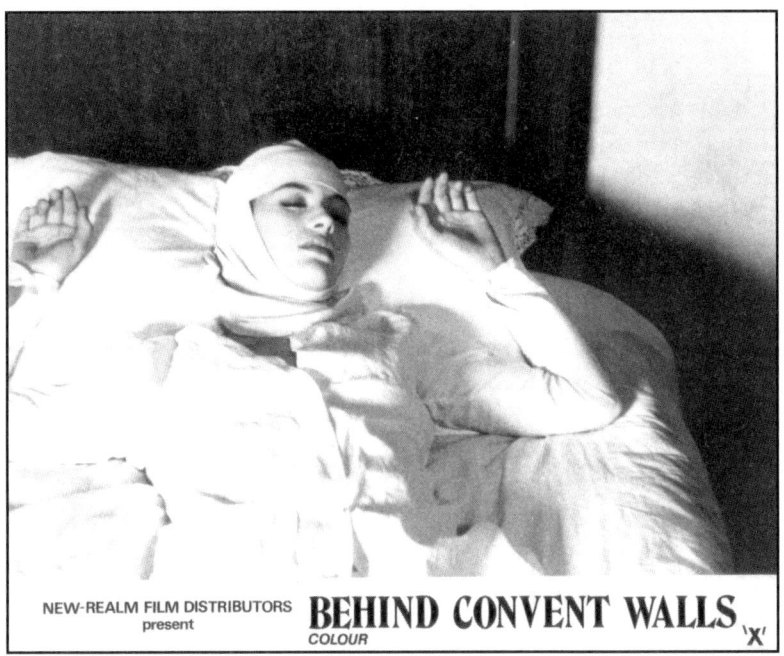

CZECH REPUBLIC | FINLAND | **UK** | NETHERLANDS | JAPAN | USA | FRANCE | SPAIN | UNDERGROUND | REVIEWS

NEW-REALM FILM DISTRIBUTORS present **BEHIND CONVENT WALLS** 'X' COLOUR

NUN #1	[*excited*] Sister Agnes! Come on!
MANAGER	You can do anything you like with it.
NUN #2	Do you think I could suck it?
MANAGER	Well, I'm a man of my word, Sister — so go ahead.

Silent since the opening scenes, church organ music now returns.

NUN #1	Take it all in.
MANAGER	Look at her lapping it up! Sister, join in! there's enough for both of you!

Other nun moves in to kiss Manager. Cut to the nuns performing fellatio on the Manager on the bed. Still dressed in complete habits, but with bottoms exposed.

MANAGER	Don't be shy. Work on the balls — it'll do you good.

Cut to lobby. Telephone rings. A 'creative' edit emphasises the 'drama' of the ringing telephone by cutting in for a close-up of the object. Bellboy goes to answer it.

BELLBOY	Hello? [*suddenly noticing the scene on the CCTV*] Cor! Oh, I didn't mean you, sir! Call it seven. Okay, I've noted that.

and artists who also sought to attack and ridicule religion, often by sexualising it. The Belgium-born artist Félicien Rops (1833–98), created a number of works against the Church, including one drawing entitled *Sainte Thérèse*, which depicts a young nun masturbating. Less of a political bent can be found in the movies of Euro directors like Jess Franco, Joe d'Amato and Walerian Borowczyk. Works such as *Love Letters of a Portugese Nun* (1976), *Images in a Convent* (1979) and *Behind Convent Walls* (1977) may muster some arthouse pretension but fall firmly into the realm of sexploitation and porno. Curiously, there are also a number of Japanese lensed films set within sexy Catholic convent walls. So popular a subgenre are sleazy movies depicting the cloistered life that they have their own tag: nunsploitation.

Continued on p.39

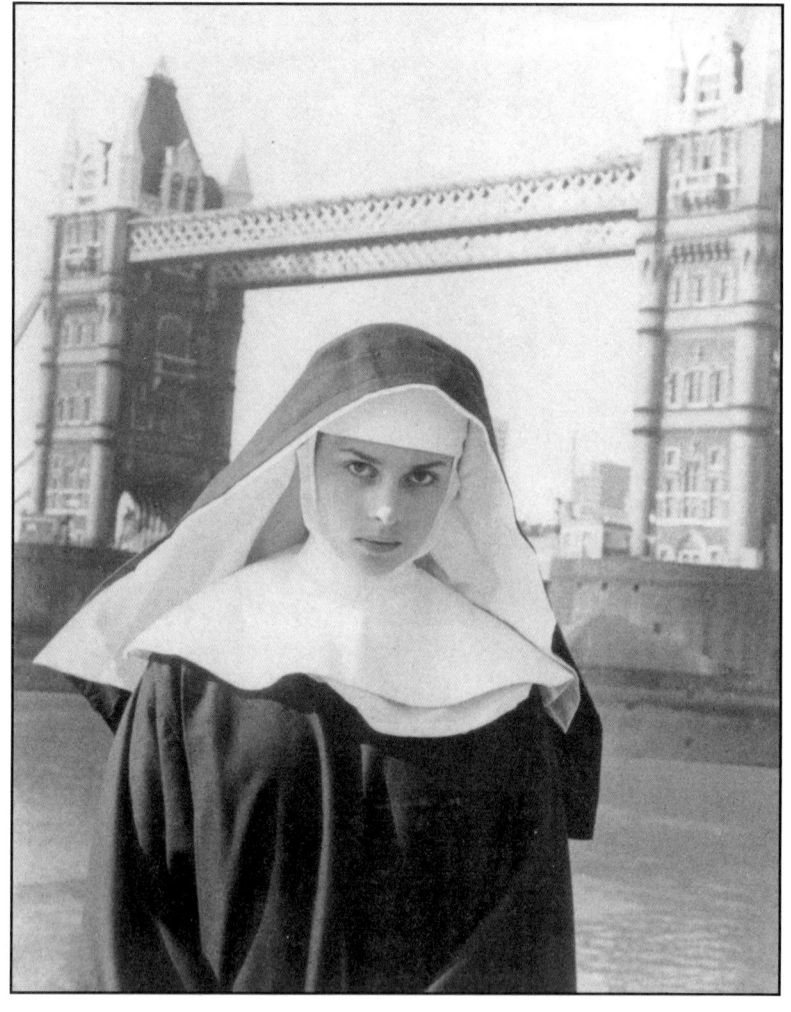

THIS PAGE Natasja Kinski publicity shots for Hammer's flawed but under-rated final film, *To The Devil A Daughter*.
NEXT PAGE Still from *Kane* magazine's *Naughty Habits*.

**Manacled
Mormon
Nympho
Nuns**

Bellboy puts phone down and goes up to the nun's room. He walks in, pulls his penis out and proceeds to sink it into the first nun's vagina. Until now, no one has even bothered to acknowledge another presence in the room.

NUN #1   *[reacting to the penis inside her]*: Hello! How I dreamt about this at the convent. Give me more!

NUN #2   Oh, Sister Mary, we must be the chosen ones to receive such a blessing!

Cut to nuns nude now, except for their headgear, large crucifixes around their necks and stockings and suspenders. Both are straddling the men, who are naked except for their socks.

NUN #1 If I'd learned about this before, I'd never have joined the convent.
NUN #2 Well, they've seen the last of us there!

Cut to different sexual positions. Music changes to a more uptempo 'contemporary' beat.

NUN #1 It's so good! [...] I could ever want it to stop.
NUN #2 Good, eh?

Cut to what looks like the vinegar stroke approaching for the Bellboy. Crucifixes are banging against naked breasts. Nuns make a concerted effort to keep the crucifixes in clear view.

BELLBOY Can't hold out much longer! I'm gonna shoot all over your tits! [*This he does*]

Film ends.

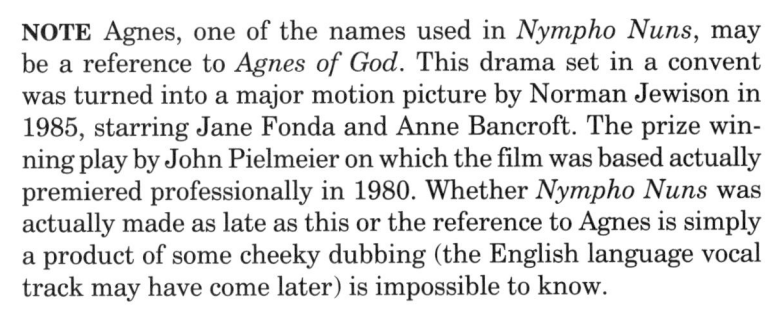

NOTE Agnes, one of the names used in *Nympho Nuns*, may be a reference to *Agnes of God*. This drama set in a convent was turned into a major motion picture by Norman Jewison in 1985, starring Jane Fonda and Anne Bancroft. The prize winning play by John Pielmeier on which the film was based actually premiered professionally in 1980. Whether *Nympho Nuns* was actually made as late as this or the reference to Agnes is simply a product of some cheeky dubbing (the English language vocal track may have come later) is impossible to know.

ONE LAST THING Talking with call girl 'Diana' about men's fantasies and dressing up:

Films and TV series often stimulate weird fantasies in many of the punters, says Diana. "After that series about a nun *Body and Soul*, men came to me asking for a nun's rig-out so I had to go out and buy one. One punter wanted me to stand over him in my nun's dress while he tossed himself off."

Quoted from *Working Girls and their Men: A Candid Investigation of Prostitution in Britain* by Sheron Boyle (pub: Smith Gryphon, London 1994) ∎

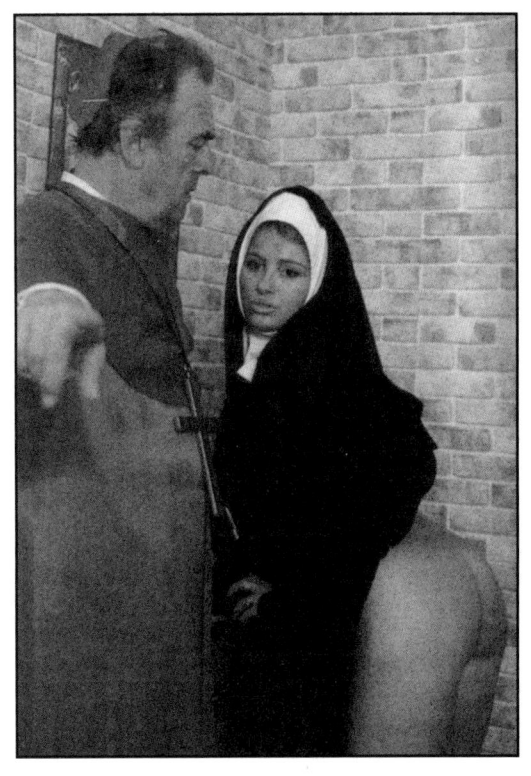

Nympho Nuns isn't the only seventies porn loop to feature a wimple. Some others include *The Horny Monk*, *Merciful Nuns* and Lasse Braun's *Casanova and the Nuns*. The British shot-on-video fetish production *Naughty Habits*, by the people behind Harrison Marks' *Kane* magazine, is a film that crosses nuns and spanking. It features one nun being flogged whilst reciting the Lord's Prayer, a scene that is replicated almost verbatim in the controversial low budget sci fi fantasy, *Original Sins* — though the makers of the latter state that they are ignorant of any such scene independent of their own, which, if true — and likely it is — undoubtedly points to some deep rooted psychological yearning inherent in all of us… ∎

Advertisements

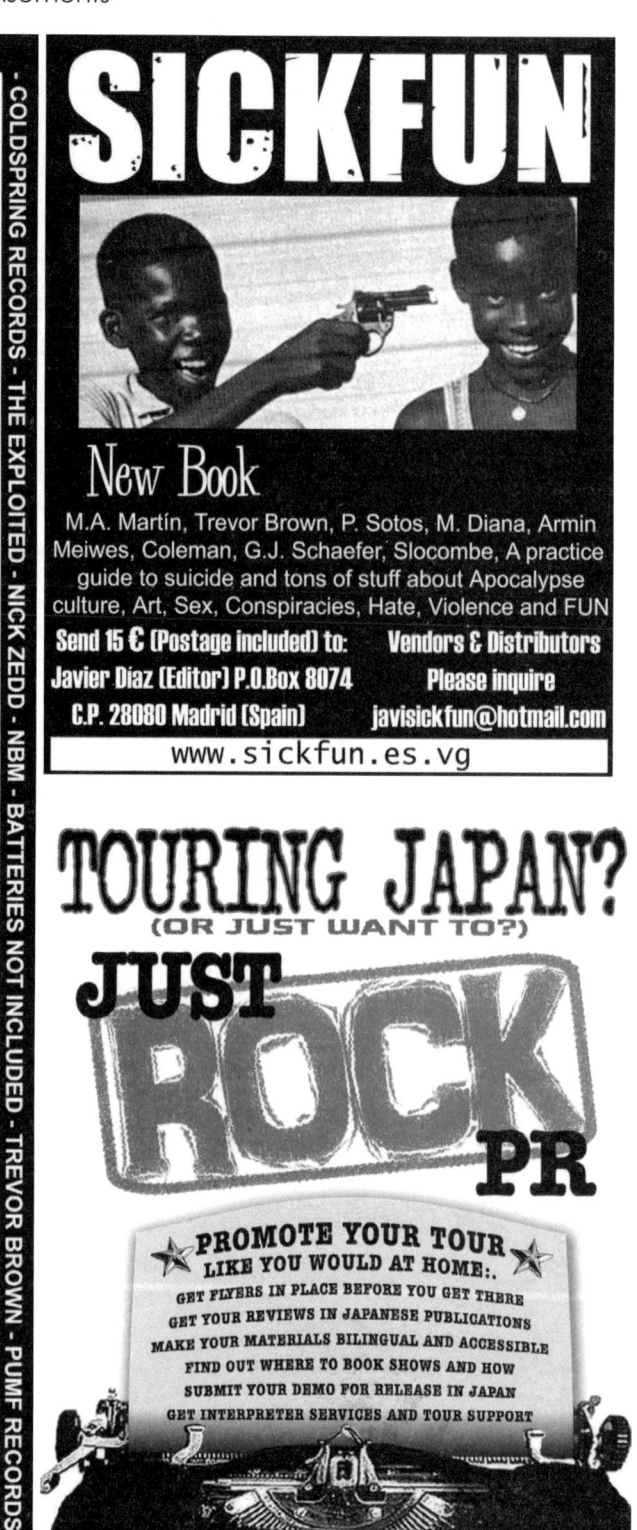

"I have been barred from them all"

Photo: Rick Caveney

POETRY IS A VIBRANT, emotional and valid form of literature that is easily, all too often overlooked. Not really recognised as a form of entertainment down your local pub, yet many people over the years have been attending performance poetry events all over the world where they could have a pint, listen to some varied poetic styles and tune into a different kind of night out.

These poetry nights can be found in most cities and it seems smaller towns too are catching on to the act. For those who have yet to experience one, they usually consist of a compere poet, maybe a couple of guest spots by other more experienced poets and then the icing on the cake, public open spots. These can range from the tragic to the hilarious, the political to the ridiculous. One thing is for sure, anything can happen.

Chloe Poems, the Liverpudlian born and self proclaimed socialist transvestite has mastered her craft to an art form. With two successful books under her gingham corset, *Universal Rent Boy* and *Adult Entertainment*, Chloe can have you in tears of laughter one minute and silent and resolute the next. Adopting a hard, no nonsense stance on subjects such as the Royal Family and anus probing, Chloe takes us on a magical cabaret ride to the burlesque. It's Karl Marx in a dress at a transvestite TUC conference.

I met up with Jerry — Chloe's alter ego — who was happy to tell me a bit more about it.

Poetry doesn't have to be about flowers or war or being gay — as Will Youds found out talking to socialist transvestite Chloe Poems.

HEADPRESS So how did Chloe Poems begin?
CHLOE POEMS   When I was sixteen I joined a local theatre. It's a place where I was really born as it was a place where there was no matter of class or anything. It all happened in May 1979, I was really born in 1962 but my life began in May '79. I was a geek and effeminate child who did not fit in to where I was brought up in Liverpool. I was a misfit suddenly in a room full of misfits and that was just incredible. Whatever made me do what I do now started then. Chloe Poems came about when I was in my twenties and I became part of a comedy duo called The Beige Experience, which was a cabaret act. That came to a natural end, we didn't split or anything, we just stopped doing it.

What happened next?
In 1983 I was asked if I would do a ten minute cabaret slot. I thought, 'oh my God I don't know what to do,' so I decided I would do those poems I used to do as Chloe years ago. And they brought the house down! I realised there was something in this. So I suppose this triggered off the whole birth of the character, even though I had started it somewhere else before, it really started then. I then began doing full length shows and touring them and became part of the London gay cabaret circuit around 1993 which was interesting, but limiting and seemed to be going nowhere. I was doing very well. I would tour with other gay acts and do festivals. To me it was very unsatisfying as all I had to do was say 'poo' and it brought the house down or make some reference to being gay and everyone loved you for it. It was preaching to the converted. I quickly got bored of that and decided to make a genuine attempt at entering the world of poetry. Even though I was still performing comedy poems at the time I thought, 'No, I'm going to take this further. I am to take this character of Chloe from this strange Gingham clad weird thing into the proper literary world.' I wondered if I would be able to do that?

So, I changed the style of the poetry, became much more left wing. Because I am a socialist and if I am a socialist, then I *really* have to do it. So in about 1995 I began to take the whole poetry thing seriously and started to look at what it actually means to be a performance poet and the things you can say. So the material became much more lyrical and literary as opposed to 'this is a poem about taking it up the shitter' which is what it used to be, and really still is (laughs).

This was to you a natural progression to leave the gay cabaret circuit and begin something new.
Yes. I was totally disillusioned with the gay scene at the time. I knew that audience couldn't sustain me and take me where I wanted to go.

Since those days, ten years have passed. Do you still feel the same about playing to gay audiences?
I have to say it has gotten worse. I can actually say that the gay scene and press haven't helped me at all. In the early days when I was doing funny poems about being gay I got a lot of press as it was unthreatening and not harming anyone. Not that I do go to deliberately harm, but only to tell the truth. Then I did a poem called The Queen Sucks Nazi Cock at a mardi gras gay festival and they haven't invited me back since. That year I did gay pride festivals and now I have been barred from them all.

Did anyone from the festivals confront you?
People who work for these festivals have said to me we can't touch you because you might do something really outrageous. I argued that the gay scene was based on a radical and free thinking politic, and was shocked to be told that I was not allowed to be free thinking and political. That was the conversation.

This was a first experience of censorship for you?
Yes, ironically the gay scene is my first ever experience of being so blatantly censored, of course I have had people say 'oh you can't say this, or do that' and I have though ok, that's fine. I was to be completely shut out of the gay strata, which has what has happened. At the time I had done a brilliant set of introducing acts I have no interest in and trying to make it buoyant and gorgeous. So, when it came for me to do my piece I thought I'd go for it with The Queen Sucks Nazi Cock. I had done three hours on that stage and afterwards there was a party thrown by the organisers who told me I couldn't come in.

You chose that poem deliberately then?
Oh yes. It was one of my proudest moments. The audience did like it, I remember them roaring and it was the organisers who seem to have a problem with it. I left Mardi Gras with a feeling that it was one of the most political poems of its generation and it was a an effeminate homosexual who did that, not some nasty disco diva who doesn't give a fuck about anything and is only there to sell records. It was a radical homosexual telling everyone the Queen is a fucking Nazi, come on and wake up!

It was the first time I felt there was forces working against me. I knew as an artist there were things I couldn't do, such as the five o'clock poetry recital at the Women's Institute. I knew that. So I guess in a sense one censors one's self.

Have you every experienced anything else similar?
I was doing a street festival, performing The Queen Sucks Nazi Cock. I was told that the police were after me for it. I was just about to finish the poem when I noticed the police coming towards me and I told the audience 'excuse me everyone, the fuzz are after me' and I ran to a café toilet and got changed in less than a minute then went back on to the street where the police were questioning people around, asking them if they have seen me! I just walked past, slowly as though nothing had happened. I found out they had even questioned the organisers about me.

You do like to confront taboo in your poetry: sex... religion... do you also write about death?
Death is the ultimate censorship isn't it? When you can no longer speak anymore. I am from a family of ten where six of my immediate are dead. If you look in my work there are all kinds of bleak references, which are subtle. I actually like death; I'm terrified of it like every normal human is. I do like what it does, where it takes you, how it makes you think and feel. When my best friend died of AIDS my initial feeling was 'oh my God, I loved you!' and I have never ever been able to feel love in this intensive way. It was over-whelming. I know I love people and I know I am loved, but I have never been given it as a whole gift in my life. I remember feeling elated and people were around me crying and I felt overjoyed. I had to leave the room pretending to be upset, but underneath I was overjoyed. Of course I grieved.

As a child I became used to death. My brothers died in quick succession. One of my first memories was being in a massive black limousine with a street full of people looking at me. It was like being the President. I'm looking out and everybody waving at me. I thought it was amazing. I do have a healthy respect for death. I like the idea of when I die of being burnt at sea with all my friends blowing horns. ∎

I Don't Have A Cunt
by Chloe Poems

I don't have a cunt
nor too much up front
why even a guide dog can
tell you I'm a man.

I don't have a fanny
I'm like a childless nanny
just take a little poke
it'll prove that I'm a bloke.

I was born with a cock
and as my balls ran amok
I realised with a shock
I had to wear this gingham
frock.

Am I a contradiction?
Do I deserve conscription?
Why must they all frown
upon me and my gingham
gown?

Minority in minority
no-one's priority
I hope against hope
and I pray to the pope
that Prince Edward might
be a transvestite.

I don't have a beaver
for I'm a firm believer
in taking things as they come
right up my bum.

You may think me base
you might think me tacky
you could be forgiven for thinking that I'm quite wacky but
fully dressed or in the nude I'm
just a queer with attitude.

Taken from Chloe's first book *Universal Rentboy*. Reproduced with kind permission.

Amsterdamned

THE CALL CAME UNEXPECTEDLY, OUT OF THE BLUE AS they say. Kev, my old mate back in Leeds, once considered an extreme example of terminal bachelorhood, was getting married and a 'stag weekend' was to be arranged — was I interested in partaking?

Location: Amsterdam, notorious pleasure zone of Northern Europe and the source of many a blistering lesion on a husband-to-be's cock. This event held much promise for amusement, potential enlightenment and total psychic annihilation.

How could I resist? Even if it involved an arse quaking amount of travel for me to get there, it had to be done. The journey to Leeds where it would all start was four hours of buttock pummelling tedium courtesy of Virgin Trains, giving me ample time to ponder what might be in store for our witless band of fools. A piss up in Leeds city centre of a night is one thing but risking the same on mainland Europe was a different prospect altogether, even more so in a place so steeped in debauched mythology as that ancient shipping port, that gruesomely stained receptacle for humanity's wretched lusts and residues. As the train ground its way through the industrial hinterlands of my foul home city I said a silent prayer for my own safe passage through the fevered hours that lay ahead.

The Band of Brothers was assembled at Kev's house:

Kev   Hairy heavy metal bastard whose imminent wedding in Gatlingburg USA was the reason for this adventure.
Andy   Formerly hairy heavy metal bastard, adding substantially to the 'Big Lad' quotient.
Big Daz As the name suggests, not a midget. His dabblings with Goth had triggered an unfortunate and unplanned resemblance to Ozzy Osbourne.
Seb   Son of York and lager warrior supreme.
Dave   A cultured aesthete. If this were a war film his character would be played by David Niven, only not so camp.
Russ   Only here for the beer.
Nigel   (aka Nidge) Russ' younger brother and a seasoned veteran of Amsterdam's darker & narrower alleyways.

And, of course, yours truly, acting in a UN Advisory capacity.

Yes, a right shower of bastards, basically. A drastic redefinition of the term 'motley crew', a pirate ship full of bravado, naivete and

The setting is Amsterdam, notorious pleasure zone of Northern Europe. Rik Rawling is on a stag do.

good old fashioned stupidity sailing under the flag of the White Rose.

The collective mood was high as the minibus hauled our sorry asses across the Pennines and onto the turf of the auld enemy. Predictions were made, bets were laid down and before even a drop of beer had been consumed we were all swearing like troopers. Like Olympic athletes warming up beside the track, we were pumping our vocabularies full of profanity in preparation for the big event — our chance to shine and represent our nation (Yorkshire) on foreign soil.

Amazingly, as soon as we crossed the border into Lancashire the skies darkened and fist sized raindrops pounded the bus. It's as though even the elements were against us as we brave Argonauts headed out on our quest (for dodgy Europorn, smelly fingers and a dose of the squits), as the Gods saw fit to use us as mere pawns in their eternal chess game.

Liverpool Airport (sorry, John Lennon Airport — incorporating the Yoko Ono Toilet Facilities) cowered under black clouds as we sat in Burger King devouring one of the first of many unwholesome and unsatisfying meals that we would endure in the next twenty four hours. Big Daz had bought *Viz*, a good sign and a valuable totem against the evils that awaited us. The airport was full of rowdy Scousers and Barnsley meat heads, beered up and jetting off to Dublin, Alicante and, inevitably, Amsterdam. The plane was only half full so we spread out. We were all sat with our legs splayed as wide as is possible, falsely assuming our balls needed that kind of room to swing. We clocked for the only unattached females on the plane, dismissed the munters, and focussed our best stalker's gazes on every curve, every flowing tress. The strumpets kept getting out of their seats, reaching high into the overhead luggage bins to collect totally superfluous bits of shit, offering a flash of t-shirt pulled taut against what Kev refers to as "teeny brists." And if they weren't stood up they were bending over, thong straps peeking over waistbands, jeans pulling tight against pie padded buttocks. It was a case of too much, too soon and already the squad was getting excited. Grown men were tugging at their crotches, opening up room for sudden tumescence.

Amsterdamned

Speech patterns became more guttural, fur started to grow and the air suddenly smelt of blood and barnyards. We couldn't be descending into madness this early could we?

Flying over the coast of Holland the clouds parted and blazing sunshine hit a land as flat as a fart. And not one fucking windmill in sight. Big Daz pointed out some 'dykes' but in our advanced state of arousal it took a while before we realised that he was not somehow possessed of Peregrine Falcon like vision and hadn't managed to spot a couple of Sapphic beauties fisting in a cornfield.

BANG! The pilot made a shit landing. Spines were fused and sphincters twitched like poisoned mice as our winged sardine can bounced along the runway like Zebedee out of Magic Roundabout. Back on solid ground we encountered our first language barrier. The Dutch folk may understand English, or at least the variant spoken by Hugh Grant and Jeremy Paxman, but they do not understand Yorkshire. This is how I ended up with a ticket for Rotterdam. I distinctly said "Amsterdam" but Clogboy clearly had other ideas. I pointed out his mistake and he rolled his eyes and gave us shit. I was tempted to remind him who had won the war and liberated his Tulip munching ass but in the spirit of European partnership I held back.

Impressed as we were by the ruthlessly efficient public transport we couldn't help but notice again that Holland is flat. Very flat. Fucking flat. I pondered what kind of psycho-geographic effect this must have on the population but it was a starter for ten wasted on men who just wanted to bum prozzies and drink lager until they fell into the canal.

The train dumped us at Centraal Station out of which we stumbled into bright hazy sunshine. Kev had booked us into a hotel in the heart of the notorious Red Light District and his keen nose for such things gets us to our room. Eight men, two rooms, one of which was only a double. The two brothers got the double room which meant six sweaty arsed oiks were going to be sharing a homosexually tight space. We bagged our bunks. I got the lower one nearest the sink, which meant I could end up with an early morning face full of piss if some lager bolloxed fucker tried pissing in the sink. Not good.

The TV went on. Russ charged in and instructed us to get Channel 24 on, now! Hmm, it's a Euro game show so what's all the fuss? We flicked on through the channels and, Wha-hey, number 38 offered a taste of things to come — tits. A shapely brunette pouring sloppy bubbles onto her tits, to be precise. Kev was immediately engaged by the spectacle, thrusting his crotch at the screen and grunting "Come on, ya Bitch." This sensitive and articulate epicure was to be married in three weeks time and once again I was forced to doubt the sanity of his betrothed.

The girl on screen was really giving her norks a good wash but with little sign of any actual shagging about to take place we soon got bored. A flash of genius suggested we try another channel. Flick.

The ensuing pre-drunken roar could be heard as far away as Belgium, when the screen was suddenly filled with the gratuitous closeup of an enormous Eurocock pistoning away inside a gasping blonde's gash. This is more like it. We laughed like fools and congratulated our amazing talent for finding porn on a TV in a Dutch flophouse. The bonhomie cancelled out the more negative aspects of our surroundings — the crusty deposits in the sink, the suicidally steep stairs that Ranulph Fiennes himself would balk at (especially at 4am when he's off his tits on Amstel and busting for a shit) and the angry thunderhead of blowflies that hovered like an insectoid mothership outside the communal toilet, ready to descend on the next faecal deposit. Before the vibes could get anymore fevered and hysterical we headed out into the heat of the afternoon and off down the throbbing streets of the Red Light District. This was it, we were going in.

How to describe it if you've never seen it? Basically it's York, on acid, with its tits out. The first streets we went down were an olfactory overload of fried meat and pot smoke. Frazzled hippies slumped in café windows, melting like Dali's clocks after twelve spliffs too many. Then we saw a sex shop. Then we saw another. And another. Next door, and utterly surreally, there was a butchers. Then another sex shop. And then there was another place selling deep fried rat in a bun. The streets were full of bewildered tourists and crusty, unsavoury types and earnest looking college professors on bicycles, flicking at their bells like it was the clit of their 'star pupils'. My first impression was that it was just Too Much: the urban melting pot about to boil over. But as a veteran of the world's major cities — London, New York, Paris, San Francisco, Vancouver — I have to say there was none of the air of menace, no glint of a threat in the bloodshot gargoyle eye of even the most scabby and ruined of urchins. Whilst I remained on guard for the ever present threat of feral gypsy pickpocket kids and AIDS dripping crack heads I relaxed enough to enjoy the spectacle.

The sex shops were incredible. Being a man of the world I'm fairly unshockable but a bright shop front gaily displaying vibrators, anal love beads, gimp masks and even a golden dildo bounding on a string is not something you see even in the heart of Soho. Next door was a 'sex theatre', the entrance to which was framed by a display of one foot square stills, presumably from the films on offer inside. These images were not sly come ons with maybe a hint of breast or thigh to entice the punter in — no, it was sloppy blow jobs, double penetrations, rimming, elbow deep fisting, gooey facial cum shots, piss gargling and nipple clamps. Not my bag, none of it, but I admired their total lack of subtlety. Once again I was forced to see such places on a par with cathedrals. They inspire the same sense of awe in their adherents but are never satisfied with the congregation that comes willingly. Always on the lookout for more lost souls to join the flock, they resort to tactics that draw on man's deepest and most ancient insecurities and longings. The choice between a dead hippie strung up on a tree or a busty brunette in black nylon with a fourteen inch cock up her arse is, as it always was, yours.

We ploughed on, deeper into the Belly of the Beast. Bars opened up onto the streets and pumped out a bewildering mix of shit pop, country & western, gay disco and heavy metal. The sun beat down and the beer looked good so we parked our arses in a 'beer garden' by the canal and ordered. In Leeds it's Tetley's or you're a puff. In Amsterdam it's Amstel or you go thirsty. Fortunately, Amstel is one of the few lagers on Earth that doesn't taste like the diluted contents of the late Queen Mother's colostomy bag so we quaffed heartily and the die was cast for the next twelve hours. Our vantage point provided ample opportunity for girl/freak watching. Alas the ratio was 20/80 in favour of the freaks but these specimens were so fucking strange that we didn't mind. It was like being on the set of a David Cronenberg film and I've never seen so many Travis Bickle wannabes in my life, not even in NYC. Army surplus jackets, bandanas, string vests, brothel creepers, skull rings, spider web tattoos and the baked and glazed expressions of people who've stuck their head inside a microwave oven and pressed 'cook'. One dude had only half a jaw. Another had so much metal in his face he looked like a cheese grater. Suddenly a gang of teenage girls walked past — young, firm, ripe and wholesome. Like a bag of cherries glistening with dew and juice. The lads gave a collective growl and Kev summed up our feelings succinctly: "Fuckin' 'Ell!"

This vision (and the beer) put some squad members in a confessional mood. Familiar names, too damning and libellous to repeat here, were evoked as men clearly singed by the flames of experience relived the pain and ecstasy of lessons hard won in the field of coital combat. Despite our knowledge that these incursions were often wrong — deeply, desperately wrong — I got the feeling that given the opportunity again all wisdom and regret would be cast off as quickly as a pair of crusty boxers and, as the theme to Dambusters

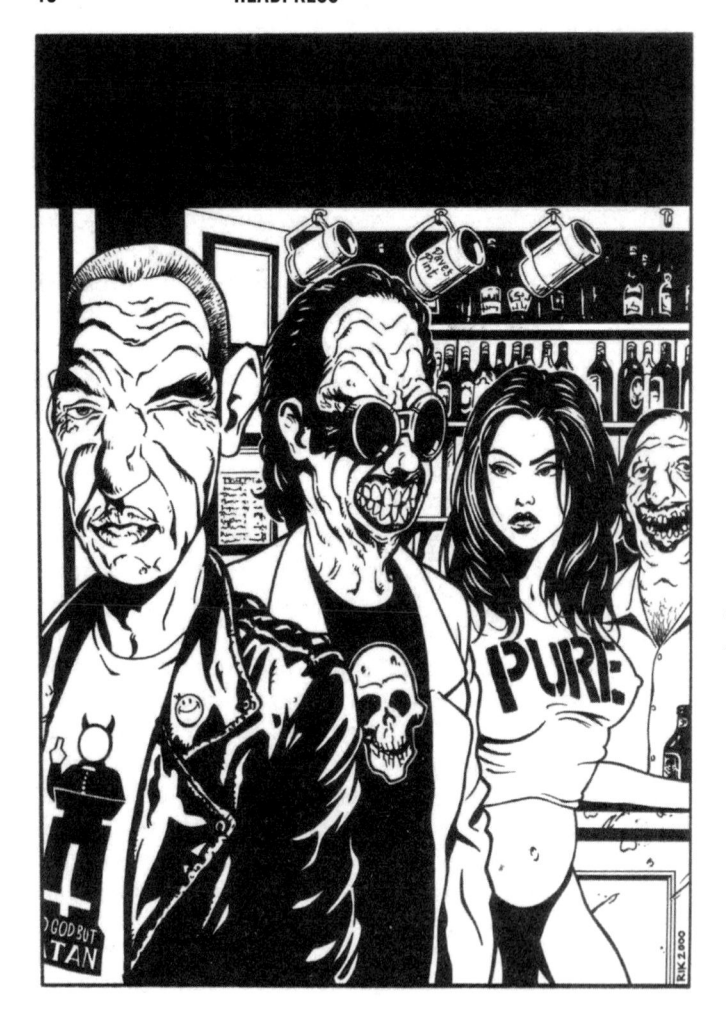

All art this chapter: Rik Rawling

Amster-damned

rang in our ears, we would once again be flying in dangerously low to unleash our Bouncing Bombs. Details of those past missions must remain vague for reasons of national security but after one especially insightful debriefing we had a new distress signal for the night: "oh please, oh please, oh please."

Beered up, louder, cockier. As the sun set we headed off in search of woman flesh. My prediction before we arrived was that the night would degenerate into drunken patheticness on a scale not previously witnessed outside of Oliver Reed's dressing room: eight grown men, giggling and pointing at gap toothed semi naked crack whores from the more blighted arse end of the former Eastern Bloc. How wrong I was.

The streets and alleyways of the RLD are, for the most part, very narrow. As twilight descended we could suddenly see dozens, hundreds of narrow doorways glowing red like a constellation of dark rubies. Drawn like moths to the flame we stumbled over broken cobblestones to come face to face with... my mother, wearing Ann Summers cast offs and a *Planet of the Apes* mask. Urggh. I recoiled in horror, nearly falling into the canal. What kind of sick pervert would want to fulfil his fantasies within the sweaty folds of such a specimen?

Well, maybe this guy right here — a jittery Turk with a pot gut and a white jacket. He poked his head around the door, she named her price (fifty euros, that's about £30 if you're interested, fellas) and he was in like Flynn. She drew her curtains and the rest was mystery, at least... for a while.

Surely they can't all be that ugly, I wondered. Kev had assured me these women were gorgeous, making the girls in *FHM* look like 'The Fat Slags' in comparison. As blandly beautiful and sanitised as those alleged goddesses are, this remained a bold claim for any man to make and based on what I'd seen so far I was about to call him down on his shit. But my faith in the Crown Prince of Beasting should not have been so easily shaken.

Like a heat seeking missile Kev led the pack down a dark, narrow alleyway. Freudian interpretations aside, this was the kind of forbidding ginnel one wouldn't dare to enter in any other city on Earth, not even in Dingly fucking Dell. And yet here we were, laughing heartily, squeezing our girths past seedy Arabs and apocalyptically pissed Mancunians, about to run a veritable Gauntlet of Gash. Both sides of the alley were lined by doorways that glowed with scarlet promise. And the girls behind the glass were all suddenly, unexpectedly beautiful. Gorgeous. Fucking stunnas.

It's worth repeating.

Fucking Stunnas.

So attractive that you literally did a double take. Wank fantasy Playboy models with perfect hair and equally perfect skin barely contained within the skimpiest of lace underthings, the kind you see on sale in Victoria's Secret but, due to the awful gravity of reality, can only ever expect to see hanging off the cottage-cheese-arse of some Razzle faced pig woman. Here the fantasy you always hoped for is made flesh.

Everything is taut and buxom and wanton. High heels, mascara and a temptation older than time. The dick mustard started boiling like lava and a collective case of penile dementia had the lads reeling pinball style down the alleyway, licking windows and whimpering like dogs starved of Winalot for a week and then offered steak fucking Diane.

Kev picked out one especially lovely creature wearing a vivid bikini top and hipster jeans hung so low on her pelvic bone that her artfully trimmed bush peeked just over the splayed zip line. With a dazzling display of dexterity Kev indicated his designs on the girl's person using a series of complex hand gestures that, to the uninitiated, could have been interpreted thus: "I'm hungry. Please can I have a bacon sandwich and a sausage?"

Another of our squad chose a slender Teutonic specimen in black leather, stirring dark fantasies of Nazi torture chambers and black plastic whip handles. He seemed genuinely tempted and before you could say "Ich Komme!" he was in. A round of applause almost went up. While our boy did the business we paused to contemplate the other wares on offer. One doorway had two girls behind it, both wearing virtually fuck all except come on smiles and a keen eye for profit margins. I entertained the notion of splashing 100 euros to have these two at the same time — that most unfeasible of acts, especially for a man of my advancing years.

Only at age fifteen are you fuck hungry enough to physically deal with two girls at once, ball lightning arcing off our genitals every time you see a bit of tit on Channel 4 and a prostate gland like a log flume. Sadly, at that age, coercing two seventeen year old strumpets into bed with you requires a degree of silver tongued sophistication that even James fucking Bond couldn't muster up. And a weekend job at Sadler's Butchers won't get you a bus ticket to Scarborough let alone the dosh required to buy in some whoremeat. This is one of life's towering ironies and it's why man invented the Smith & Wesson and the Tomahawk missile.

You know I'm right.

So, two girls, both possibly young enough to be my daughters, willing to fuck strange men with bad hygiene and cocks like the last sausage on the barbeque that no one wants to eat. As gorgeous as they were I wasn't getting wood. Once again it seemed my rational brain was in full control and I was approaching this from an aesthetic and philosophical perspective.

> Motorhead on the jukebox and assorted seedy types with facial injuries and scars aplenty...

One man who wasn't taking such a stance was the pissed meatball who had just exited stage left from some harlot's fuck dungeon. Clearly disappointed by the quality of service or, more likely, his own performance, he was determined to ensure no other customers suffered his fate. "Don't go in there lads. That's not what you call value for money." This one man *Watchdog* was on a mission but somewhat ruined the value of his case with his final outburst, blurting out "She's a fucking whore!" before stomping off into the night.

No shit.

Our own brave spunk warrior returned from his solo Suicide Mission, all ammunition spent and the target eliminated. As we regrouped in the Excalibur bar he breathlessly recounted his daring raid behind enemy lines. "She makes you strip off, socks an t' lot. She strips off n'all. Gives t'cock a bit of a suck. Then you put a bag on and fuck 'er. Did 'er doggy style. Fantastic. Oh aye."

ciously homosexual options like Smirnoff Ice or sticking with pints of unspecified lager that had the expected effect on speech patterns and logic but began to taste like they'd been scooped straight out of the canal. I've learnt to measure the true quality of these establishments from the condition of the toilets. Excalibur offered none of the hallmarks of the true scuzzbucket — the doors were intact as was the bog seat and there was no spray of diarrhoea against the wall. There were no huge clumsy drawings of spurting cocks or pentagrams amongst the graffiti and the sink even had some soap! There was, however, a sinisterly large amount of space in the cubicle and an inexplicable and wholly alien stench that seemed to be oozing up from out of the toilet bowl which, taken as a whole, conjured images of gang rape. I pissed quick and got the fuck out before some big hairy motherfucker with an eye patch and a penchant for pink virgin man ass locked me in and introduced me to Big Jake, his pet snake.

Thirsts quenched we needed to look for more whores. Inspired by the previous victory other troopers now wanted to chance their arm. We cast our patrols wider in the quest for ever more exotic flavours. This inevitably brought us to what became lovingly referred to as 'The U Bend', a semi-circular street of dingy doorways that harboured the darkest of erotic delights. It seemed this entire crescent was designed to cater for the man who likes his ladies big and black. One after another the African Queens spread their thighs like the banks of the Congo river itself, ushering the transfixed onlooker onwards into the true Heart of Darkness. Alas, we were all repelled by such blatant voodoo tactics and made faces like we'd been told the pie we had just ate was full of mashed up spiders. Unlike the superior specimens down the Street of Dreams these mamas wouldn't

The Excalibur bar conformed to the biker bar aesthetic as defined by a million straight-to-video shit films. Skulls, Harley D gas tank with airbrushed naked lady cavorting with skeleton, gouged wooden walls, sticky floor, Motorhead on the jukebox and assorted seedy types with facial injuries and scars aplenty. They even had a couple of non horrific women in skimpy tops leaning against the bar. Anywhere else they would have been strictly second division skank but here they seemed to shine like diamonds in a pile of shit.

The Excalibur also failed to offer Amstel which left us resorting to suspi-

Amster-damned

take no for an answer. With voices last heard from the brush wielding housemaid in *Tom & Jerry* they called to us like jungle sirens.

"Hey, Sweetie! Come get the pussy."

They tapped on the glass with deadly talons and bared their teeth like angry junkyard dogs, not the classic idea of a come on in anyone's book I don't think.

Pausing to use the amazing street urinals (that help prevent the entire city from smelling of piss and spoif) we then ventured across the canal into previously uncharted territory and it was here that we found Ladyboy Street. That street name wasn't on any map but one walk up to the end and back confirmed our worst fears. Certainly not lacking in prettiness these lads had cute enough East European cheekbones and pert tits but judging by the disturbing bulges in their well padded thongs they had slightly more to offer than the conventional whore. One guy, christened 'Ivan', caught the eye of our Sergeant who was drawn time and again past the basement boudoir where he conducted his strange variant on the term 'giving as good as you get'. The clientele down here were clearly from a unique branch of human evolution — everything from wizened Yoda-esque midgets to leathery faced gyppoes — the kind shipped off to the colonies in Australia back in the day. Troubled by the notion that these weird fuckers might be hot for some she-male shenanigans we hurried back into the comfort zone of heterosexual harlotry and ordered another round.

Details got blurrier the further the night went on but what I am sure of is that one more from the squad took the plunge in to the foxhole, only to emerge triumphant.

The hours seemed to melt into a miasma of beer and whores and pissing in the street.

At one point Sarge did have cause to inform me of a piquant observation he had just made. "Rik, I've decided, you are a very sick man." I asked him to show his research behind this radical statement but he was not forthcoming.

I also recall playing the new game of Dodge the Dealer. The very shiftiest looking of bastards, Amsterdam's equivalent of dodgy scallys with anorak pockets full of bad E, kept trying to tempt us with this enticing prospect. "Cocaine Ecstasy Viagra."

I'm here to tell you that if you need either of those prospects during a night out in Amsterdam then you have got no fucking imagination. Who the fuck wants to be on cocaine whilst reeling through the arteries of that corner of Babylon? Imagine being on E when you've got stunningly beautiful whores licking their lips and dreaming of setting your credit cards on fire? As for the Viagra option… you'd be dead within the hour, bleeding profusely from the crotch down, fucked to death.

By about four AM it was no good. The bars were closing up and as dawn threatened along the horizon we finally had to admit that we were bolloxed. Two ugly bitches offered to come back to our rooms to put on a show for £10. Seemingly a bargain but we were sober enough to make two crucial observations:

(1) They would have emptied our wallets and legged it before discarding a single clout.

(2) They were pig fucking ugly.

Instead we put porn on the TV and tried to kip but were way too wired and Kev's hilarious attempts to sleep in a bed from which two of the legs had been removed had us laughing until tears ran down our dirty faces.

So we went back outside. With the bars closed we had no choice but to ride the Tunnel of Tramps once more. Fuck only knows what rates those lasses are on but even down the U-Bend they were still hard at it. You wouldn't get that sort of commitment down the chicken stuffing factory so maybe there was something in this whoring business? Certainly, with no pimps and no obvious signs of addiction to crack ruin it was a more progressive career curve than that of their scuzz sisters back home in Blighty. And at an average rate of £50 every fifteen minutes the truly stun-

> Our vantage point provided ample opportunity for girl/freak watching. Alas the ratio was 20/80 in favour of the freaks…

had a hangover like a bullet in the head, cured only by paracetamol and Ribena. We tried to find more conventional thrills on the other side of the Amstel River as certain squad members searched for perfume to appease the womenfolk back home but our attempts to rise above the caveman were pathetic and of no consequence. We downed a medicinal Guinness and hopped on the train, but not before narrowly avoiding a participation in some fatuous street theatre where a deranged Benelux cretin juggled chainsaws and balanced a bicycle on his cock. A twat, and we told him so.

We had no choice. We still had unfinished business down in the RLD. Sarge, Kev & myself volunteered for this perilous mission, each with his own agenda.

Sarge wanted to check out the Russian girl with the cock one more time — and buy a glass dildo, I needed to make a closer study of the wares on offer in the sex shops and Kev wanted to buy a load of 'bacca to sell for profit back home. Sadly Ivan was not at his/her/its stall so we went into a shop called something subtle and ambiguous like 'Fuck Hole' or 'Wank Palace'. I don't recall exactly what it was but that detail is irrelevant. What was important, and continually amazing, was the utterly blatant window displays and the sheer wealth and diversity of product on offer. Every, and I mean, every taste has been catered for and if it hasn't been then it means humans aren't doing it and can't do it.

The videos and DVDs were all racked in order of studio and subject matter. The degree of specialisation is bewildering at times. How many she-male videos can a person use in their entire life? Seemingly that amount is INFINITE judging by the ENTIRE WALL of she-male videos for sale in on shop. Butt-Slammin' Bitches. Chicks With Dicks. Sluts With Nuts. Fucking thousands of them. Nature can't be allowing that many genetic fuck ups to

ning girls must be raking it in.

Still, you wouldn't want your wife or your daughter doing it and there's the rub.

We finally staggered into bed at six AM and passed out into various comas, serenaded by the lilting music of mad Koreans arguing in the street below… only to be woken at twenty minute intervals by Sarge's Richter scale snoring.

When we finally roused our exhausted arses from our pits it was almost eleven AM and we were shit out of luck as far as breakfast was concerned. The room was as hot as an opium den and stank like the bowels of the behemoth itself. I

Amster-damned

slip through the net can it? It's either that or it's the same freak performing in every film!

Other categories include: S/M, Pain, Bondage, Anal, Pissing, on and on it goes. Black cocks in white chicks. Dwarves. Grannies. And in one suitably shadowy corner, shelved opposite copies of laughably innocent-by-comparison Fiesta, were the shit videos. Part of the infamous 'Choc' series the titles were a blatant come on to coprophagist dung diddlers everywhere: Shit Lovers, Shit Time and, inevitably, Shit Fuck. The cover 'art' invariably looked like someone had been careless with a bar of Galaxy left out in the sun for too long but on the reverse there was no misinterpretation. Greedy looking fellas wearing shit like warpaint Mel Gibson Braveheart style scooping handfuls of Angel Delight out of Eurobitches arses and chowing down. Hey, who's hungry?

One step even further beyond was the bestiality videos. These just looked foolish and staged but on closer inspection of the cover the images revealed the grainy texture and gutter level production values of the Real Thing. Ugly middle aged German housewives licking the end of horses' cocks. Possibly the same woman cavorting on a bed with a shaggy black canine. And maybe her daughter licking the balls of a fluffy white Malamut husky. Just look at those titles: Hot Dog. Horse Cock. Cum Doggie Cum. All that's missing is a commentary from David Attenborough and this is a BBC ratings winner.

Of course, as you might expect, there's always another level you can sink to. An orange A4 binder sat on a stool offering product too dark for display in a shop even this shameless. Bold black type on the cover told it like it was: RAPE. Uh Oh.

As unaroused as it's possible to feel without actually coming from another planet my prurient sense of 'what the fuck?' was triggered. I opened up and leafed through the clear display pockets filled with video box covers. Lots of women looking scared, men in gimp masks, fake blood, knives from army surplus shops and pained expressions in close up. Arms bound with electrical tape, torn blouses... pretty much what you'd expect but when taken as a whole... the effect is disconcerting. Like going on a picnic with Peter Sutcliffe. One of the covers even featured power tools.

Oh shit. I looked around — the lads had abandoned me, repelled by the extent I'll go to in the name of research.

For light relief we went into Private, part of a chain of upscale Euro sex shops that look like a branch of Next — only this time the cocks & dildos are for sale, not working the till. This was a more relaxed and sophisticated shopping experience but still managed to cater for the rich and varied tastes of European masturbators. Everything was neatly arranged according to deviancy and there was a refreshingly friendly and welcoming air to the place that you just don't get in the more downmarket scud parlours where after a while the walls (of porn) begin to gradually close in around you. As I perused the wares on offer Sarge sized up the dildos. He was looking for a sleek and wholly artistic glass number, pretty much the Ferrari of vaginal stimulators, something no self respecting suburban slutfreak wouldn't want wedged between her sugar walls. Kev, meanwhile, was shocked and horrified by his latest find — a DVD, the title of which made the Ronseal 'Does Exactly What It Says On The Tin' sales pitch sound like a John Donne poem translated by Roky Erikson in comparison. 'Girls Who Fuck Guys In The Ass.'

"I wonder what that's about?" I said.

Kev was unamused. "What's the fucking word? Why would anyone want to do it?"

This radical new perversion had just slammed into his head Killdozer-style and he was having none of it. What did he think all those strap on cocks were on sale for? There aren't that many dykes in the world who secretly crave the thunderstick.

Welcome to the dark side of Planet Freud, dude.

As for me, I was in full Desmond Morris mode, observing the naked ape in all its glory. The shoppers in this store were a much more varied bunch than that found in your average Soho sludge dungeon. London's wankers are all sweaty men in anoraks and professional types wielding briefcases full of teen porn and mouldy bananas.

Here, inside Private, was your classic societal cross section — buffed bummers in the Gay section and pocket billiard playing ferret faced fools down by the Straight magazines, thumbing copies of Maximum Perversum and trying not to gasp or grimace. In the section reserved for fetish wear there was a middle aged woman with a pack of Anal Lube and a scud mag under her arm, gingerly fingering the hem of a nurse costume. Next to her was a younger woman, maybe twenty or so, skinny, dark hair, dressed like a student, carefully browsing the full range of gay male DVDs on display. She showed one selection to the older woman — it might've been Meat Packer — and that's when the penny dropped — this was a mother & daughter team shopping for porn! What the fuck went on in their house of an evening?

Sarge, meanwhile, had spotted a tall, vaguely Goth tart buying rubber knickers at the counter and asking the wench behind the till for her opinion. It was starting to get too surreal. Kev was looking menaced by the plastic fists — it was time to bust a move and cop our flight home.

Before we set off there was one more pressing matter — the obligatory lavatory visit. Fuck knows what the Dutch make of us now we've gone but I'm sure the toxic waste dumped in the hotel lobby was not appreciated. The paint started to peel, the windows started to melt and birds fell from the sky. As a testimony to journalistic accuracy I am forced to report the following: Kev made blancmange, Russ sank a Brown Bomber and Seb laid an alien egg which is now probably being studied deep under the desert floor of Area 51 as you read this.

Fuck wit Englishmen that we are we thought we'd caught the wrong train. Panic dissipated when Sarge spotted hippies dancing gaily in a field. Who cares? Fuck it.

Now we can stay for another night! Exhaustion was taking its toll and the skyscraper weight of accumulated madness and debauchery was bearing down upon us. Picture eight men slumped in a heap in the departure lounge, teetering on the edge of coma when suddenly — shit, were we hallucinating? — four teenage girls hoved into view.

Where were their parents? Where were their clothes?

The lead strumpet had a too tight t-shirt and canvas baggies slung low out of which her pubic bone was bursting forth like the bow of a ship.

Kev: "Fuckin' 'Ell!"

Sarge: "Do they realise how close they are to getting us arrested?"

We were suddenly wide awake, hit by a collective lolita speedball.

You could almost hear our thoughts drowning out the tannoy.

More clump. Must have more clump.

We were not going to make it.

The gods smiled upon us and offered frisky coffee skinned air hostesses in tight uniforms and trampy young mothers in t-shirts stolen from their daughters.

Then we saw her... the debauched Delilah of our dreams. The lilith our libidos longed for. Blonde hair dishevelled like she'd been gang raped in the bogs by a rock group. Tits like puppies scrapping behind a flimsy boob tube. Mini skirt cut to mid-thigh with a slit up the back and big fuck off Tank Girl boots.

"Make her bend over," hissed Sarge. "Knock that fucking teddy bear out of her hands and let's see that split do its job."

No one had the energy for sexual assault so wanton fantasy would have to make do.

We flew back in a stunned silence, lost in our own private reveries.

As the minibus raced back towards Yorkshire we dreamt of food that didn't smell like genitals and wouldn't hit your colon like Little Boy falling on Hiroshima. We dreamt of soft white beds unstained by foetid ass crack and the fever dreams of a hundred, thousand masturbators. We dreamt of the warm embrace of our soul mates, to be lost in the soft folds of their understanding and sympathy for our biological curse to always be imbeciles.

In our hearts we knew we were not bad guys — just another set of misguided fools washed up on the shore of our inadequacies, surrounded by the bleached white bones of our adolescent fantasies and the terrible litter of our realities.

We saw the polaroids of our souls taped to a glass door, bathed in red light that shines forever in the darkness of our ignorance.

And we knew we were home. ■

Carmilla Tamaki and all-day shifts at Ruby

CARMILLA TAMAKI IS THE very antithesis of the majority of Japan's traditional SM practitioners. Although when I first meet up with her she's working within 'the system', paying the rent by doing all night shifts at Ruby, an intimate (i.e. basically one room) SM bar in Ikebukuro, and a weekly live show at Tokyo Jail in Roppongi (both places she has since left), she is also working with punk band Auto-Mod ("the fathers of Japanese dark wave" according to their singer Genet) providing vocals and something more… an SM performance may either be incorporated into their live set or the music may halt for fifteen minutes while she takes centre stage.

What follows is collected from several meetings with the somewhat schizophrenic performer (everyone tells that she's a different person each time they meet her, which personal experience bears outs to seem quite accurate, while Genet more specifically offers: "She can be a very normal pretty girl… or a devil woman!"), the initial one taking place at Tokyo Jail, a venue that serves as a good example of commercialism at work within the Tokyo BDSM scene.

Carmilla Tamaki is not like the rest of Japan's SM practitioners. Miles Wood finds out why.

When I arrive a short dance routine is already underway as a prelude to Carmilla's act (which she will perform two or three times during the night, though I only stay for one as I'm informed each additional one will rack up my bill), which is fairly light and routine, marking the venue as one where the clientele is more the general public looking for a little risque eroticism rather than SM otaku, and where general admittance, performance fee, drink and snacks (not to mention a drink for the girl of your choice to idly chat with) will soon run you beyond fifty pounds for a couple of hours. For those just wanting a sample of Tokyo's SM scene, it's comfortable and totally unintimidating even if you don't speak a word of Japanese, but the more hardcore will find time and money better spent at an event like Sadistic Circus, the smaller SM shows often staged at Loft Plus One, or at Steve Osada's intimate and welcoming Studio Six.

Interview

PREVIOUS PAGE
Carmilla Tamaki at work in Ruby.

THIS PAGE
Carmilla (left) in Deseo. Photos: Miles Wood

Carmilla Tamaki

HEADPRESS How did you first become attracted to SM and what were your first experiences?
CARMILLA TAMAKI I can't remember. But when I was three years old my father broke his arm and he had a fever and was sleeping. I kicked him and he cried out in pain but I just laughed and ran off. So I knew, and he knew, that I was a Sadist at a very early age.

How does the 'system' work at a place like Ruby?
Hourly pay, the charge of nomination, and the show tip serve as remuneration to me. In SM bars clients pay a limited

time cover charge and buy a drink; after maybe an hour they must pay again or leave. Of course they must pay more for any extra services. Sometimes clients just turn up, while others may telephone beforehand or send email for me or the club. Some clients state specifically their own desire, others may just wanting to know some things, and some say "please do everything whatever you want!" I'll never act out something what I don't want just because it's what they desire. However, there are times I cannot play as hard as I wish, either because a client cannot bear it or due to the restrictions of the club. Very often the distress which I give them will be too severe, but then I expect it; there are many whose actions do not follow their words. Even if someone says "I like whipping!" usually they cannot bear it any more after I whipped them only three times. And, since normal clients are also often visit, we have to take care not to have to become too unpleasant, or they may be put off when they see what we do at that time.

Many bars such as Ruby lack any privacy, or any additional rooms or space for 'play'. Do clients not mind that there are probably others (staff and other clients) watching?

Maybe they don't mind so much about others, because they know that others are interested in SM too. Sometimes there are those who care but I tell them "don't mind, you are friends who like same thing." If I and someone want to have some time on our own, we must use other places and other time.

Are you surprised that there seem to be more and more of these clubs opening, especially, it seems, ones catering for male submissives?

I think that they increase too much, but I don't really care about those things because it is are unrelated to me. However, it seems, there are more ones catering for male submissives, like you said. I think it's due to uneasiness to various things—economy, politics, and other many things—and this is one way of forgetting them. Did obedient Japanese increase in number? Did the Japanese who want to depend on others only increase in number?

How do you respond to the commercialisation of SM, through the ever increasing number of 'mistress bars'. Have clubs made it like a form of prostitution?

I regard it as very deplorable. But I also think it's a fact that if there is such no places, then many people will be troubled without a way to fill their desire. But I'm never 'mistress', ever. I'm just a sadist. Women called 'mistresses' in Japan are almost prostitutes. They are just working in order to fill a client's desire. But I'm not so. I'm doing it just filling *my* desire as sadist. I want to control and govern them. A face and a cry in pain makes me happy.

Do you prefer to dominate men or women? Presumably all your clients at somewhere like Ruby will be men, while when you do shows such as the one at Jail your 'victim' will be female.

I don't care for my victim's sex, just if the person is a good victim for me. However, in the case of the partner of show, a female has a better appearance. I'm always making an effort to perform the show to make different style from others. Almost all the people that have seen my show at Jail recently were surprised; they enjoyed themselves and were struck with admiration!

Tell me about your relationships with your slaves.

I met them at my shows. Almost every one came to see my performance again and again. It entreated for their wanting to become my slave first, and only those who thought that I could make him my slave out of the persons were made into my slave. When I played with one of my older slaves (he was eighty three years old!) he said to me: "I want to die just now. I don't want to die in the hospital. If you are able to, I need you to kill me." Then I thought I wanted to kill him. But we know that, I cannot do it. That problem often afflicts me and make me lament. I love my slave like I love my cats and dogs. I love them but cannot sleep in the same bed. Slaves are at the bottom but they are important because what's at the bottom is important. ■

Extreme Modulation

Marie Shrewsbury is in sync with the dark heart of New York City.

"OK CINDERELLA, ARMS UP, ANY SHARPS, KNIVES, needles, guns, bombs," asked the doorman at the Webster Hall.

"Like no," I laughed. As if I'd own up to it if I had. Zenwarp was the name of the dance/techno goth night that I'd arrived at. Much that my second Friday night in New York City was turning out to be rather dull, it was considerably better than the previous Thursday, when I'd ended up on the floor at a VNV Nation gig. The first few days had been frenetic, full of adrenalin and new sights and sounds assaulting the senses, from the wide roads and massive buildings to the omnipresent yellow cabs and steam rising from the pavements. The noise was like nothing I'd heard before, not the rumble of traffic like in central London, but more of a low background hiss, pink noise, low and filtered with subtle fluctuations within it. For the first few nights it did an excellent job of keeping me awake. By Thanksgiving I was feeling pretty damn lousy. It had taken me three days to discover the hard way that you can't live exclusively on black coffee and bagels. The afternoon's parade had been exhausting as I'd stood on the corner of Broadway and 42nd St unable to move for people while a crazed man from Brooklyn shouted to everyone about how someone had been stabbed on that very spot the previous year. Well I simply couldn't not go out on Thanksgiving night, so I slipped on my black velvet frock and my flowery headdress, covered my face in UV make up, and exceeded the prescribed dose of my medication just a little on the off chance that it might improve my temperament.

VNV Nation were playing at The Limelight, which was only two blocks away from my hostel. When I went out I was pretty giddy, somewhat drunk on the prospect of being a super British Goth in Manhattan. Giddy though, in an edgy kind of way that's only a hair's breadth from hysteria. With that attitude it didn't take long for things to go sour. As I queued outside the converted church, I made my first critical error in being overfriendly with some grade A assholes who mercilessly made fun of me for the next twenty minutes. My psycho girl routine wasn't helping much either.

Cash Reward
$10,000.00

For information leading to the arrest and conviction of anyone shooting a NYC Police Officer.

You *do not* have to give your name. You will be given an "ID" number.

COP SHOT
Citizens Outraged At Police Being Shot

Call 1-800-COP-SHOT

All photos this chapter: Marie Shrewsbury

Extreme Modulation

From there it could only go downhill. I had my work cut out for me bluffing the bouncer that I was over twenty one, it's standard practice to check your ID even if they really obviously don't need to, then they give you a wrist tag that the bar won't serve you without. It wasn't even like I was going to drink anyway. The door charge was $25. When I got to the bar a pint of coke was $6, and half of that was ice. Something told me that my liquid intake would not be extensive. There were a few good moments of distraction with a woman called Deta who was down from Boston for the night, she told me about the scene there, and introduced me to her parents-in-law, nonetheless I was on a downward slide. When the support act Icon of Coil had finished playing, I was sat on the floor in the chill out room desperately trying to pull my head together. A French guy came up to me and asked me if I wanted a drink. He squats down beside me and introduces himself as Stephan. He's cute. He's got short dark hair and a bit of a beard. He tells me that he's staying in Chinatown. All of a sudden my evening is looking up spectacularly, and I am so sure that I'm about to pull — anything in fact, to distract me from my present state. I play with his hand and ramble inanely at him for the next ten minutes. Then he tells me that he's going to the bar and he'll come right back. He didn't. So then I'm really pissed off, and kicking myself for waiting for him because I've lost my place in the hall and can't push through the crowd to get a good look at VNV Nation. Dehydration is setting in a bit, only I'm buggered if I'm going to pay another $6 for a coke so I go in search of the toilet. The first big surprise is that it's a communal loo, with both men and women using the same room. There's no urinal, just a row of cubicles. I suppose it kills the age old tradition of boys using the ladies because they need a mirror to put their make up on. Getting to the sink should be the easiest thing in the world, except they appear to have posted an attendant, a Puerto Rican woman who hands people paper towels. Over a sink is a marker pen sign that reads 'Tips only — Please be generous'. Culture shock has attacked me in the strangest places, but never before in the privy. After a while I get sick of sitting around so I decide to leave, only I can't find the exit and I'm starting to get claustrophobic. A vile feeling sets in at times like this, like I'm only a micron away from completely freaking out and screaming my head off. It never quite makes it the last bit of the way. It just feels like it's going to. I want to say goodbye to Deta, but no amount of wandering will bring me across her. Eventually I find my way out of the building. Even walking the two blocks home isn't simple. I get accosted by this chap on a bike. He's too thin and wears a grey suit and a hat that doesn't look quite right on him. As soon as I stop, he starts hurling some story at me about how he's a theatrical costumier and he's locked out of his flat and all his clothes are hanging up outside. He talks fast, a verbal machine gun, spewing out details incessantly, like the name of his boss and the company he works for. It hardly matters, it hasn't taken me long to figure out that he's trying to get me to go to his house to 'watch his clothes' for him. I'm so edgy that I stand there and protest, "Leave me alone, you're scaring me." He mutters a sarcastic "thanks" and cycles away. I return to my hostel, exhausted and freaked, to whine at my roommates about what a lousy night I had.

My dormitory was shared with two other women. Meagan was in the top bunk opposite mine, and was down from Canada to go to art school for a few weeks. We got on pretty well from the start, she was an immensely funny character and within half an hour of meeting she's giving me tips on how to pull straight women. Jane comes in much later, looks at me, and announces that she is so incredibly drunk. I'm shattered from a long day's flight, and retort with, "That's ok, I'm completely off my head on antidepressants." Jane becomes suddenly even more animated, "Are you on Prozac?" she asks, "Can I have one?" I keep telling her no, and she keeps on bouncing up and down going, "Oh please, can I have an antidepressant?" For an encore she asks me if I'm a guy. In the morning she remembers all of this, though insists that she was joking about the pills.

Meagan was perky and entertaining, her cropped bleached hair lent her a boyish charm that she carried off with a certain panache. We shared a similar sense of humour that made it easy for us to get along. One evening she came in and announced that her art class had finished early because they'd run out of acid. I teased her mercilessly before she got to say that they were doing resist etching on metal. She's amazingly talented at sketching, and continually draws people and objects in a little note pad that she carries. One night she drew me lying there trying to sleep, and even though I'm a lump in the covers, it still looks like me. On my second morning there I'd sat up in bed just in time to see her pull her blanket back and watch a dozen cockroaches go scurrying out from beneath. I'd never seen one before so I'm immediately grossed out. I'm sat there going, "Oh my God, you've got cockroaches in your bed, oh God, oh God." Jane gets edgy and says "Stop saying that" and I've lost it so much that I ask without thinking, "What, stop saying oh God or the other thing?" It's occurred to me by now that there might be 'roaches under my own blanket too, and I'm not sure if I'm more afraid of looking or not knowing. There aren't, but I'm so spooked that I jump out of bed and pace the floor in only a t-shirt going, "Oh shit, oh shit, oh shit." Both of them try to reassure me that 'roaches are entirely harmless, just gross.

Jane is harder to get on with — maybe it's my head or maybe she's suspicious of me, or something. I can never quite touch base with her. She's working in NY in real estate. She's been looking for an apartment for a long time. She hasn't found one yet and is getting incredibly cheesed off with living in hostels. The hours that she works must be strange, because she rises late and stays out until the small hours. Sometimes she talks to me about a man that she's seeing and how she'd like to settle down with him, and this subject seems to mellow her out a bit. Otherwise I think she's highly strung.

One night I came back from a club and shut my bag in my locker. Think metal lockers like you have at school. Almost immediately I realise that the locker key is in my bag. The door has enough give in it that it can be bent open a little without damaging it, so I keep on trying to bend it back far enough so that I can reach into my bag for the key. I have to pull various items out so that my bag will drop low enough to reach. Several tops come out, followed by a very resistant copy of *Time Out* and a pink feather boa that almost gets stripped. It's an effort, and I keep having to rest and remind myself to stop hyperventilating. Meagan watches from her bunk and keeps telling me to leave it until the morning, only I know I'm not going to rest until this is sorted out. Eventually I manage to wedge the door open with my *Rough Guide to New York* far enough to reach into my bag. Then I sit there for a moment, sweating and swearing, amid a pile of clothes, magazines and pink feathers.

A man comes around the next day to spray the room for 'roaches. When I go back later the room smells of chemicals. I hope that it's safe. It brings back memories of when I went to the Whitby Gothic Weekend and my travel sickness pills reacted with my medication. I spent the entire morning finding pillar boxes incredibly attractive and telling my friend Teresa about how when the sun shines it feels like it's snowing inside my head, tiny flakes that glisten in the sunlight. Teresa said something like, "Stop it Marie, you're scaring me." The snow thing was kind of cool actually. I had that a few times, and once it even snowed cherry blossom. Like my passion for pillar boxes, that thankfully has passed.

Friday morning finds me vowing to have a quiet night in lieu of the previous day's shenanigans. Friday evening finds me manic again and rearing to go out. I forget the actual night I was thinking of going to. On the way out I stop in the kitchen for a coffee. It's lousy and gut rotting but its one redeeming feature is that it's also free. Cordellia arrives, an English woman of Chinese extraction, and tells me how she'd returned to NY for the Thanksgiving day parade. There's a hippy looking guy in his forties sat by us, with untidy hair, dungarees and a tie-dye guitar case over his back. After we've chatted about nothing much for a bit, he takes out the guitar and performs My Favourite Things. We both sit there and grin at him inanely. He continues to entertain us for a little while. By now I've relaxed sufficiently that I decide to stay put. Meagan arrives, and gets sufficiently excited by what's going on that she goes away, to return with a friend plus guitar. She plays some. Then I ask Derry if he knows any Lou Reed. As it is, he knows Heroin, only he can't remember all of the words so I agree to join in. It's the first time I've sang rock music in company, but between the two of us we muddle through, and I don't care that my singing's lousy. It's not like I'm trying to perform a classical piece, I just keep it low and dirty. After that he does Walk On The Wild Side. There couldn't be a more appropriate end to the evening for a bunch of exhausted misfits winding down in a Chelsea hostel, somewhere around midnight.

If there's one thing above all others that came as a surprise to me about NY, it is how friendly the locals are. They're reputed to be brash, but the truth is that they just don't care. If they're loud or forward with you, it's out of a gentle ambivalence rather than maliciousness. In all of my time there I get no street hassle at all, there's the occasional laugh or friendly banter, but nothing threatening. I am shown a respect that my own city does not afford me. The subway too is completely different to the place that which I'd imagined. One thousand bad movies had led me to believe that it was a place where the danger of being knifed or thrown onto the electrified rails lurked around every corner. It's grotty but it's spacious, and there are people around at all hours, even all through the night. I feel far safer than I ever would on the London underground. Best of all is that the people aren't afraid to talk to each other, you can strike up a conversation with virtually anyone and they'll talk back. If you tried that in my capital they'd probably ignore you or look at you like you're insane. One day I met a chap on the platform who, perhaps enticed by an untoward smile, became animated as he told me about how he was going to be Santa Claus at Macy's, and how he planned on writing about it.

Extreme Modulation

He smiled at me to an unnatural degree. I think he must have been on something, or maybe that's just paranoia on my part. We continue our conversation on the train. When he gets off, a woman who's been eavesdropping tells me that he's actually one of many Santas at Macy's, and he's only doing it because the previous year a well known journalist had written about what it was like to be an elf.

Saturday night was a serious improvement. I'd remembered to eat, managed to relax a bit and, more importantly, dropped my English Goth Psycho Chick pretensions. The Batcave had come highly recommended to me by a good friend. My first vivid memory is of a man in a dinner jacket and flat cap sat at a table drawing Goths. He doesn't speak to anyone, and ignores you if you speak to him. He just sits there and draws Goths. Later on someone tells me that he's there every week, though no one knows what he's called. I meet a chap called Chris, and several women friends of his. Chris is what I'd think of as a fairly classic NY rocker, if you'd put him in a stripy shirt he could have walked straight out of The Ramones. He seems to imagine that England has the most amazingly advanced Goth scene ever, though he doesn't look too disappointed when I tell him that the Batcave is pretty much like home. We go through to another room, which plays more traditional gothic music. Partway through the night I start flirting with a woman who's stood close to me, she's small and cute and reminds me of something avian. There's a certain disarray to her that I find appealing, she wears jeans and a t-shirt pulled in at the waist by a studded belt. When I tickle her under the chin she chirrups like one of the little dinosaurs from Jurassic Park. I borrow her fan when I'm hot. I can't remember precisely where we went from there, but somehow we end up snogging and touching each other all over before we've even passed two words with each other. She seems to like it, especially when I hold her by the wrists and pin her against the mirrored wall. Somewhere between the heat of our bodies, several hours disappear. By 04.30 we're sat in her car outside my hostel. I'm not allowed guests, and Julie lives with her folks on Long Island, who I'm assured I do not want to meet. She says that she wouldn't have taken me home even if I were a guy. We talk for some time, and I share all of my dirty little secrets with her. She is completely unphased. We touch some more, gently. My fingertips trace the lines of self inflicted scars on the inside of her forearms. I show her similar ones that I did many years ago on the back of my arms with a Stanley knife. We kiss, and for a little while, the promise of affection fills me with a certain fragile optimism.

Perhaps this is a good point to say a few words about my present mental state. It's not good. It's never been brilliant, but now it's got so bad that I've sought solace with the Selective Serotonin Reuptake Inhibitor (SSRI) class of antidepressant drugs. Prozac is the most famous of these, and while it was the original SSRI to be developed, it's now one of many options. I've used tricyclic antidepressants before and found them very unpleasant, they gave me the feeling of looking at the world from inside a glass case, or of watching my life on television. Citalopram Hydrobromide is my drug of choice, so to speak. To say that it can make you feel pretty weird at times is an understatement. The first week that I was on it I couldn't sleep for toffee and didn't seem to need it. The second week I did nothing but sleep. One of the earliest effects is that you can't think straight, and even when that lets up, it's an effort to seriously focus your thoughts. Sometimes I can't even think out loud to myself. Not entirely a bad thing, considering the sheer amount of crap that normally goes around in my head. Then there are more ridiculous things, like when you suddenly feel ecstatically happy for no reason whatsoever. The opposite end is when you feel a phenomenally oppressive kind of down, like you're being held underwater, not so much a literal suffocation, more like it's your mind that's drowning. The first few months are pretty rough really, the ultimate in love / hate relationships, after a fashion. Sometimes it's almost like a physical sensation, like a serpent coiling itself up around your body, you can almost feel it moving across your skin, drawing itself tighter, even looking out of your eyes, and much that you want to shake it off, you know that it's not going to happen. Just when you hate it more than anything else in

Extreme Modulation

the world and are vowing to stop taking the tablets as soon as humanly possible, that's when it sinks its teeth right into the back of your brain, with a sharp, flooding burst of pleasure so intense that you can almost pinpoint the precise spot where the venom has entered, so intense that it borders on pain. You hate liking it in the most twisted way possible. That mostly passes after a while. Other things endure, like when I want to cry but it won't happen. The sensation wells up inside, but instead of turning to tears, it just sits there like a blunted, shapeless mass until it settles down again. At times it feels like the emotional equivalent of being staked out, other times I'd liken it more to being an electrical storm in a jam jar, lots of energy, but with the limits of movement strictly defined. A friend at work once ribbed me that maybe my GP had prescribed me LSD as a sick joke. What is possibly the strangest thing of all happened to me on the Statten Island ferry. I'd walked down from Chinatown via Pier 17, which is far less interesting than the guidebooks would have you imagine, and at this time seemed to be the only place where Christmas was happening in a big way. There were trees and carol singers everywhere. It was grisly. When I got to the ferry terminal I was sweating, so I boarded and headed straight to the bow, which is in the open air. As the boat pulled out and the warm dry air of Manhattan gave way to the sharp harbour breeze, I felt myself gradually merging and becoming one with the wooden deck of the ferry. I've had things like this happen before and they're not always particularly pleasant, this one however was oddly comforting, so I offered little resistance. I felt like I too was made of wood, a figurehead, ploughing through the water, impervious to the cold wind that rushed around me. Elation and purpose sit alongside a numb obliviousness, a bland comfort in being without reason. I don't try to analyse events like this. It was quite sufficient just to experience it.

When I meet Julie again it's Sunday evening at The Raven bar in Alphabet City. The Raven has a run down kind of cosiness to it, most of the seating is old settees where one can lie back and relax. Julie drops several volumes of her poetry into my lap, which I flick through. We snuggle up together and touch some, interspersed with the occasional snog. Now and again friends of hers arrive, and after being introduced, we totally ignore them for the rest of the evening because we're so into each other. Barring the occasional trip to bar or toilet, all we seem to do for the next seven hours is be together. She has long dark hair that I keep playing with, untangling it or winding bits around my finger. At some point I burst into tears for no particular reason, and Julie hugs me and strokes my hair and tells me that everything's going to be ok.

Towards the end of the evening my head is pleasantly fuzzed up. I sleep intermittently with my head on her lap. Eventually she drives me home. We agree to meet up later in the week at a Helmut Newton exhibition.

The Chelsea Hostel shelters an array of colourful characters under its roof, who I periodically meet in and around the kitchen. There's a guy of Mediterranean appearance who claims to be Puerto Rican. He repeatedly attempts to talk to me while keeping his headphones on full blast. I get so sick of this that I start moving my lips silently, just like the scene with the deaf woman in Fawlty Towers, much to the amusement of everyone else in the kitchen. There's an assortment of misfits of various nationalities, races and genders. The most odious of these is a man who tells me that he used to be with Osho, the Indian guru. The first time we meet is over breakfast. He tells me a bit about his time with Osho, then asks me if I like sex, followed by "Did your father beat you or rape you?" For some people, it's just never too early in the day for that kind of thing. Then he asks me if I'd like to have sex with him. I decline. I don't know why I bother to talk to him, maybe just because I'm so out of it that nothing surprises me, save for the fact that I bother to talk to him in return. He gives me the best shoulder and neck massage that I've ever had, then persuades me to do the same for him. I suppose at least Osho taught him something useful. Later he tells me that he's been in eleven different mental institutions.

I'm late for my meeting with Julie, and for a while I loiter around the gallery, wondering if she's later than I am or if she's been and gone. When I get tired of waiting and take a walk, I hear her yelling at me from the other side of 42nd street. The Helmut Newton exhibition is pretty much what you'd expect of it, curious, and more often than not more than slightly perverted in quite original ways. From there she takes me on a tour of the East Village and shows me all her little haunts. There's a laid back cafe called Alt.coffee, and another place that stocks a range of otherwise unavailable English products, like Lucozade, Jaffa Cakes, and a drink that she calls 'Rib-en-a'. She takes me to the tackiest cafe ever (it alleges to be a restaurant) which has different vinyl seat covers on every bench, mostly with bad retro fruit or flower patterns. After there we're wandering near CBGBs when we stumble across a peculiar frontage. It's all opaque glass, and there is a wall that screens the inside from spectators. A sign on the door reads:

'REMOTE is operated by Controlled Entropy Ventures ("CEV"). Upon entering these premises your name, image, voice and likeness may be broadcast over the Internet or recorded and replayed at a later time by CEV or its designee for advertising or any other purpose.

By entering these premises you hereby waive the following rights:

To privacy. You agree that you have no expectation of privacy for any acts or statements made on these premises.

To publicity. Any and all audio conversations made on these premises are the sole property of CEV who retain the right to profit from said recordings. You agree that you enter voluntarily and will not receive any compensation for CEV's use of your name, image, voice or likeness.

To bring a claim against CEV. You agree that CEV will not be liable for any damages, direct, indirect, consequential, incidental or special associated with the recording or broadcasting of your name, image, voice or likeness. You further agree that you will indemnify CEV in the event that a third party brings a claim against CEV as a result of any act or statement made by you on the premises.'

An attraction to the strange and unusual is a trait we both share, so naturally we couldn't resist going inside. Each table has a console on it, which looks like a 1950s vision of 2001, with a screen and controls on each side and two cameras on the top. From any console you can not only view what any other camera in the building is seeing, but can control the camera with a joystick. Given some of my weirder fantasies about being manipulated and controlled, I am in a cyber heaven. It's A Clockwork Orange meets The Prisoner in a debauched embrace of black velvet. We sit in an alcove and snog while the bar fills up around us. Julie keeps trying to keep our camera on us so that she (and anyone else) can watch us grope each other. She is disappointed every time control of the camera is seized by someone who would much rather look at the ceiling than at us. As I say to her later, most probably no one there couldn't care less about what we're doing, it's just the idea that anyone or everyone could be watching you that makes it so kinky. More than once I find that I've stopped touching her, and have to recoil when it feels like my body has momentarily turned to wax. Despite our physical closeness, I feel numb to the core. I think it's the drugs messing with my head. Julie takes it pretty well, if it bothers her she doesn't let on. We snog some more, then without warning Julie delivers the perfect end to the evening when she politely announces that "I'm having a wonderful time but I feel suddenly nauseous".

Coney Island was one of the bleaker parts of the city that I visited. God only knows how many stops out from Manhattan, through station after station, and a huge cemetery full of white headstones for almost as far as you can see. It's famed for its amusement parks and rides. November finds the fairgrounds closed up and the big wheel stationary. I don't know when the summer season normally ends here, but a sign on the mesh fence tells me that this year it ended early, in those ominously familiar words, 'due to the events of September 11th'. There's something particularly desolate in the landscape of empty rides, set against a background of run down apartment blocks. One building has colourful signs outside advertising the various exhibits of a freak show. I stroll along the boardwalk for a while, then out along a pier. The pier branches out about half way along, where I find a shanty town made out of bags and bin liners, with maybe twenty or thirty homeless people sheltering beneath them. The Rough Guide tells me that these are known locally as 'Hoovervilles'. Its residents watch me quizzically. I'm nervous enough to turn back, there's enough people around that I'm not too worried, but it's still creepy.

Perhaps my favourite museum moment was in the American Museum of Natural History. They have a vivarium which is home to a number of species of exotic butterfly. There's an airlock at each end to make sure that nothing escapes. The heat and humidity inside is bordering on the oppressive. All around you flap butterflies with colours that wouldn't be out of place in a bag of sweets. The smaller ones are mostly orange or yellow and black striped. The larger ones tend to be more exotically patterned. I'm snapping away at these like crazy, when I look down and see a huge specimen that's landed on my crotch. It's about six inches across with dark grey wings. Its head is furry, and its huge proboscis wave at me. The best I can do is to put my hands in the air, close my eyes and yell "Get it off of me!" Fortunately the museum is prepared for such scenarios, and a woman equipped with an ostrich feather on the end of a stick wafts it off of me.

The museums are a strong point of NY. The Guggenheim is an experience in its own right. What is indescribably shaped from the outside unfolds upon entry into a dimly lit ascending spiral with the main exhibition, dedicated to the artwork of Brazil, on the spirals outer face. There are wooden angels that captivate me, a Christ that looks worryingly like Fu Manchu, and a gaggle of Pentecostal figures that might be his grisly little helpers. Galleries extend from the spiral, crisp and white against its gentle darkness. At the top there are works by modern artists. One exhibit consists of a number of brightly coloured masks with things over the eyes. The final exhibit I see is the likeness of a bathroom wall, with tiles peeled back to reveal a gaping hole five feet square spewing entrails and gore. Slices of wall sit around the room, with edges raw and sanguine.

One day I took the subway all the way up to Washington Heights, at the extreme upper tip of Manhattan, to visit a museum called The Cloisters. It's set amidst a park on top of a large hill, the views of New Jersey are supposed to be amazing, but there was such a heavy fog down that all I could see was a slither of river. The Cloisters itself is a mock period building which is host to numerous exhibits of medieval art. Some of the carved angels in there were quite amazing. Sadly, no flash photography was allowed, and my attempts at shooting without flash gave blurred results. There was a shop where I bought a small psaltery type instrument to try and keep myself sane whilst my keyboards are several thousand miles away. You can play anything on it, just as long as it's in G major.

Sometimes I'd just wander around the city, or walk instead of taking the subway to get a look at the scenery. Union Square is good for craft stalls, I bought a velvet cape there covered in celtic knotwork. Washington Square, as Julie assured me, is good for bad dope deals and getting busted, as David Lee Roth once found to his expense. Times Square is a completely different proposition to several years ago, the sleaze and sex shows have been moved on to be replaced by Easyeverything, a Disney store and the Hello Kitty shop, which sells nothing but Hello Kitty merchandise. Several large signs tell us that this is all thanks to 'Official Times Square Redevelopment Project Sponsor Britney Spears', while above the words Ms Spears poses next to a can of Pepsi. Chinatown positively throngs with life. Some of the scarier shops have trays of water outside filled with still living aquatic creatures of unknown taxonomy, for sale. It's still one of the best and cheapest parts of town to eat. I'd meant to go to Sheridan Square for a drink in the (in)famous Stonewall pub, though somehow never got round to it.

By the end of the second week I really feel like I'm losing my mind. I even think about rebooking my plane ticket and flying home. On Sunday I go out to the Metropolitan Museum of Art and spend maybe two hours in a half hearted attempt to appreciate its contents. I know that what I'm looking at is good, but I'm too messed up to actually appreciate anything. When I get back to my hostel at 5pm I eat and go for a lie down. Somehow I doze off and sleep until 10pm. I'm awoken by two women arriving, both in their late forties, who are on their way back to the UK after travelling the world for a year. They're both vociferous, and tell me all about Australia, in between whinging that this is the most expensive hostel that they've ever stayed at. Somebody please tell them that they're in the ultimate city. I can't help wondering if they're lovers. Perhaps that's judgemental of me, considering that not so long back I was discussing with Meagan how we didn't believe that there had be such a thing as gay / straight or otherwise. I get up, feed and rehydrate myself, then go back to bed. When I find that I can sleep no more, I get up and go out to The Raven, arriving there around midnight, just in time to find Julie rushing out. Some friends of hers are publishing a magazine which is lacking content, so she has to dash home and spend some quality time with her word processor.

I get talking to Julie's friend Mia, her boyfriend, and another guy who's with them. I've forgotten his name, it's something obvious, so for now we'll call him John. Mia tells me that when she was in her teens she spent some time in a psychiatric hospital. It's not too surprising that we get along just fine. We stay there until 2.30am then go on to Justine's, which is a fetish themed bar. Mia has the most amazing Spanish Coffee, which the barman sets fire to and uses the flames to melt a layer of brown sugar stuck to the rim of the glass. On the monitor a naked anime female is being raped in every conceivable orifice simultaneously by a man equipped with an array of tentacle like penises. I have to look away as a tentacle the size of a fire hose snakes down her throat with the subtlety of an express train. Fetish posters cover the walls. At the far end of the room is a large wooden X-cross and a whipping bench. The barman tells me that anything goes except actual nudity. John appears to be having undue trouble staying awake, every so often I notice his head nodding forwards.

From there we move to a 24 hour cafe on the corner of Avenue A and 7th Street, rather originally called A7. The interior is painted in bright colours and smothered in fairy lights. Mia and her chap have some emotional stuff going on between them, so myself and John sit at a different table. We chat about nothing much for a while. He buys me a fruit salad. I keep wondering if he's trying to come on to me. When I comment on how tired he seems, he tells me that he smoked some dope before he came out. Later he tells me that he'd also had a line of heroin. This should gross me out, but an unnatural calm seems to have settled upon me. He talks enthusiastically about how heroin makes him feel relaxed, and how he never uses it more than two days running. Once he took it on fifteen consecutive days. Apparently the withdrawal was so bad that it was worth doing just to appreciate why you should never do that again. I wonder if he'll invite me home to try a line. Tiredness is catching up on me, and with it some strange sensations. The purple fairy lights have become a shade of purple that I've never seen before in my entire life. There's something just a little bit too sharp and crisp about them. Then I realise that the entire room is too sharp, and all the colours a little too bright to be real. It's like I've entered a Technicolour movie. It's a classic SSRI moment. I used to feel guilty about moments like this, that there was something about the way that they were just a bit too good that must be immoral. Now I take it as simply a counterbalance, for such moments have their dark reflections which can sneak upon me with equal stealth. I describe how I feel to John. He tells me about his ex who was on Prozac, and the time that she did some heroin with him then became intensely depressed for a week afterwards. I figure that if he was thinking of inviting me back, I've just given him a red light. He recommends some good restaurants in Brooklyn to go to. When I ask if he wants to meet up at one he declines. Maybe it's because I'd mentioned somewhere in our conversations that I hated sex, or maybe he was never coming on to me at all. When we leave A7, my friends hail a taxi back to Brooklyn, while I get the subway to Easyeverything to see if I can get online while my distant friends five hours in the future are around. I'm feeling kind of manic, and for reasons that are not entirely clear to me, I email my former line manager Sue Lavez-Vous, to tell her that I'm completely out of my mind on drugs, having an affair with a fluffy female goth and breaking down in tears at least once a day. From there it's back to the subway. The train is full of commuters, soberly dressed and half asleep, their bleary eyes survey me as I stand there in my pink feather boa and a ludicrous smile. I get to bed at 8am.

I sleep most of the day, for which the two women give me a good ribbing. We talk some, and I make the mistake of telling them that I'm going to see Britney Spears on Wednesday evening. She teases me about how Goths aren't supposed to like Britney, and how I must keep it secret from all of my friends. I tell her about the time that my friend Kerry found her CDs in my collection, and I spent the next ten minutes trying to persuade him that it was 'research'. I eat, then head out to CBGBs gallery for Alchemy, their Monday evening gothic night. Upon arrival I am introduced to their resident cat, Fish, a huge old stripy creature who cares not much for people or for the tenderest of ministrations. He has five fingers on each front paw, which appear disproportionately large. It is while photographing him that my film jams in the camera, and in my clumsy attempt to fix it I expose the film containing some of my best shots of the club scene. Julie arrives comparatively early. She's anxious about the articles that she'd submitted to the magazine, and tells me about how maybe they weren't as desperate for submissions as they'd led her to believe. It's worrying her that the publishers are appraising her articles elsewhere in the club as we speak. She relaxes some, and invariably we end up having a bit of a snog.

Central Park is a place interesting enough to warrant a mention of its own. It's a great place just to wander, and in several hours of such meandering I don't think I've seen even a quarter of it. There's a zoo there, which has a reptile house, aviary, and various other animals which don't look too impressed to be there. There's an otter which seems quite entertaining as it swims up and down its pool, until you realise that all it can do all day is swim up and down its pool incessantly. The polar bear doesn't look too chuffed either. General wanderings keep bringing me across an assortment of lakes, statues, bridges and other structures that have issued forth from the fevered mind of architects. My personal favourite is a huge fountain, dry at the moment, on top of which is an angel covered in pigeons. I like angels. I feel a certain empathy with them. I come across a man playing guitar and singing to perhaps one hundred people sat on a hillside. They seem to know all of his songs and sing along enthusiastically. My presumption is that this is some sort of gig, then I ask someone who tells me that he is a famous busker known throughout NY as 'that guitar guy in central park'. He's played there every year for the last ten, this year he's been lucky to find the summer season stretching into the first week of December. Best of all is the bronze statue of Alice in Wonderland. It's the expression on Alice's face that makes it, as she stands with her arms out, one of blissful ambivalence to the lunacy that is ensuing around her. She sums up how I feel at the moment better than anything else in the whole world. I want to photograph it but when I first see it it's covered in children. I want to try for a clean shot, but since I've left my Zyclon-B at home, that means waiting. The obvious plan is to go away and come back just before dark, when the children will have gone. I do, but they haven't. I wait while night falls, managing a couple of partial shots, but not a full one. Some other people are waiting too. When the last child leaps off and disappears beneath the huge mushroom, they begin to clap and cheer me on to photograph it, shouting "Now, now!" More often I seem to see the outside of Central Park where it meets Museum Street.

One afternoon I'm wandering around the Museum of Modern Art when the strangest feeling comes upon me. It's like I've finally reached the bottom of the rabbit hole. It's like the last shot has been fired and you're looking down on the battlefield from a great height surveying the damage. Where others would see fields and trees and houses, you see mile after mile of craters and mud, littered with bodies. There is something magnificently vile in the first moment when you see yourself clearly and appreciate just how far your self hatred runs.

Somewhere during my stay I decided that it would be a great idea to get some violet contact lenses, I kind of figured that since I was feeling so otherworldly, I might as well look the part. I'd never worn contacts before and I'm generally squeamish as hell, but I was so into the idea that it overcame my inhibitions. I went to an optician who did a few tests then ordered a pair for me. My first attempt at putting them in was a complete nightmare, I must have had about twenty tries, my eyes were sore and watering and I was so grossed out by the whole thing that I thought I was going to pass out. In the end I made an excuse to go to the toilet and sat there trying to pull myself together, taking deep breaths. The shop assistant suggested that I come back and try again the next day.

I spent most of the next day psyching myself up for the opticians appointment. It was my second last day in the city, and the day of Britney Spears' gig, at which I was determined to 'christen' my contacts. This time I managed to get them in after only half a dozen attempts. There was just time to nip back to my hostel to freshen up before the gig. Outside Madison Square Garden, the first whiff of excitement came as I saw the gigantic digital sign advertising the event. In the lobby were dozens of stalls selling Britney merchandise. I bought myself a hockey shirt with 'Slave 4 U' on the front and 'Spears' on the back, tying it around my waist for the evening. The inside of the venue was huge, with stadium seating extending back hundreds of yards from the stage. I had a good seat, about a dozen rows back, directly in front of the stage.

The support was a boy band called O Town, apparently the winner of the US version of Popstars. They were abysmal. Even SSRIs couldn't make those guys look good. The arena had filled up to capacity, and in the dark thousands of coloured glowsticks were being waved like a starry night. When Britney came on, she made her entrance strapped to a knife thrower's wheel, bursting into 'Oops I Did It Again'. I shoved forward to the front of the stage along with most of the stalls, but unlike any rock concert I've ever been to the security seemed to take offence at this and systematically hassled people back to their seats. It took them about half an hour to get through to me though, so I got a good view in the meantime. The sound in Madison Square Gardens was dire, all mushy and distorted. I knew that I should be having a better time than I was but I was plagued by the feeling of detachment that I get at times, like nothing around me is quite real. I just couldn't quite get into it. After doing her set, including no less than eleven costume changes, she played out with an excruciating version of 'Baby One More Time', accompanied on stage by a special effects wall of rain. They'd obviously tried to rework the song into something a bit more avante garde, in the process they seemed to have lost most of the musical content of the track, all I could make out over the PA's mush was the intermittent peal of drums. It was a lousy end to the gig, I mean, I've heard toilet circuit bands do better covers of that song.

I went back to my hostel and emailed Julie, hoping to meet up with her before my flight out the next day. She emailed back to say that she was busy and couldn't meet up with me. It was a real disappointment, I'd been looking forward to seeing her one last time, if only to say goodbye. After having a final wander around the city, I headed out for JFK airport. The security coming in had been lax to the point where by bags weren't even x-rayed. Going out it was tight as hell. I guess after 9/11 they weren't so much worried about who was coming in as who was going out. One of the staff asked me why I'd rebooked my departure date, and I told him it was to get to the Britney gig. He asked me if it was good and I told him about the lousy

Extreme Modulation

sound. "Yeah, everyone says that" he told me. I couldn't sleep on the plane so I spent most of the flight playing Ghosts and Ghoulies and watching bits of Hedvig and the Angry Inch, before arriving back at Heathrow in a haze of elation and exhaustion.

Perhaps the funniest thing anyone said to me there happened on my last day, when I went down for breakfast. A man that I did not know laughed at me in the kitchen, then told me that I was 'exactly the type of weirdo that you expect to come across in New York City'. Perhaps I should have felt oddly at home.

Afterward

Six weeks on and my trip is at once like a distant memory and a close friend. For all its lunacy, joy and disappointments, I'm not likely to forget my first trip to the US. A little contact has been retained with some of the people that I met, by email. Frustratingly little. My tender moments with Julie have faded in quality to the point of being intangible, elusive, and ultimately unrestorable. As to myself, my temperament has improved somewhat since my return, though I still find my moods intensely variable and still annoyingly detached from life around me. The more that I feel better in myself, the clearer I see myself, and the worse the image looks. I have the dubious pleasure of knowing that I hate myself to work on, coupled with the undermining doubt that there is nothing that could ever make me genuinely happy, or even content. As the classic line goes, I don't know what I want, but it's not what you're giving me.

Farewell NYC, for now. Farewell the Batcave, Julie, St Mark's Place, CBGBs, non-stop noise, steaming pavements, yellow taxis, walk / don't walk and subway sandwiches. Welcome back to the haze of working life, to my office full of drugged admin. support, to my cat that gets jealous of my keyboard and pisses on my duvet in protest, and to my friends, who, for all my whining and darker moments, make my life worth living. Welcome back to the familiar trinity of normality, banality and reality. ∎

Dead on the Inside

Jan Bruun visits the mütter museum — Philadelphia's still life freak show — and talks to its director, Gretchen Worden.

PHILADELPHIA'S MAIN TOURIST ATTRACTION, APART from the South Philly cheese steak sandwich, is the Mütter Museum. The museum is like a still life freakshow, crammed with old skeletons, foetuses, human heads cut into thin slices and graphic depictions of horrifying diseases. They have a plaster cast of the bodies of siamese twins Chang and Eng, with their actual liver displayed on a shelf right below. Chang and Eng were connected through the liver, and they were autopsied right in the building that now houses the museum.

I came to town straight from the world's first ever Sideshow Gathering, in Wilkes-Barre, Pennsylvania. Veteran sideshow and circus fan Rob Houston was kind enough to let me stay at his place for a couple of days, and he took me to the museum, and introduced me to its director, Gretchen Worden. Worden took some time out of her hectic schedule to talk to me about their exhibits.

She has worked at the museum since 1975, and been its director since 1988. When I talked to her she had just finished the first ever book on the museum, and she seemed to have an encyclopaedia like knowledge of dried and pickled corpses worldwide. She dished out answers complete with names, dates and locations in a deadpan, matter of fact manner, but with an obvious intense enthusiasm for this strange subculture of nasty diseases and misshapen human remains, whether placed within the realm of medical science or in more lurid settings like the sideshows. She gets a little excited when she hears that I'm from Norway:

Gretchen Worden: "Did you ever see Julia Pastrana's corpse?"

"No, the ape woman is kept away from the public in a vault in the Norwegian state hospital, but I helped out on a book that came out about her in Norway. The embalmed corpses of her and her equally hirsute son was owned by the Norwegian Swedish travelling fairground Lunds Tivoli for many years."*

Jan Bruun and Gretchen Worden. Photo: Rob Houston

THIS PAGE
A cabinet displaying sliced up human heads.

NEXT PAGE
An overview of the museum.

Photos this chapter courtesy the Mütter Museum, unless noted otherwise.

Dead on the Inside

HEADPRESS Could you tell me about the origins of the museum?

GRETCHEN WORDEN   The College of Physicians started out in 1787, and in 1849 they started a small collection. And then, in 1858 or 59 they signed an agreement with Dr. Thomas Dent Mütter to get his collection, and that's when it became the Mütter Museum. By 1863 they had moved the collection into the new College of Physician's building. I generally use that year as the start of the museum, because that's when it really became part of the college. That history is in the book we're putting out now. It'll show what the initial collection consisted of. Dr Mütter also gave away $30,000 and that was to add to the collection. They bought a lot of material from Joseph Hyrtl from Vienna, when he was retiring, and they got a lot of other collections, because they thought it was going to be a real teaching museum, and it really never was that, because at the same time, the other medical schools were developing their collections.

So what's the purpose of the museum?

It was meant to be for young medical students and physicians, but now it's mostly for the general public. A lot of student age kids, every college kid that comes to Philly wants to come here. We also get groups from the public schools. In the fiscal year of 2002, which ended in June, we got 47,000 visitors, which was 17,000 more than the year before. About half of the visitors paid student admission price.

Your reputation is growing?

Yes, and one of the main reasons is TV programs. Especially an hour long program on Discovery, which was shown internationally. It was first shown in November 2001, and they keep airing it. I got an email from someone in Taiwan who saw it, and everybody who sees it wants to come here. We're getting a virtual tour of the museum on our web site, which will help too. Ripley's Believe It Or Not wanted to do a tales from the vault bit, where they go down in the basement to look at stuff, but I don't think we want their approach with all that smoke and spooky music. We don't need that. We can afford to be choosy. The guy who did the Discovery program is now doing shows on other museums, like the Fragonard anathomical exhibits in a veterinary school outside of Paris.

[At this point she shows me a book and I think it's the plasticised corpses of Gunther Von Hagens.]

No! This guy is eighteenth century.

These corpses are dried?

Yes. He was the brother of the painter Fragonard. There's a lot of artistic overlay. I think he had some secret formula to dry the corpses.

But are there any other museums open to the general public, that show human

specimens in formaldehyde, often deformed, like you've got here?

The National Museum of Health and Medicine in Washington. That is now out at the Walter Reed Army Medical Center, so it's outside of the city. It began as the Army Medical Museum in 1862, a year before we opened. There's another one, the Warren Anatomical Museum, a part of Harvard Medical School. A couple of years ago they put all of it in storage, but they're now trying to bring it back to life. There are other medical museums, but they're mostly instrument collections. We came out of the nineteenth century teaching museum tradition, but most of the old collections are history, although some schools might show a few specimens in the hallways.

My impression is that in Europe, in the places that do have collections like these, they're only available to medical students.

Yes, and they do have fabulous collections in Holland. In Utrecht I think there's a collection that actually is open to the public. In Leiden, Holland they have an amphitheatre with skeletons. There's a collection of congenital anomalies in Amsterdam that you kind of can get into, but it's on a floor of a big modern medical centre, a fully working hospital, and might be tricky to locate. We have a few cyclopian specimens here, but they've got seventeen different kinds. It's just not fair. But they got started out in the eighteenth century, specialising in that. I'm going to a meeting in Paris soon, of the European Association of Museums of Physical and Medical Sciences.

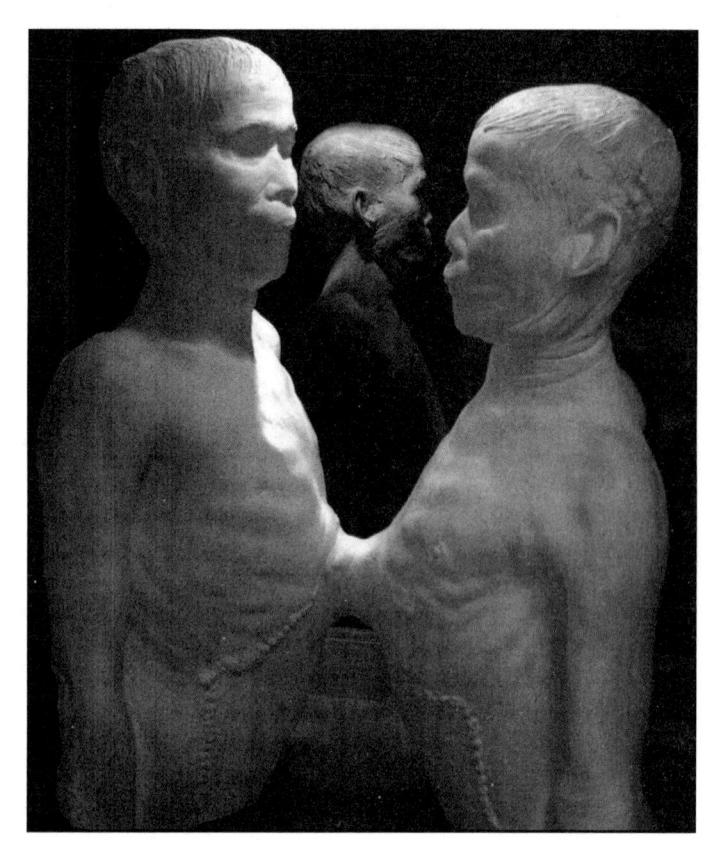

THIS PAGE
The plaster cast of Chang & Eng, whose autopsy was performed at the Mütter. The museum got to keep the liver, the part that connected the brothers.

NEXT PAGE
A wax display of eye diseases.

Dead on the Inside

I've just been redoing our congenital anomaly exhibit, writing new text. It's fascinating, I've been getting a lot of info off the internet, on the different syndromes. But you can't just go to one website, you have to check out about five, they all have a little different information.

What is congenital anomaly?
Birth defects, deformed babies. Now we know so much more about medical genetics, so we're trying to figure out what exactly we are looking at. The last time we changed our labels we used all the latest books, but a lot of that knowledge has been expanded now. But some of these syndromes, they still haven't decided which is what.

Science is always in flux, you'll never have the final answer to almost anything.
Exactly. So we're always gonna be rewriting labels.

Do you have any medical education?
No. Physical Anthropology, but that's strong in the biological sciences.

[The phone rings, and Gretchen has to attend to the business at hand for a few minutes.]

When did you start putting out the calendars? That must've helped to raise the public's awareness of the museum.
The calendar for the year 1993 was the first one, and we published until 96. Then we stopped for three years and came back in 99 with the year 2000 calendar. I think it had a huge effect, visitation really started picking up. The first year it came out there was a big article in the *Wall Street Journal* about it. But the 2002 calendar is the last one. It's so much work for the publisher, Laura Lindgren , whose idea it was in the first place. She does all the design, she gets the photographers, she does mailings to the individuals and the PR. She's one of the best book designers in NY, so she has lots of other work to do. So we thought, we've always talked about doing a book. People want more information about the museum than you can put in a calendar. We did the calendars because we had all these big name photographers coming here taking pictures, so we thought how can we get something back from what they're doing? And the calendars were perfect at the time. The book is not the ultimate book, that's gonna be the whole history of the museum and all of its collections, but it's a lot more information than anyone's ever got about the museum, all in one place and with all these fabulous photos. There's photos in there from all the seven years of the calendars, and we had a couple of new photographers take pictures that haven't been

published anywhere. We also went back to our historical collection of photos, which we always used to pick from for the November page in the calendars. Some of the early photographers were fine arts photographers that were doing work for the physicians. Gorgeous shots.

Do you change your exhibits around, to highlight different themes?
Not really. The current exhibit on conjoined twins has been up since the late eighties. Our temporary exhibits tend to go on for a long time. I just put out some new stuff on a pair of conjoined brothers. We have such big files on conjoined twins that every time someone does a documentary on them, we're in it. The Learning Channel just broadcast one on siamese twins. They use us for historical background. A lot of those still shots were ours. Every time there's conjoined twins in the news, we get the calls. Our staff is just two people. We don't have the resources to do anything special unless I can get interns to work on them. And a lot of the interns I do get have not been doing new exhibits as much as redoing old exhibits. But in the gallery section we change it around. Now we have an exhibit on infectious diseases, and the next one is on Lewis and Clark. That'll open in February 2003 and go on for about three years. We're doing a lot of planning now in terms of what the future direction of the museum is, how we can re-

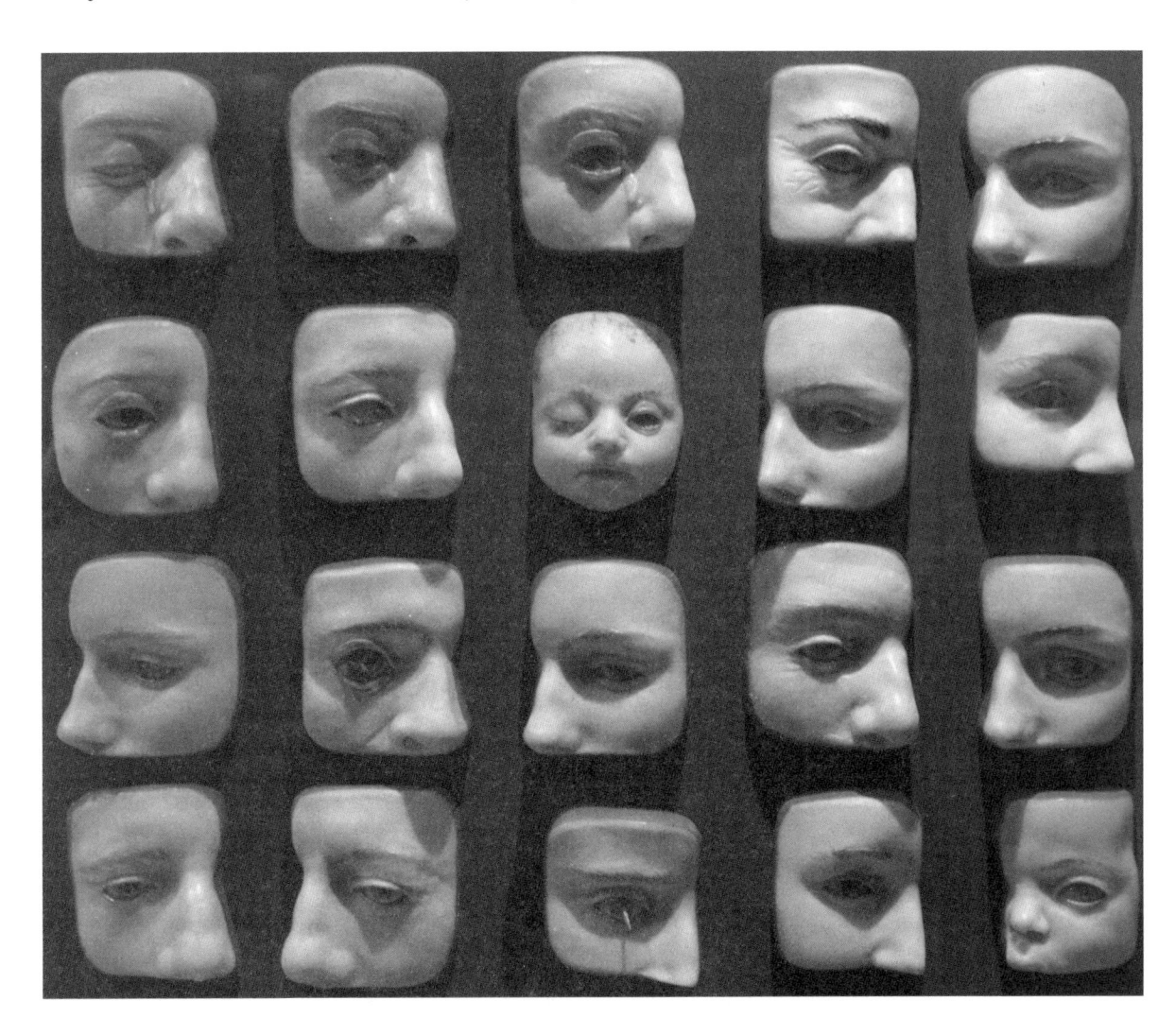

* The book by Christopher Hals Gylseth and Lars Toverud later came out in an English edition: *Julia Pastrana — The Tragic Story of the Victorian Ape Woman* (Sutton 2003).

Mütter Museum of The College of Physicians of Philadelphia By Gretchen Worden. Photography by Shelby Lee Adams, Arne Svenson, William Wegman, Joel-Peter Witkin and many more | Pub: Blast Books, NYC 2002 | Hb with color and b&w photos | 192pp | ISBN 0-922233-24-1 | [w] www.blastbooks.com

Dead on the Inside

ally take advantage of the collections and show them off to the public better, and taking into the account that we're getting different audiences now. We used to get a lot more of the medical health career people and now because of the publicity it's more from the general public.

So you're trying to make all the medical terms understandable?
Up to a point, but I also want people to get used to the vocabulary of medicine, because when they go on the internet, not every term is going to be explained. They have to know 'polydactyly' mean a lot of fingers and toes. So we're not at fifth grade reading level.

Any specific plans for the future?
That's what we're sort of rethinking. When we did a renovation and reopened in 1986, we took all the cases out and reinstalled the exhibits, putting a lot less material out there than what had been out before. So there's a lot more in storage, in particular instrument collections that are very fascinating. And some of the exhibits, like on internal medicine, there was just stuff thrown in there so we could open in time. I'm going back now to redo some of them. And some of the things we have on display are probably not that interesting to the general public, and should be put into storage so we could make room for other things that are more interesting. Also, we haven't really done a proper cataloguing of our collections. We just got a grant to do just one collection.

Well, someone once said: never trust anyone with a tidy desk... [Worden laughs and looks around her cramped basement office, with looming piles of documents, folders and books filling every square inch of her desk and tables. She points to a tiny bare spot:]
I spent weeks clearing just this small area, and managed to get down to bare wood. This area though, (pointing to a twenty inch high pile of documents beside her) it's gotta go, I've found five, six, even ten year old stuff in here. It's hard just to keep up with all the current business from day to day. Right now I'm having one of my employees scanning images of Chang & Eng's autopsy for a TV series called The Day They Died that deals with the deaths of various famous people.

Do people still donate things to the museum?
Yes, sometimes. Look here.

[She takes me through a basement corridor.]
This is what the museum looked like when I first came. Bare concrete floors painted green. These are unfinished cases. Right now we call this the tumour room because we moved a lot of the wet specimen back here. A lot of them are in a deteriorated condition.

[She gestures towards a roomful of glass jars of twisted tumours in cloudy formaldehyde, moves towards a door and lets me into the museum for free.]
This is the lower level, which tells you what a medical museum is all about...

THE EXHIBITS are housed in nice wooden cabinets with glass panels, and you need to set aside two or three hours to get a good look at all the mind blowing stuff on both floors. It's not everyday you can see a human head sliced up as a piece of loaf, the liver of Chang & Eng and dozens of differently misshapen skeletons and skulls. Don't miss it if you're ever in Philadelphia. Nice gift shop too. ∎

[w] www.collphyphil.org/muttpg1.shtml

Gretchen Worden died in August 2004.

Fantastic new & recent books from Headpress

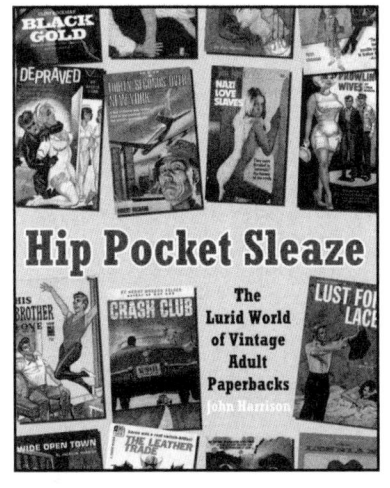

Info & secure online ordering: www.headpress.com

An SAE/2xIRC gets a catalog: Headpress/Critical Vision, PO Box 26, Manchester, M26 1PQ, UK

A Short History of Outlaw Motorcycle Clubs in the Media

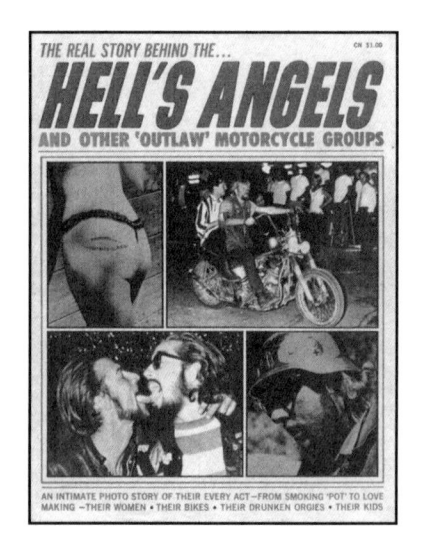

Tom Brinkmann unearths COLORS, a motorcycle bad mag from the seventies.

THE OUTLAW MOTORCYCLIST HAS BEEN A PLAYER ON the American landscape at least since the end of WWII, getting their first taste of national recognition in Hollister, California in 1947 with the July 4 celebrations and motorcycle hill climb that attracted cyclists and clubs from all over the state. It turned into forty hours of lawlessness and a drunken 'takeover' of the town by rowdy motorcyclists and was the basis for the Marlon Brando/Lee Marvin film *The Wild One* (1953).

The Korean War took a lot of the clubs members into the service which caused them to be more or less low key in the early fifties. But by 1955, a couple of years after the war ended the ranks of the outlaw clubs began to swell again. Throughout the late 1950s and early 1960s incidents in various California towns involving clashes between townspeople, law enforcement and the seemingly growing numbers of outlaw motorcycle clubs, were reported in local and national magazines and newspapers.

On March 15, 1965, California Attorney General Thomas C Lynch issued a fifteen page report, based on ten years of study on, 'HELL'S ANGELS AND OTHER DISREPUTABLE MOTORCYCLE CLUBS.' This report was the basis of most of the information that the press had to go on concerning the outlaw clubs.

First, Hunter S Thompson's article, 'The Motorcycle Gangs, Losers and Outsiders' in *The Nation* (May 17, 1965), started the ball rolling for the national press coverage of the outlaw motorcycle clubs, particularly of the Hell's Angels Motorcycle Club who were one of the original clubs in California and the most infamous among law enforcement.

Another incident which brought the cyclists to the forefront of media attention was the Weirs Beach riots in Laconia, New Hampshire that took place on June 19 and 20, 1965, during the Forty Fourth Annual New England Tour and Rally and made the national newspaper headlines, as well as *Life* magazine. Thirty four cyclists were arrested in the incident and seventy people were injured. Until then the outlaw clubs had basically been considered a West Coast phenomenon. By 1966 outlaw motorcycle clubs had reached the peak of their media coverage, and become rebel anti-heroes to some.

Secondly, there were the magazines and books. The outlaw cyclists, mostly the Hell's Angels, had gotten some coverage in men's magazines like *True*, *Modern Man*, and *True Detective* in August 1965, but the *Saturday Evening Post* of November 20, 1965, sported a Hell's Angel on the cover — who was summarily kicked out of the club — and an article on them that became the main introduction to the club, and outlaw cyclists

COLORS MOTORCYCLE MAGAZINE

Vol 1 No 1 [top], May 1970

Vol 2 No 3 [above], Winter 1971

$1.00 | 56pp

Colors Magazine
PO Box 143
Dobbs Ferry, NY 10522, U S A

in general, for the public at large. The magazine *The Real Story Behind the Hell's Angels and Other 'Outlaw' Motorcycle Groups* was published in 1966 by Angels Publishing Co, and depicted their parties, runs, and lifestyle in general, as photographed by Bob Grant. The mag had limited distribution but did sell well enough to warrant a second printing, although it was mainly sold through mail order ads in the back of some 'adult slicks' as well as in *Real* magazine which had had two cover stories on the Hell's Angels MC that same year, also with photos by Grant. *The Real Story Behind the Hell's Angels and Other 'Outlaw' Motorcycle Groups* can be considered the first outlaw biker lifestyle magazine.

Hunter S Thompson's bestselling book, *Hell's Angels* (1967) — which had its genesis with the article written by Thompson for *The Nation* — ended with his befriending and hanging out with the Hell's Angels Motorcycle Club for over a year, but not as a member. That was until Labor Day 1966 when he got stomped and was sent packing. *Freewheelin' Frank* (1967) by Frank Reynolds and Michael McClure also helped to familiarise the population with first hand tales of outlaw life. Two other more obscure paperback originals were *The Sex and Savagery of the Hell's Angels* (1967) by Jan Hudson (pseudonym of George H Smith) and *A Place In Hell* (1968) by H R Kaye, a biography of 'Wild Bill' Henderson, a former member of the Hell's Angels MC.

Thirdly, the crop of biker movies cranked out for the drive-in movie circuit, started in 1966 with Roger Corman's *The Wild Angels* starring Peter Fonda, Nancy Sinatra, Bruce Dern, Diane Ladd, and members of the Venice, California chapter of the Hell's Angels Motorcycle Club. Titus Moody's *Outlaw Motorcycles* was also released that year. Although it was a short documentary with a couple of acted scenes thrown in — and not widely seen — it truly depicted the outlaw clubs milieu in Los Angeles at the time, filmed while smoke from the Watts riots rose in the background over LA as seen in a couple of the scenes.

Hence, the onslaught of numerous magazine covers and articles that featured the outlaw clubs from 1965 on, put the images of outlaw motorcyclists in the forefront of popular culture and imagination.

In 1969, the release of the popular film *Easy Rider* shifted the focus from the outlaw clubs to the lone wolf, or stoner biker as portrayed in the film which caused many to take up cross country motorcycle trips to discover America on their Harleys.

In 1970 *Colors* magazine was born, essentially starting the genre of outlaw motorcycle lifestyle magazines.

COLORS WAS — AND STILL IS — A very hard to find, short lived mag, and predated *Easyriders* summer 1971 debut. It was founded and edited by Phil Castle, a biker who ran a fuel oil delivery company in New Jersey while he tried to make *Colors* a success.

Bad Mags

Colors was primarily focused on the East Coast outlaw bike clubs and events, as that was its home turf, so to speak. But, the money ran out before *Colors* caught on, and by the end of 1971 it had folded after only five issues. It also suffered from poor distribution, as some newsstands, hypocritically, wouldn't carry it and the first issue was banned in a few states, as mentioned in one of Castle's editorials below.

Colors was a hands on production, by those concerned, for the love of their motorcycles and non-conformist lifestyles. It went against the odds, flying in the face of a hostile reception by some newsstands and motorcycle shops.

One of the original contributors to *Colors* was John Herlihy, aka Rogue, who contributed photographs and also wrote a few articles for the mag. Rogue was a one time Airforce gunner and photographer and was also the International President of the Huns Motorcycle Club of Bridgeport, Connecticut for four out of the ten years he rode with them. He was also instrumental in organizing bikers in the fight against the mandatory helmet laws in Connecticut, and was successful. Rogue is on the cover of the second issue (Fall 1970), on his bike 'Crazy Horse', featured inside. Rogue went on to work for Paisano Publications after *Colors* folded and helped them launch *Easyriders*, which did catch on and spawned many imitations. Rogue now lives in Florida, is a well known photo journalist in the motorcycle field, and has contributed photos to many mags, including *Colors*, *Easyriders*, *In the Wind*, *Biker*, *Choppers*, etc.

On *Colors*, Rogue comments:

Colors was a good magazine, especially considering the people involved were *bikers*, not journalists making their living from publishing. The idea was to have a voice, and 'Tell it like it is.' Let people know what was going on, and in many cases, the other side of the story. The stories and information released to the news media by law enforcement and the government was often times misleading or untrue.

It was also going to be a tool to support our efforts in repealing the Mandatory Helmet Laws and other injustices to motorcyclists. And in a way, it did do what it was intended to, by being imitated by larger publishers. The format carried over, and we were in an even better position to inform the bikers of America what was going on.

As the title *Colors* and the side bar 'Motorcycle Club's Bible' (later changed to 'The Non-Conforming Motorcyclist Bible') make clear, it was oriented to, and focused on, the outlaw clubs. It was filled with an abundance of b&w photos of various club colours, bikes, club members, mamas, hangouts, and it even had some tech oriented articles. In the first issue (May 1970), *Colors*' statement of purpose and format, are given as follows:

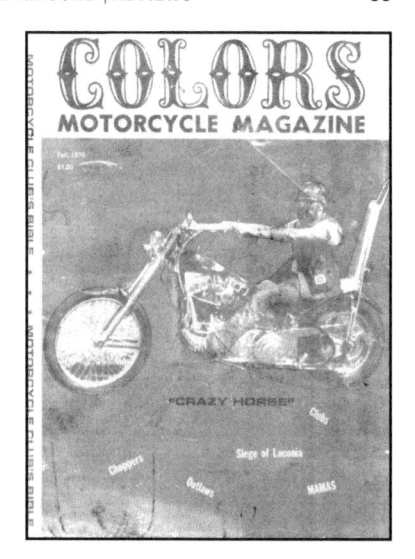

Vol 1 No 2, Fall 1970 [top] and
Vol 2 No 2, Summer 1971 [above].

If you enjoyed Colors, get the BAD MAGS book where hundreds more obscure periodicals are discussed!
www.headpress.com
or see p.160

This is your magazine. That's right, at last someone has come out with a magazine that is not afraid to be called an outlaw magazine. We will not hide behind technical articles or motorcycle manufacturer's sales talk on those foreign bikes. COLORS magazine will not have a 80% AMA background.

We do not care what citizens won what AMA sanctioned race or event. Instead we will feature stories, articles, pictures, and so forth of so called outlaws and clubs.

We will not exclude all foreign bikes from our pages so long as they are directly or indirectly connected to a club, as there are some pretty hot foreign bikes that have been made into some beautiful custom jobs. Nor do we want to feature only choppers as there are many outlaws who do not ride choppers.

We will print any news of your club that you would approve of, as well as pictures, articles and events having to do with clubs.

COLORS will also feature interviews, technical material and some cheesecake for you red blooded studs. COLORS will be glad to print any gripe you may have or any pictures of your bikes, club or its members if you will send same to us.

This is a general idea of the format of COLORS (your) magazine, its success depends on your help and patronage.

Another *Colors* editorial explains further:

Why do motorcyclists ravage the countryside, beating, raping, destroying? NOT TRUE. The news mediums pick a few isolated incidents of vandalism (and what-not), and blow these into movies or headlines. Fights are often started by non-riders testing the patience of the cyclist. As for rape; don't tease the lion in his den, you won't get clawed (old Chinese saying!). Cyclists do not commit more sexual crimes than other groups of society. They do not rove the streets looking for virginal daughters to rape. It's not the bikies bag. As for destruction of property; people are confusing cyclists with extremist bombers and rioters. All one needs is to see a bike near the vicinity of the scene, and they scream, "motorcycle gang!" Why does COLORS glorify the outlaw? We aren't. We're simply tired of a false image pushed on outlaws by ignorant citizens. Aren't you?

Are these cyclists really as tough as they seem? Ask them.

An excerpt from an editorial by Phil Castle from the second issue discusses the problems with getting the magazine sold:

John "CRAZY HORSE" Herlihy

All images in this chapter taken from Colors *magazine. © respective copyright holder*

We included certain things in our mag that might be considered off color in our efforts to make it more entertaining, and if we went too far we apologize even though our mag is aimed at a mature audience of bikers. Motorcycling is no place for the faint hearted.

If we wanted to exploit the outlaw we would depict him as they do in these cheap movies and so called men's adventure mags because this is what people like to read about cyclists: violence, depravation [sic], sex, and all that rot.

… by coming out with the format we presented in our initial issue, we encountered the following problems that tend to disprove the exploitation accusation.

Our first issue was banned in New Jersey, Mass., parts of Pa., Conn., and Delaware to mention a few states.

The cycle shops refused to sell our magazines, except for a few righteous shops who did not fear the establishment. Advertising offers were refused even from shops whose major sources of sales were outlaw and customizing people, not to mention the cycle manufacturers. Last, but definitely not least, we were turned down by many newsstands in the states where we did get distribution. When we questioned the reasons for their objections we were told because of its contents. I noticed the shelves of these very same stands were full of books that would make the Marquis DeSade blush and Hitler gloat.

The main coverage the outlaw clubs had gotten until *Colors*, had been from the straight press and the sensational men's magazines that regularly featured them in fact and fiction. In the editorial above, Castle makes the astute observation that the very same newsstands that refused to carry *Colors* did carry the usual men's adventure and girlie magazines which were overflowing with torture, sadism, and plenty of sex, and ironically, sensationalized accounts of the outlaw bikers themselves.

Having said that, there also seems to be some ambiguity and second thought at work with Castle, on the one hand, he tries to distance *Colors*, and the outlaw clubs, from the sensationalized accounts of rape and pillage portrayed in the mainstream media. On the other hand, he occasionally uses the term 'outlaw' to describe the clubs, as that is what they called themselves. But, the very term 'outlaw' describes someone outside the law, someone who breaks laws. The less controversial phrase 'nonconformist' is used by Castle also, as a way to help distance the clubs from the sensationalism.

In the first issue there is also an article called 'Good Guys vs Bad Guys', which is about the reports of gang rape leveled at the outlaw clubs in various tabloids and newspapers, some of which give graphic descriptions of the sex acts involved. It mentions several incidents from around the

Breed

WOP—Pres. of mother chapter of Breed

Many thanks to Rogue for his generous cover scans and inside info on Colors Motorcycle Magazine.

NEXT PAGE *Some sample* Colors *pages.*

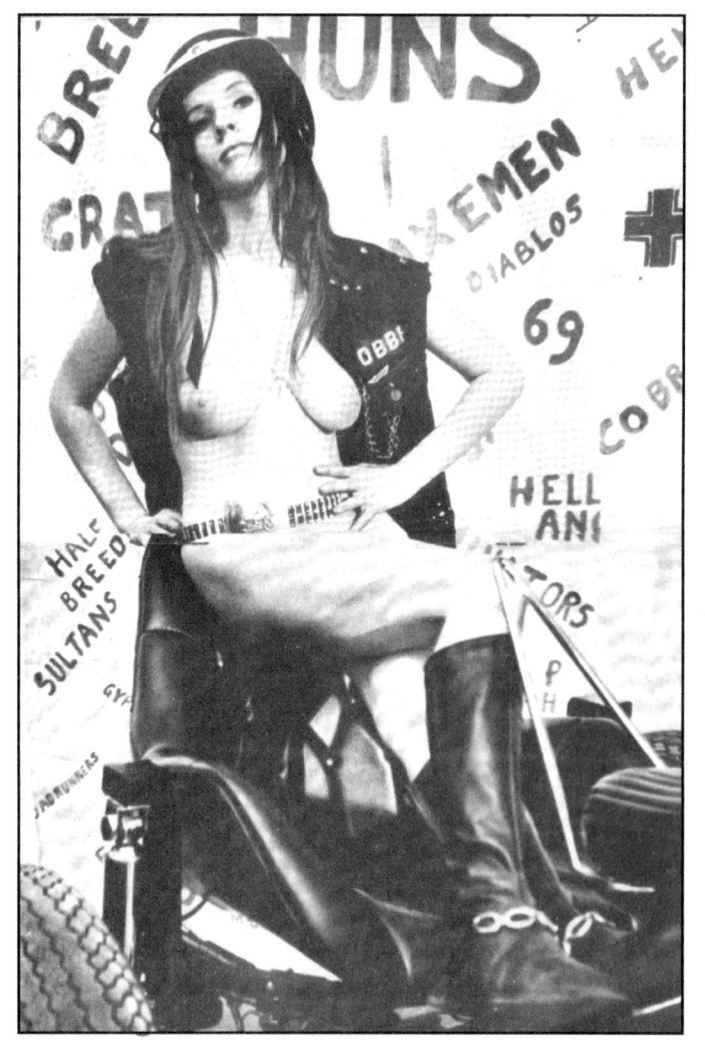

country involving 'outlaw gangs' and explains at the beginning, "We object to the word 'gangs' as most of these outlaw clubs are as well organized and recognized as some of these AMA clubs." But the writer then goes on to use the term 'gang' throughout the article, until it concludes with these thoughts, "So it seems that the law abiding motorcyclists are declaring war on the girl stealing outlaw clubs. It's like the days of old when Knights fought over the fair Damsels only to find out that the Damsels weren't so fair." And lastly, "Let's face it, hard as it is to believe, there is a certain sexual attraction about the outlaw types. But then who could ever understand the female species anyway!"

The annual motorcycle races at Laconia, New Hampshire and the general biker party that surrounds it each year is well covered in *Colors*. Members of the staff would also go on runs with various East Coast clubs and feature articles on them.

Colors was pivotal in that the focus was on the outlaw clubs and their lifestyle as all the biker mags that had come before were technical specs articles on customizing and repair, etc. It was the magazine closest to the outlaw segment of the biker population at the time.

One feature in *Colors*, at first called 'Potpourri', then later changed to 'Rogue's Gallery' — from which Rogue got his nickname — contained interesting photographic portraits of the bikers, their women, their colours, and their bikes. If collected together in book form, the photos themselves would make a great photographic essay of the reality of the outlaw bikers at the time.

Another of the many interesting features contained in *Colors* was the 'Entertainment Review' which had bikers themselves reporting on biker movies and the popular media's portrayal of the outlaw clubs. In the first issue's reviews they covered episodes of the TV series *Adam 12* and *Then Came Bronson*, both of which featured bikers. In the *Adam 12* episode, they were portrayed in an idiotic way and the *Then Came Bronson* show is likened to *Route 66* and mentioned because the character James Bronson rides a Harley Sportster. But the two most interesting, and revealing reviews, are of the then current movies *Naked Angels* and *Easy Rider*.

Of *Naked Angels* the reviewer says:

> That's just what it is, a lot of naked angels, the female kind that is. Aside from

the bare breast & buttocks there is a lot of action in the form of fights between gangs and among the main group themselves." And, "We believe this picture to be as realistic as we've seen without the over playing of the sensationalism angle. We liked it.

Easy Rider is, not surprisingly, given two thumbs up. The review starts, "Easily the best cycle picture we have seen in a long long time and why shouldn't it be. It is produced and written by outlaw type people, for the outlaw type audience and the like." It concludes, "We can't praise this one enough. If you haven't seen it do so as soon as possible."

Colors did have some technical articles, usually one or two per issue, but they were not the main focus of the magazine. Although the other cycle mags on the stands did cover choppers and customized bikes, they shied away from coverage of outlaw motorcycle clubs, with an occasional mention of them when the owner of a featured bike belonged to a club.

Colors also had a 'Club List' at the back of each issue, which was a list of the outlaw clubs from around the country, and the list got longer with each issue. After the movie *Easy Rider* the focus on the outlaw bikers shifted from the clubs and focused more on an outlaw biker lifestyle, generally outside of the clubs, but still connected to them in spirit.

Colors proclaimed itself the 'Motorcycle Club's Bible', which caused some to consider it "the grungiest [motorcycle mag] of them all" because of its outlaw slant and its cheesecake feature, 'Mama of the Month' when compared to the other cycle mags on the racks at the time such as *Big Bike*, *Street Chopper*, *Chopper*, etc.

Colors was maverick, different from the rest, and it paved the way for all the more club friendly cycle mags to come that had taken a lot of ideas from the *Colors* format including biker fiction, nude cheesecake photos, and the outlaw lifestyle focus in general. ■

Pigalle Place Paris

Joe Scott Wilson goes to France and takes the Metro to the sex shops

IF YOU HAVE NEVER BEEN TO FRANCE HERE IS A TIP: try to learn one or two words before you go. It is only courteous to make an effort and communicate with foreigners in their own tongue when abroad. They appreciate it and buy you drinks.

Well okay, forgetting the drinks part, the courtesy won't necessarily get you far in France. Take for example the time I went to Paris in September 2002. On landing at Charles de Gaulle airport at around 10 PM I had to make my way to my hotel in the city centre. The train seemed the best option but by late evening the Charles de Gaulle train station stood almost empty except for bewildered tourists like me.

There is an information desk in the train station where a queue had formed. I joined the queue disheartened to see that the guy behind the desk was impolite. His off handed directions seemed to have left the people in front of me bewildered, but before I could get to ask him my question — "How do I buy a ticket if the ticket machine won't accept my credit card?" — his shift was over and he was replaced by a woman who then sat with her back to everyone, reading a magazine. She replied to every question with a curt "Paris" without bothering to look up.

That was the information desk at de Gaulle train station.

I wasn't the only one in the predicament of not being able to buy a ticket, and consequently I joined a small band of rebel commuters who boarded the Paris bound train without tickets (but every intention of paying upon arriving in the city).

I felt pretty fired up jumping the turnstiles, especially given that three guards stood nearby. But they failed to react in any way and looked rather bored.

On arriving at Gare du Nord in Paris we left the train to find the platform empty. There was no place to buy a ticket and the turnstiles here couldn't be jumped. Neither would they budge under force. But a kindly ticket carrying man on the far end of the platform held open one of the gates for us and we bustled through.

The Parisian public transport system is notorious for its pickpockets and I got to see one in action within minutes of stepping foot off the train when a street urchin attempted to lift the purse of the woman in front of me.

I parted company with my new travelling companions and got a taxi the rest of the way to the hotel.

The next day I started to make a mental tally of the number of derelicts or miscreants riding the Parisian Metro system. Although it is illegal to beg, beggars are everywhere hopping from one car to the next. Other transients just wander through carriages offering a demented soliloquy. With few exceptions, every single car I board on every single journey has somebody who wants my money or wants to tell me something important. The immigrant problem is pretty bad, and women exhibiting babies and forlorn children for loose change is a common sight. One woman I encounter more than once

Photo: Joe Scott Wilson

on the Metro jumps from car to car dragging along a little girl of no more than eight years old and a karaoke rig. Without hesitation, the girl bursts into a piercing rendition of New York New York to a backing tape, while the woman — her mother presumably — encourages the captive audience to show their monetary appreciation.

During my brief visit to Paris — a trip that combines business with pleasure, as I told customs on arrival — I want to spend a little time roaming Pigalle Place, the red light district of the capital. In fact I had no excuse for not visiting the Pigalle, seeing as my hotel was in Montmartre, only one stop away.

In the Pigalle you have the Moulin Rouge, the world famous club that draws wealthy tourists — or those that can afford champagne at £80 a glass. An adults only tour bus was pulled up nearby while I was in the area. Further down the road is a museum of erotica, while in between and all around are strip joints, X-rated cinemas and sex shops. Slap in the middle is a bar in which the staff view their clientele with clear disdain, and on a side street the café that was used in the movie *Amélie*. I wouldn't have recognised the place, even with the huge *Amélie* poster on the wall, but I happen to bump into one of the rebel commuter families who point me in its direction.

I systematically move from one sex shop to the next. I like the porno culture and the people it draws and I like the counter staff in these places, a lot of them in France being Oriental. Some of the staff are elderly, gentlemanly types who seem ill suited to the job of smut, while others are pushy, with no charm or patience. One rough and ready Asian guy has long hair and a big moustache and reminds me of the gun totin' extra who always appears in Hollywood action films (like *Die Hard*). He tells me it isn't important to know the price when I ask him the price of his DVDs; what *is* important, he says, is that I find something I like — we'll worry about the price afterwards. Yeah, like when I get my credit card statement, you sicko. (I don't actually say that.)

He digs out his "*stock de spécialiste*" after I have studied the films on open display.

He is my new friend, he tells me, and will do for me a special price. Many of the films are around the £20 mark by my calculations, but even DVDs that have a price tag of £70 he obligingly drops down to as little as £30.

In another shop I happily barter with one guy until he suddenly refuses to talk anymore and snaps the film back into the rack. Elsewhere one sex shop guy asks me if I want any 'gadgets' — I don't, and if not for the labia on open display I feel as though I could have just been asked if I would like fries with my burger.

Tourists peek through the curtains of the sex shop doorways. Elsewhere two German ladies deliberate over a cabinet displaying dildos. They handle the toys without any hint of joy or fun.

No one bothers me in the French sex shops. But it is late evening and I must be getting tired by now. I walk into one place and say "*au revoir*" and in another place I say "good morning" — to which the guy behind the counter responds, with no hint of a friendly greeting, "good evening."

Porn shop people like to guess the nationality of the punter and are generally pretty good at it, but I am almost always mistaken for a native Frenchman. When I shake my head they guess again: Italian? American?

A fair bit of the pornography on display in the Pigalle is bestiality material. The rest is pretty much typical of the kind of stuff you'd find anywhere else in the Western world. I only find one place that bothers — or dares — to openly sell more edgy stuff than the other shops in the area, with racks devoted to simulated rape films. As I'm digging through these, the counter guy leads me elsewhere to another section, where he tells me in heavily accented English, "Fisting." He makes a fist and denotes that the penetration goes very deep. "Blood. Very good."

Back in the night air I spot a neon sign over a club down a side street that reads Lolita. I imagine that such a provocative invitation equates to nothing more than very expensive drinks.

And with that I head back to the hotel and deduce that I will need a corkscrew for the cheap bottle of wine that awaits in my room. But first the Metro that doesn't disappoint: a woman in my car gets up to make an announcement, "Ladies and gentleman…" — but that's as far as my understanding of French will take me. ∎

ZOMBIE ZOO PRODUCTIONS & CONFECCIONES DRACULA
THE WILD WEEKEND
GOGO GUIDE 2004
Three Madcap Nights of
Wild Foot-Stomping Fun

Wild Weekend

IN THE REAL WORLD IT IS THE RUN UP TO THE US presidential election but Spain doesn't recognise senator John Kerry as a candidate at all, if the novelty rubber facemasks here are anything to go by. If the election was fought and won in the souvenir shops of Spain, George W Bush would lose by a landslide — his visage outnumbered three to one by that of the Osama Bin Laden mask. The full face limp rubber novelty item strikes me as quite funny, but such is the current climate that I cannot imagine anyone in the 'free world' wanting such a thing even as a joke. I contemplate the sheer terror it would bring to an airport lounge, and the likely outcome of the wearer being banged up in a prison cell with an honorary mention in the Big Black Book Of Dissidents. Heck, even the thought of wearing such a thing in the privacy of one's own home is an uncomfortable one.

Other tasteless souvenirs include a toy soldier set packaged under the name 'First War Of The Century', which depicts Bin Laden on the box and incorporates accessories such as a barrel of nuclear waste.

Miss Nailer and myself have not travelled to Spain for Bin Laden or the US presidential election but for the fifth Wild Weekend — our first visit to the almost annual sixties garage music event. The Casino Mediterraneo, the rather grand sounding venue for the weekend's main festivities, is hardly the walk away that we anticipate. Rather it is six or seven kilometres from the city centre on a bus that travels once an hour (if it bothers to stop).

Benidorm is ideally suited to host the Wild Weekend. With any semblance of good taste and modesty hidden beneath ex-pats and the allure of tourists, the city is a giant seaside resort selling tat on stalls around which Oriental salespeople hover. I pick up a pocket watch bearing a five euro price tag. I smile and ask the young salesperson at my side the price anyway. I am primed to barter but my query does nothing but alert a second, clearly more experienced

Benidorm, Spain
Nov 19–21, 2004

Three nights of non stop sixties garage music and go go dancing. David Kerekes is on another planet.

salesperson who materialises with a no nonsense sales pitch glare.

I don't buy the watch but later, when Nailer realises that she will require sunglasses in Benidorm's winter noonday sun, I put my bartering skills into high gear.

"How much?" I ask in English.

"Nine euros," says the young man.

"OK," I reply and hand over a ten euro note.

There's nothing out there

OUR HOTEL is the Hotel Las Vegas. The sliding door leading onto the balcony doesn't lock. Quickly deducing that it wouldn't take much of an athlete to traverse the divide between balconies and empty our room of its possessions, I take the three flights down to reception. The receptionist says that the door is meant to be like that — all the balcony doors in the hotel are like that — it's a health and safety issue. I find this unlikely but with nothing to back up an argument to the contrary, we keep the room.

We need to get to the casino between seven and nine pm to collect our Wild Weekend passes. The organisers are very adamant about these hours — any later we are advised and the ticket office will be closed for the duration of the festivities. Having travelled so far, we don't want to chance it and so endeavour to arrive around seven o'clock. This means giving up on the bus (which will only take us one way anyway, the return service stopping around nine thirty) and opting for a taxi. I have a piece of paper with Casino Mediterraneo written on it, which I show to the taxi driver.

Taxis will be our one dependable mode of transport to and from the casino over the weekend. Given that the prices remain the same after midnight (approx eight euros each way), this isn't such a raw deal.

We arrive shortly before 7 PM, the great big neon lettering of the casino rolling into view on our ride down the motorway. The place is in the middle of nowhere, flanked by a busy motorway on the one side and black hills on the other. Straight away we hit the reception desk for directions. Actually, we hit a couple of young people who are preparing a banner in the foyer. "Wild weekend?" I ask excitedly in English. Their expression is one of mystification.

The woman behind the reception desk puts us straight. In an unnecessarily animated manner she points us in a direction that takes us out of the casino altogether. "You have to go outside," she says. *But there's nothing out here!* As per her instructions we leave the main entrance and go around the side of the building. A security office. Further on, in the darkness, the fire exit for the casino itself. That seems to be it... except for some tiki in the vegetation, which leads us to an oversized beer tent. We walk in. A stage draped in tinsel, beer pumps, wall to wall primitive paintings and a bored looking man in a chef's hat suggests that we are in the right place. No one is on the door and it's seven. At twenty to eight there is still no one on the door, and the tent remains empty apart from a couple of engineers and a drummer working on a soundcheck.

We meet Mark who has just travelled from Belgium for the event, the last leg of his journey guided by the lady on the casino reception. He wears a striped t-shirt. He has no ticket and wants to buy one on the door. We hate to upset him but a placard behind the door of the tent states that the Wild Weekend is sold out. "Oh, no," he says and goes to have a look.

I anticipate 100 people. Why this figure, I don't know. Mark is familiar with previous festivals and reckons there will

---

NEXT PAGE
The Stags — in a promo shot that doesn't appear to reflect the line-up of the band on the WW night.

Wild Weekend

be around 800. At this moment in time, stood in the empty hall and being the only souls around except for staff and crew, even fifty people would seem an unobtainable figure.

Spaniards take things nice and easy, we are quick to discover. They have long lunch breaks and the shops don't open till late in the day. This isn't a particularly good environment for adhering to a schedule fixed in a less lax climate (like London, base to Wild Weekend organisers Josh and Babs). Barely off the starting block, the Wild Weekend has fallen way behind its allocated timetable. A two hour wait for doors to open, we discover, is not unusual. Come Sunday, N and myself will break even this record with a three hour wait in a hotel lobby.

A coach rolls up and people pour from it in high spirits. They number at least fifty. The evening is underway.

It is very important to buy beer at this point, but the bar staff don't answer to hard cash — coupons are required for all beverages and snacks. These are obtained at a desk in the hall, from which a considerable queue has formed.

The coupons are valued at two euros, which will get you a packet of crisps, three euros, which will get you a glass of beer, and five euros, which will get you spirits. I buy a bunch of five euro coupons, but promptly have to return them as the folks behind the bar don't give change nor will they accept a higher value coupon for a combination of drinks.

We anticipate the time to be much later than it is, but without a watch the weekend dissolves into a Gaussian blur with small bursts of reality, thanks to the digital time displays flashing above shop fronts around the town.

Wheelybag, the portable DJ, starts to spin some platters in the hall on his self contained, highly colourful rig in a box,

Wild Weekend
dir: John & Karen Bentham
[w] www.jettisoundz.com

This is a record of the Nov 2003 event and features a couple of numbers from each of the bands that played — an entirely different line up to that of Wild Weekend IV, and includes The Nederbietels (Belgium), The Bristols (UK) and Saturn V (USA). The quality isn't too hot: the camerawork is largely static and the sound appears to have been recorded within the audience. A segment shot inside a car travelling to the casino with the radio playing, adds to the home movie feel. I came away from this DVD thinking that (a) there were a lot of chick fronted bands in 2003, (b) France isn't a country conducive to rock, and (c) the Gonuts are a really disappointing headliner, coming over as a novelty act with their outfits and staged food fights.

The samba version of I Feel Love by Count Indigo, however, is great.

This DVD would be a great souvenir for those who were there, but that's about it. If you are in two minds whether to attend Wild Weekend and come to this film for guidance, you may be disappointed. Hell, don't be in two minds about attending the next Wild Weekend — just do it. [David Kerekes]

Casino Mediterraneo at night and (below) the Smartest Man in Spain. Photos: David Kerekes

Wild Weekend

but through choice or design winds up outside by the entrance in the cold. He seems happy enough, working his deck and announcing records.

We see Mark has managed to get in.

The Stags, the first band of the evening and hailing from the UK, get things underway nicely, firmly establishing the dream like feel that will adhere to the whole smoke machine and fairy lighted weekend. Coming over like a frat band, with a go go dancer on each of the two podiums on stage, I'm really glad that I've not yet managed to down too many of the strong lagers on offer tonight. Their set incorporates a cover of The Sonics' Have Love Will Travel, which I'm surprised doesn't feature in more of the weekend's song lists.

In between the bands, one of the several international DJs will play top tunes (with the exception of Wheelybag, who appears to have placed into storage his own equipment once the ceremonial introduction to the event is over). Some dancing goes on. One guy in denim performs some fancy Northern Soul footwork, while another — stocky, smartly dressed in Chelsea boots — performs some natty spins and has the sixties arm waving, finger snapping business down pat. He won't stop dancing for anything. I refer to him from this point foreward as the Smartest Man In Spain, because I remember an ad of the young George Harrison modelling a pair of fashionable boots that carried that wording.

One track mind

I'M REMINDED of something else when The Knickerbockers' One Track Mind — a song credited with out-Beatling the Beatles — suddenly blasts from the speakers: browsing in an independent record store in New York one day, I asked the guy behind the desk if he would play tracks off a Beatles bootleg I hadn't seen before, *Soul Sessions,* which comprised outtakes and alternate mixes of material featured on the *Rubber Soul* album. The clarity was amazing, and the person behind the desk remarked, "that's nice" as McCartney strummed his way through an acoustic demo of We Can Work It Out. The moment was split by the voice of a disgruntled record browser who couldn't understand the pricing structure on some of the CDs in the shop. "Hey man, what gives!" he yelled, in an attitude that suggested he had been mulling over his problem for several long and arduous minutes before opening his mouth. "Man, these fuckin' discounted used records ya got over here ain't that fuckin' cheap!"

"Dick!" — came the curt response from behind the counter.

Anthony Newley

IN THE GENTS TOILETS, I come to the realisation that if the young men at the Wild Weekend — with their bushy hair and big sideburns — are representative of Spanish males in general, then all the men in Spain look like they just stepped out of *The Cannibal Man*. Initially I liken them to the diminutive, hairy actor Sal Boris in *The Beast in Heat*, but that is cruel and besides, unlike *Cannibal Man*, *Beast in Heat* is not a Spanish film.

The Imperial Surfers are up next, a Spanish surf instrumental trio from the Dick Dale school of motoring — twangy guitar licks and a drummer who shouts out each song title.

The quantity of spirits that a five euro token will fetch is quite amazing. If this was Burger King, Nailer would be knocking back half a Go Regular measure of Malibu with each round of drinks.

There follows the second dance routine of the evening and one of many that will feature over the course of the weekend, as performed by the Actionettes and the Action Men. There is generally a theme to each of these routines, reflecting the fancy dress theme of the night. Tonight is high school night, which explains why all the gals in the dance troupe on stage look like Olivia Newton-John in *Grease* and all the guys are dressed like high school nerds. Having seen several of these guys wandering around earlier in their thick rimmed spectacles, white jerseys and beanie caps, I had no idea that they were an 'act' and was impressed by what seemed an almighty case of fancy dress synchronicity.

But dancing, dancing. Too much dancing.

Godfrey's I Must Be Mad hits the turntables. No matter how familiar some of this stuff is to me, whenever the opportunity arises to hear it at a respectable volume it brings to the songs a whole fresh dimension. The guy in front of me thinks so, too. It's the Smartest Man In Spain, who spins on his heels and makes with the moves. I decide he reminds me a lot of the young Anthony Newley, which then reminds me of the time some twenty or so years ago when I couldn't shake the song Windmills Of My Mind out of my head: I went to a local market stall that sold collectible records and asked the guy if he had a copy of the single Windmills Of Your Mind by Anthony Newley. He pondered the question for a moment. "I don't think Anthony Newley ever sung Windmills Of Your Mind," he replied, then added, "Well, he may have sung it in the shower, but I don't think he ever released it."

I was convinced it was Anthony Newley, though later I found out it was Terry Jacks who released the popular one hit wonder.

Anthony Newley, who is now the Smartest Man In Spain, shakes his hips.

The Embrooks take to the stage. The UK trio — modelled unashamedly on Brit acts like The Small Faces and The Action

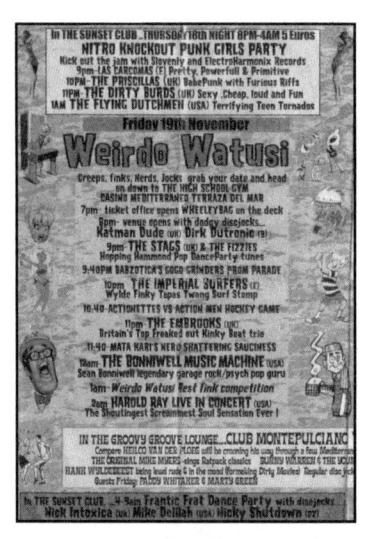

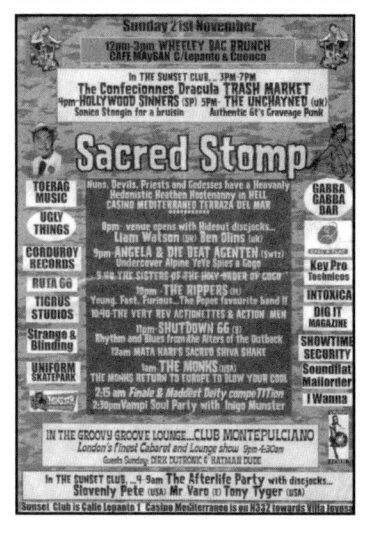

— blast out some incredible freakbeat noises, with superb bass riffs and jagged valve amp chords. It is impossible not to be swept away on The Embrooks' energy and the crowd laps them up

By the end of their set, the cigarette smoke has become close to unbearable. My eyes are hurting. Everyone it seems has a cigarette in one hand and a mobile phone in the other, taking dinky pictures of whatever happens to be on stage.

We don't hang around for original sixties outfit The Bonniwell Music Machine or Harold Ray, the artists who will round off the evening, deciding instead to preserve our energy levels and alcohol capacity (and our eyes) for the following day's festivities.

Do you speak español?

Wild Weekend

OUR ROOM AT the Hotel Las Vegas is sandwiched between a room inhabited by two Spanish guys who talk on the perpetual cusp of an argument, and another in which a couple of girls, who don't talk particularly loudly at all, can be heard clearly all the same. So clearly in fact that when I am awoken in the early hours by their conversation, half asleep I momentarily deduce that strangers have walked into our room. I have no trouble at all keeping up with all their dirty little secrets.

When finally I nod off to sleep, it is time for a marching band to pass beneath our balcony, resplendent with fireworks going off. This isn't a dream, rather a Saturday morning tradition in Benidorm, I feel. The band makes their way to the old part of the city where they regale the tourists and locales with fiesta type music.

Breakfast at the hotel provides a good self-service selection, with frankfurters, bacon, scrambled eggs, beans, bread rolls, cereal, juice, hot drinks and plenty of cakes. One of the waitresses sings to herself as she goes about the business of clearing tables. Elderly passers-by peer in from the streets, looking anxiously in on the scene, thoughts propelled anew to their own next meal.

The food is good but the walls are thin. And I notice a lit cigar on the stairwell.

We take our time heading off to the Sunset Club where Saturday's festivities will commence at around 3 PM with a trash market and live music. (We miss the Wheelybag brunch at the Café Maysan.)

The walk along the beach front brings to us the sight of discreetly topless sunbathers and The Last Supper sculpted out of sand. The figures in the sculpture have fingers that are all over the place, evidently a demonstration of the artist's skill but the result makes for a wonky sight and gives the impression that the artist can't do hands.

The bars on the front are many and the food on sale comprises almost entirely of burgers, or cake and coffee for one euro.

It has gone three, but the Sunset Club is still closed.

In a nearby bar I think I convince Nailer that the song playing on the jukebox — Joe Cocker's version of With A Little Help From My Friends — is actually by a band called Monty Bongo & The Naval Paraders.

Two hours later we return to the Sunset Club. While it is now open, the first band is still setting up.

The trash market itself is a bit of a disappointment in that it's small and not particularly trashy. But then the Sunset Club is small and sweaty so I guess it's appropriate. It's also expensive for drinks: six euros for a glass of beer and a coke. Little wonder there is a guy in the gents who keeps asking me for change…

When eventually the 3 Delicias — a Spanish three piece with a stand up drummer who plays his heart out — do get up to play, I am very impressed by the fact they do a cover of Leave My House. The audience loves the 3 Delicias. Indeed the Spanish audience has an element that treats each band with unbridled party enthusiasm, bouncing around, turning one another upside down, placing things on their heads. I'm not convinced that the bands necessarily appreciate this heightened degree of frivolity, and I do fear for the safety of two beered up revellers when a loop of plastic tape, normally used to secure boxes, finds its way around their necks.

The Playmobils are up next. The White Stripes have a lot to answer for, and I'm happy that this Swedish duo keeps their songs like their set: short.

We didn't manage to catch the Wild Weekend bus to the casino the previous night but tonight we are determined to save ourselves the taxi fare. There is a hairy man outside the Sunset Club who has the same idea. "Is the bus going to the casino?" he mumbles in a manner that suggests he is acutely drunk, before asking "Do you speak *español?*" I reply no, but he repeats the question in Spanish anyway — before the channel from his brain to his mouth is submerged completely in booze and all intelligible dialogue ceases. I think the man is asleep on his feet. He snaps into vague consciousness with an answer to a question directed at somebody else in the club doorway.

"So what do I play? I play the fuckin' radio man."

Minutes later he is in the road stopping traffic, looking for a taxi, extending his hand toward any car door in close proximity. Understandably no one is willing to hang around long enough to let the staggering hairy man into their vehicle.

The coach rolls up and the Wild Weekenders hop on board, including our hairy friend who promptly falls asleep on the shoulder of the guy seated next to him. He stirs only once during the journey to the casino and that is to make a single disparaging remark directed at someone with an American accent seated behind us.

"*Danger zone?*" He mimics the words accurately. "What kind of accent is *that*?"

And then he is asleep again.

Arriving at the casino on time, there is no sign of the organisers and the bar isn't yet open, but there is a soundcheck taking place — we choose to wait in the cold because of it. I'm not sure why but there is something terribly disheartening about hearing a soundcheck: the thump-thump-thump of a bass drum or the jangle of a guitar, repeated with slight sonic variations ad infinitum.

Tiki-Man destroy puny humans

THE WILD WEEKEND scene is quite an incestuous one, with band members and dancers constituting a good portion of the audience when they're not performing.

Saturday night's theme is 'Tiki Twist' — with fancy dance comprising of beach bum outfits, sailors, savages and hula chicks. But one particular fancy dress stands head and shoulders above everything else — literally. It is a man wearing a tiki head mask, some two feet in height, its mouth a down turned black hole.

Like one of the giant effigies on Easter Island it expressionlessly surveys all that passes beneath it. It's a Jack Kirby monster come to life. *TIKI-MAN DESTROY... PUNY HUMANS!*

And then he starts to dance! Very creepy.

The next time I see Tiki-Man he is at a table surrounded by empty beer glasses, chatting to a sailor with a wooden Popeye pipe. I hope I get to take home more than just one memory of this whole weekend, otherwise I fear that this will be it.

I make a drunken note: 'Tiki Man Is Scaring Me.'

What an opening band we have for the second night! The (Amazing) Staggers from Austria belt out a wonderfully tight sixties pop beat with a rich Hammond organ sound. The band look great. Then the singer erupts onto the stage. Like someone wound him up too tight, with his thick rimmed black spectacles, greased down hair and tight fitting suit, he bounces around before jumping onto his back and kicking his legs into the air. This demented Freddie Garrity lookalike

The Staggers

(of Freddie and the Dreamers fame) has so much energy that me and Nailer turn to one another with dumb smiles etched across our face. "He can't possibly keep this pace up!" But he does. And we are very glad. Through the entire set and the encore too, the singer — who we learn is called Wild Evel — doesn't slow down for anything but a refined and very deliberate swig of his beer before smashing the (plastic) glass across his head. Nothing can contain him, nothing will stop him. When he's not hollering or screaming the most inspired lyrics in the world into his microphone ("Jaguar!/Grrrrrrrrrrr!"), he is tearing the props apart or rolling around. When the guitar cuts into a track titled Do The Ripper, he whips out a novelty dagger with which he theatrically proceeds to stab his fellow band members before breaking it and shrugging his shoulders.

The Staggers score several firsts: they are the only band I have seen whose singer courteously leans into the audience to let someone take a drink of his beer. They are the only band of the festival whose set sends me screaming to the merchandise table for goodies. Next to the Monks, they are the only Weekenders who are forced by overwhelming demand to return to the stage for an encore.

The latter throws them a bit. It looks like they played all their own songs, so they opt for a cover. Wild Evel gives a nice impromptu introduction to the song in broken English, which warns the ladies in the audience of a strange man who might be lurking around the next corner. "I think you know who I mean," Wild concludes. In actuality, nobody does but then nobody cares. We all love Wild — this god-like cartoon character, whose every move is an elaborate pantomime. I have to assume that one of the Weekend stage hands is a big Screaming Lord Sutch fan, because the encore turns out to be a cover of Lord Sutch's Jack The Ripper, which sends the usually unphased figure into a mental, rocking fit.

So be careful who you are laughing about
Cos I can make you scream and shout
Waaaauuuuughhhhhh!
Wild Teens, The Staggers

Josh, the Wild Weekend coordinator along with his long standing girlfriend Barbara, is the acting MC. Yesterday he was garbed in the manner of a stereotype English school teacher, with bottle bottom glasses, a mortar board and gown, announcing that the best band in the world would be playing the festival, "all twenty one of them." Today he is a wild man in a loin cloth, beating his chest and babbling unga bunga gibberish into the microphone.

In keeping with the theme, there are a lot of fancy dress sailor outfits here tonight and also a couple of guys who seem to have come dressed as comedians Vic and Bob doing their Jacques Tati impression. I consider this and search for a connection, but can't find one.

I like the fact that members of the staff are engaged in mopping up during the course of the evening. I find it 'very continental'.

Speedball Jnr from Belgium play Dick Dale type instrumentals courtesy of a guitarist who pulls some frightening faces and a female bassist who doubles as one of the go go dancers. They are spot on with what they do, but there is only so much that can be done with a surf instrumental and so we sit most of Speedball Jnr out.

From Japan, the next band up is The Faceful, a four piece that throws itself headfirst into a short set and consequently win the audience over. Or perhaps this has more to do with the cute female singer and her tight butt that one member of the audience feels strongly enough about to jump on stage and squeeze mid song. How she restrains herself from giving the guy a slap I don't know. The Faceful for me highlights the fact that the better Wild Weekend bands aren't locked into a musical groove, rather they draw their energies from sixties garage (and perhaps one or two items of sixties clothing) but then wring it through many other styles until what is left is wholly more idiosyncratic. (A reporter at the Trash Market earlier in the day made the condescending remark that it was great these young kids from around the world were celebrating the sixties like this.)

The guitarist in The Faceful (wearing a Crime t-shirt) hammers out old skool punk chords, the bass player rips through high octane scales and the singer in a red sequined suit belts out singalongs in Japanese, carried on the shoulders of

THIS PAGE
Josh amidst the tinsel.
Photo: David Kerekes

NEXT PAGE
The Faceful live at Wild Weekend V.

the crowd — there may be elements of garage in all of this, but the band has made them their own. This is what separates the wheat from the chaff, the fantastic from the mediocre. The Faceful from Speedball Jnr.

Bringing to an end their cover of Time Is On Our Side, The Faceful singer engages the audience in a chant, evidently built around a crash diet of basic Spanish rock'n'roll. Nailer (whose own Spanish is also pretty lousy) translates:

"Me gusto cerveza" (I love beer)
"Me gusto rock'n'roll" (I love rock'n'roll)
"Vamos vamos" (Go! Go!)
"Cerveza cerveza" (Beer! Beer!)

Tiki-man wins a prize in the best fancy dress competition. Somebody dressed as a priest doesn't win anything because the priest theme is tomorrow night. Monks night. The competition event isn't fully fleshed out, and Josh soon runs out of things for which he can award the several remaining prizes. "Come on," he announces, "attract my attention."

The Black Diamonds are billed as US legends, though I have to confess my ignorance in this instance. I assume they must be an original sixties outfit riding the resurgence of interest, but if that's the case they are awfully well preserved, looking quite youthful and sharp from where I'm standing. They play 'beat party sounds', which is authentic enough in its laid back twangy rock execution but also rather dull.

Intelligent life

TODAY IS SUNDAY. After breakfast Nailer and myself go in search of the Monks.

The Monks — a band that time forgot. Five American GIs stationed in Germany in the sixties who left the army to form a band, playing gruelling shifts of up to six hours a night and honing their sound down to a primal rhythmic structure, in part to combat the language barrier between them and their German audience. And to piss people off too. Their first gig on American soil was in 1999. The Wild Weekend will be their first return to Europe — and only their third ever gig — in over thirty years.

Having spoken to Josh about it the night before, we know the Monks are staying at the Hotel Helios, which is situated in the vicinity of the Sunset Club. It proves difficult to find and we ask for directions several times — from two trash men emptying bins, a Dutch holidaymaking couple and finally a very tanned man wearing no shirt, who points the hotel out to us on the skyline.

The Hotel Helios is rather grand but the receptionist seems distracted and talks to himself. I ask him if he can call Gary Burger or Dave Day for me, the names of two Monks that happen to be foremost in my mind. He picks up a phone and, dialling, asks: "Burger? Nothing else?"

"No, no!" I quickly respond. "*Residente!*"

After this little mix up there isn't any need for him to call anybody, because in the foyer I see a man carrying a guitar case. He has the attitude of a monk.

"Gary Burger?" I ask.

"No. Eddie Shaw."

I introduce myself to Eddie and shake the hand of the man who constructed abnormal bass parts for some of the most unlikely pop music ever created.

More Monks follow and I say hello to them all in the foyer of the Hotel Helios. Eddie explains that they're off to do a soundcheck and should be back in a couple of hours whereupon they'll be happy for me to conduct an interview.

The first time I heard the music of the

Wild Weekend

Monks it was courtesy of the album *Five Upstart Americans*. It was playing in the background as myself and some friends were chatting away over beers. I was becoming increasingly distracted from the conversation by the repetitive, hypnotic beat of the music and the fact that the instruments were locked into a groove that seemed to get louder and more intense and a singer screaming lyrics that were child like and a little bit threatening at the same time.

"Have you heard this music?!" I blurted, interrupting the conversation. "It's all wrong!"

"Um, yeah. I guess." They responded.

Now I am in the Hotel Helios — which suddenly feels very much like a dream — speaking to the guys whose music has found its own special place, but who I had resigned to never being able to see play live; one more band whose time had come and gone and I had missed by miles.

Thanks to the Wild Weekend I have a cosmic reprieve.

Given the way things move in Spain and at the Wild Weekend, a mere two hours for a soundcheck seems unlikely — particularly when the sound engineer was last seen roaming the streets at eight o'clock this morning, pissed.

I optimistically arrange with Eddie to meet back in the foyer at around 4 PM. Nailer and myself make ourselves comfortable.

Into the foyer of the Hotel Helios, like most bars and cafés we visit, comes a stream of unassuming pop music with the occasional surprise. For instance, OMD, George Michael, The Bangles and a Spanish crooner are followed by the unexpected sound of This Charming Man by The Smiths. Then it's back to Shania Twain. The temperature outside is noticeably cooler today but the lack of air conditioning in the foyer makes for a warm sleepy environment.

(Suspicious Minds by Elvis Presley...)

Nailer puts on her sunglasses so that no one will notice her falling asleep. This makes her look like a rock star, which may be the reason staff don't bother us in our three hours of loitering.

The Monks! (L–R) Roger, Gary, Larry, Eddie & Dave.

Wild Weekend

I'm wide awake but last night I dreamt (for the second time this week) that I was on a strange planet. I am wearing a space suit and communicating with Earth when I notice a strange construction that suggests intelligent life — a tubular object, about the length of a cigar, protruding from a rock. (That it was probably created by intelligent beings is a dream deduction I base upon the object not actually sitting on the ground.) I pluck the thing from the rock and begin to unscrew one end. Inside is something resembling the nosecone of a NASA spaceship. I report to Earth that I am not going to investigate further as I'm unhappy about what might be inside, becoming agitated upon hearing movement from within. It unscrews itself, unleashing countless black, pin head sized creatures that fly straight at me trying to penetrate any vulnerable part of my space suit. My vision turns black as the creatures — too small to have any determinable features — completely cover my visor. I'm glad my suit is airtight. But then the tiny specs get in. I am clawing at my visor when I awake to the sound of one of the girls in the next room on the telephone: "Right… Right… Right… Aw… You'll be alright…"

Another space dream I had earlier in the week was set again on a strange planet with me wearing a space suit, but in this instance I had special breathing apparatus on account of the surface dust of the planet that came up to my chin. I waded slowly for what seemed hours until I reached a building flanked by two humanoid creatures, both deep in the dust like me. Then I awoke.

Some people say the meaning of a dream runs contrary to what is actually depicted in the dream. I am at a loss to figure the significance of my space dreams.

(Heart of Glass by Blondie... Billy Jean by Michael Jackson, a song that gets the receptionist humming... Changing Man by Paul Weller... The nature of the play list is a bit more adventurous now that the day is wearing on.)

At 5 PM the lights in the foyer come on. Groups of old people who are seated around the place — in expectation of an evening coach excursion? — are motivated by the lights into getting up, grabbing their belongings and donning their coats and jackets.

Anita — Mrs Eddie Shaw — whom we met earlier, is passing by. "They're not back yet?" she asks. "That's Spain for you!" We will see Anita again before the Monks return.

(Fame... Smoke On The Water...)

Some people are playing dominoes and card games, while a party with a film camera shoots the foyer by the reception area.

(Charmless Man by Blur...)

6:30 PM and still no sign. "That's some soundcheck!" jokes Keith Patterson, who happens along. "It'd better be something serious!" Along with Mike Stax editor of *Ugly Things* magazine, Keith tracked down and interviewed the Monks back in 1990, and so is in part responsible for bringing the band back into the public arena.

(Alberquque by Prefab Sprout, a song and a band that epitomises indie averageness...)

The Monks return. They are surprised to see us still waiting, and apologise. The soundcheck they admit wasn't great and they are tired and way behind schedule. In spite of it all however, they are perfectly courteous and the interview goes ahead. [*The Monks interview appears in Lovers Buggers & Thieves, see ad elsewhere.*]

Spanish like Paella

WE LEAVE THE MONKS and the Hotel Helios very happy indeed, an interview under our belt, and decide to have a celebratory meal — something traditionally Spanish like Paella But hearty meals are difficult to locate in Benidorm, especially traditional ones, and so some time passes as we search for any reasonably priced bistro that isn't dedicated to fast food.

Wandering the streets eventually we hit an intersection, with two familiar restaurants on the other side of the road. We'd passed these restaurants much earlier in the day whilst in search of the hotel. Located back to back, outside of each stand the same waiters as before, still politely encouraging potential customers to come inside. One waiter had offered me a business card and I had taken it despite having no intention of returning. Now here we are again, choosing his restaurant over the other because his restaurant is empty and he looks dispirited. As he sees us crossing the street towards him his face lights up — his many hours of perseverance having paid off.

We eat too much.

Hairy Man returns

IT IS SAINTS & SINNERS night at the casino. The last evening of the Wild Weekend brings forth girls wearing flashing devil horns and many guys dressed as priests (and some as nuns). There is even someone dressed as Evel Knievel, replete with Stars & Stripes motorcycle helmet that stays firmly locked on head for the duration. Given the relaxed nature of the event, there are no competitions tonight and no prizes are awarded for best fancy dress. But the winners in my books are the two guys wearing Ku Klux Klan outfits. They manage to turn a few heads. (The sensitive issue of racism is topical news following the football match earlier in the week where Spanish supporters derided England's black players for ninety minutes.)

Angela & Die Beat Agenten from Switzerland are the first band of the evening. They are completely out of their depth and are the one real dud of the whole weekend. Their playing, combined with their song introductions, regulation sixties outfits and pistol packing spy antics, come across as horribly laboured.

The Rippers from Italy on the other hand play hard R&B, with guitar and bass players pulling faces and attacking their instruments as though

Three Monks in Spain: (L–R) Eddie Shaw, Dave Day & Gary Burger. Photo: Miss Nailer

Many thanks to the Wild Weekend organisers, Josh and Barbara, for putting on such a great show, the crowd and of course the bands and performers. A big thank you to Miss Nailer, Eddie Shaw (The Monks), and Wild Evel (The Staggers), Sawa Takashi (The Faceful), and Lou & Nigel (The Stags) for the photos.

their lives depended on a good show. The vocalist belts out the tunes well enough and plays a mean harmonica, but his habit of concluding each number like he's about to collapse from physical exertion, clutching breath as though he has just run a marathon, is irritating. Is this supposed to be an endearing trait?

"Plenty of entertainment all night, I think," says Josh up on the stage where he will later propose to his long standing girlfriend and Wild Weekend co-ordinator, Babs.

I am thrown for a moment when I encounter someone in the audience who looks like Ollie Reed in his puffed up final days. I am thrown again when two identical faces stare blankly into the audience away from the stage, the white clown makeup of French mime artists posited on the back of two heads.

I could watch the Smartest Man In Spain dance all night. He dances with his girlfriends but is focused on all that is around him. I like his funny shape.

Mark is still here, wearing the t-shirt that he wore two nights ago. His friend from Belgium tells me a story about a drunken man he met in the small hours of this morning, who was requesting the directions to a hotel, any hotel. The description is that of the Staggering Hairy Man. Mark's friend tells me it is the strangest thing he has ever seen in his life — but then he says the same about the go go dancers and the Tiki man and the event in general.

Shutdown 66 from Australia is a good garage rock outfit, let down somewhat by a front man who doesn't really cut the mustard. A pity, as this is a band whose drummer isn't averse to picking up parts of his kit and taking them into the audience for some wayward skin bashing.

Everything on this third night of the Wild Weekend is geared towards the appearance of the Monks — their third gig since disbanding in the sixties. I would say the countdown to the Monks, the band that motivated us to travel to Spain in the first place, started not tonight but on the day we spotted the Wild Weekend flyers in a Manchester rock shop several weeks ago.

Monktime

Higgle-dy Piggle-dy
Way down to heaven,
Yeah!
Higgle-dy Piggle-dy, the Monks

FINALLY it's Monk Time. Religious chanting fills the auditorium, milking the reverent expectation of the crowd for all it's worth. The curtain opens on original band members Gary, Eddie, Dave and Larry, plus newbie Mike who is assisting on vocals and who was introduced to me earlier as a "sound manager". The drummer is a stand in, Roger Johnston sadly having died two weeks ago. All are wearing black suits and a noose for a tie beneath their Monks' habits.

Gary greets the crowd, the unmistakeable gravel of his voice no different to when he laid down *Black Monk Time* tracks thirty years ago. Eddie on bass plays the patterns we all know and love, while an excited Dave hammers his banjo like a pile driver and Larry hits the high notes with his keyboard. The band is tight, but as one song melts into the next they become tighter, played with increased confidence and gusto.

Reforming bands and playing reunion concerts is something of a mini craze these days, but for the Monks it never for a moment seems like a nostalgia trip. These are guys of advanced years on stage, no mistake, but they play with a heart and passion that sets them apart. I don't think for a moment they care a jot about reunion gigs or what anyone else might be doing in the world of popular music. That was never their concern in the sixties when they cut their hair in a completely unflattering tonsure, donned their Monks habits and noose neckties, and it isn't their concern now. Their sound remains 100 per cent contemporary, because it remains removed from any time frame.

On asking Eddie in the interview earlier whether he considered whilst recording *Black Monk Time* that here was something unique, he answered without hesitation: yes. Gary added that it seems like they never stopped playing, and that thirty years is more like yesterday. It certainly seems that way watching the Monks play tonight, blistering fuzz box and feedback, though I suspect the first few numbers in their set are affected by fallout from the soundcheck anxieties of earlier.

The Monks' set comprises *Black Monk Time* in its entirety, the single I Can't Get Over You/ Cuckoo, plus bonus material as featured on *Five Upstart Americans*. I quibble that they don't play He Went Down To The Sea, a single B-side that isn't really indicative of the Monks' sound but captures something fragile and has some great vocal parts.

The show is over far too quickly and Josh implores the Monks to return to the stage for one more number. Having exhausted their set they return to play Oh, How To Do Now a second time, a blistering version that leaves the audience baying for more. They don't get it.

Fuzzy Monday

AND SO ENDS three nights of the Wild Weekend. Equal parts surreal and fabulous, the outstanding musical moments have been the Monks and The (Amazing) Staggers. As for everything in between — well, it's left both myself and Nailer with fuzzy Monday morning heads, and I stand in the hotel breakfast lounge thinking that it shouldn't really be that difficult or complicated a decision whether I need coffee or food or both.

Complication?

The Monks. Complete respect. They did what they did for their music, their art, their craft all those years ago. Looking kind of strange and ridiculous and living the life for a 'reward' that would take a whole generation to reach them — such as it is. Mine and Nailer's waiting a mere three or so hours in a hotel lobby for an interview is no time at all to wait.

Taking a moonlight stroll later that evening, Nailer and myself wander into old Benidorm, on a hill by a church overlooking the beach. A voice calls out my name. It's Gary and Eddie. Talking about the Wild Weekend show and how fresh the music still sounds, Gary says, "We are not trying to be twenty years old. We just do what we do." We chat a little and then say goodbye.

I have had some surreal experiences in my life but being stopped in the street by the Monks ranks as one of the most surreal. This is a bizarre and fitting end to our brief stay in Spain; an epilogue to our Wild Weekend that not even Quinn Martin could have conjured up. I pinch myself. While I do on occasion dream of strange planets, I also dream of attending gigs by bands that I could never hope to see in reality, but not even my dreams would be so naïve or audacious as to have those bands stop me in the street for a chat.

The rest of the evening I am somewhat detached. In a restaurant serving paella that isn't too expensive, I ask for "*une bière, s'il vous plaît*". I know I'm not in France but I won't be in Spain for much longer either. ■

For future events, keep an eye on
[w] www.wildweekend.com

Subway Suicides

Mikita Brottman is on the New York subway system, where suicide is a regular hazard, more common than in other major cities

WHEN I WAS LIVING IN LONDON A FEW YEARS AGO, A friend called to tell me he'd be late for our meeting; there'd been a suicide on the subway. As the train was pulling into the station at Bethnal Green, an otherwise inconspicuous woman had apparently run forward and literally *hurled* herself off the edge of the platform and under the wheels of the oncoming train, horrifying the crowd of early afternoon passengers.

The train remained in the station, an announcement was made, and the platform was evacuated. On his way up the escalator, my friend saw the emergency team arriving with medical equipment and crime-scene tape. The other passengers, being British, muttered a few laconic complaints about the woman's selfishness and their missed appointments, but this was clearly a nervous and defensive response to the terrifying scene that had just invaded their afternoon. My friend and I were naturally curious about this woman and the combination of circumstances that had led her to this sudden, desperate act. Checking the local newspapers the following day, however, we found no mention of the incident.

Similar things happen in the New York subway system, where suicide is a regular hazard, more common than in most major cities. Disturbingly, however, the New York Transit Authority does not release any suicide figures, and most cases of subway suicide fail to make the news.

In some ways, it doesn't surprise me that some people elect to end their lives in the subway, especially in a city like New York; much of the subway here seems so depressing. In summer weather the heat can be quite suffocating, and in certain stations late at night the stench of urine and ripe garbage is inescapable. With its ill lit platforms, stifling air, junk strewn stairwells, and fat bellied rats clambering among the rails, it's hard to imagine a more dispiriting place for those already at the end of their tether.

Indeed, how many of us haven't had the experience, at least once, when standing close to the edge of the tracks, of thinking how easy it would be to take that extra step off the edge of the platform? I've known people for whom this temptation is so real they can't bring themselves to use the subway. This is one of those peculiar and destructive impulses best described by Edgar Allan Poe, in an essay of the same name, as the 'Imp of the Perverse.' "We stand on the brink of a precipice," writes Poe. "And because our reason violently deters us from the brink, *therefore* do we most impetuously approach it. There is no passion so demoniacally impatient as that of him who, shuddering upon the edge of a precipice, thus mediates a plunge."

Hurling oneself under a subway train certainly seems like a foolproof, if messy, means of death.

but for those members of the emergency response team whose job is to walk down the track and pick up all the pieces. If the victim is deceased, things are sadder but easier; subway workers can have the line back up and running fifteen or twenty minutes after the incident. If the suicide is not successful, the rescue process can delay trains for hours.

It is curious that in this post Kevorkian era, with plenty of advice available from groups like the Hemlock Society and books like *Final Exit*,

However, not all who do so manage to kill themselves. An eighty ton, eight car train is traveling very fast when it pulls into the station, and is certainly solid enough to cause instantaneous death, but only if the person gets hit in the right way. Some would be suicides live on in a lifelong vegetative state. Some survive with severed limbs — a horrifying outcome, not only for the victim,

people still choose to commit suicide on the subway. With the easy availability of many different kinds of fatal drugs, throwing yourself under a subway train seems an unnecessarily cruel and unpleasant means of ending your life. In fact, most of the people whose lives end this way are homeless and dispossessed, often alcoholics or psychiatric outpatients — people already inclined to self destruction, and perhaps with little access to more 'civilized' methods of suicide. The media in Toronto had a great deal to say in August 2000, when Dr. Suzanne Killinger-Johnson, a wealthy psychotherapist, parked her Mercedes at a subway station and threw herself under a train, clutching her six month old son to her chest. But little was made of the other thirty or so suicides that took place on the Toronto subway that same year. Does the fact that 'respectable' members of society rarely kill themselves in this way explain why there are far more suicides on the subway than are reported in the news?

Or are there more strategic reasons to explain why — unless we or someone we know witnesses a suicide first hand — we tend to hear very little about this disturbing phenomenon? Reliable research shows that the reporting of suicides in the press can have an impact on vulnerable people. A major 1995 study of suicide coverage in Australian newspapers found that rates of male suicide increased following reports of suicide in the press, with actual suicides peaking on the third day after a story appeared. (Female suicides are apparently less swayed by media reports.) In another famous study, the number of subway suicides and suicide attempts in Vienna dropped after the introduction of media guidelines led to less frequent reporting of suicides in these locations. On the other hand, it is a well established fact that people who are determined to kill themselves will eventually manage to do so in one way or another — that media reports can influence the *method* of suicide chosen, but not the overall number. The New York Transit System — the largest subway system in the world — is pleased to release plenty of impressive statistics about its 468 stations and 656 miles of track. But should we not be informed of its other, less triumphant statistics as well?

Different subway systems have different policies in this regard. On the London subway, a 'Person Under Train' incident — colloquially known by tube workers as a 'one-under' — are reported quite stoically by London Transport, and often included in public reports on timetable delays. It's not rare, for example, to discover that your schedule has been delayed due to 'a person under the train at Stepney Green,' information that is not considered dangerously encouraging to would be suicides. (Nor does it seem to be so: the London Transport reports two or three suicides a month on the tube, which is not especially high, though the number increases during Christmas time, with as many as three a day). In Tokyo, by contrast, subway suicide has become so common that extra guards

Art this chapter: Brianna Johnson

Subway Suicides

now patrol the platforms of twenty six suburban stations to deter suicidal jumpers — not so much for reasons of public welfare as to avoid the disruption of Tokyo's obsessively regular train schedules. In an additional effort to discourage would be jumpers, the Tokyo transit system has adopted the policy of billing the suicide's family for the extensive clean up procedures that such incidents generally demand.

In Toronto, suicide prevention posters are displayed and telephone hotlines have been installed on some platforms. Still, suicide rates on the Toronto subway remain as high as one a week, and have become such a common occurrence that subway personnel no longer call a coroner to the scene. There are practical reasons for this new policy. If a person is pronounced dead on the tracks, subway service has to be interrupted for the next twenty four hours while the police conduct an investigation; if the body is transported to a hospital, lengthy train delays become unnecessary.

So severe has the problem in Toronto become that safety experts have suggested the installation of plexiglass barriers between the beginning of the platform and the end of the subway tunnel, since the majority of serious 'jumpers' stand hidden behind the wall of the platform where the train first enters the station. Since a person waiting in this hidden zone cannot be seen by the train driver until it is too late, these plexiglass barriers would mean that anyone jumping onto the tracks would have to do so in full view of the train driver, who, with this window of opportunity, could easily reduce the speed of the train as it entered the station, significantly limiting the possibility that the suicide will be fatal. The idea is that potential suicides would at least be discouraged from choosing this violent and public method, knowing that they may succeed only in sustaining terrible injury. The cost associated with the installation of the barriers, according to safety experts, could be paid for by corporate advertisements placed on the plexiglass shields. But what company, I wonder, would choose to promote its merchandise on a suicide barrier? Prozac, perhaps?

An experiment in Budapest to install large mirrors on subway platforms has also been undertaken with the aim of preventing suicides, though the logic behind this move seems unclear. Perhaps catching a glimpse of themselves in a mirror is meant to jolt would be suicides back into the present moment and remind them of their real world responsibilities. For the elderly, depressed, or disheartened, however, a glimpse of their reflection in the mirror does not sound as if it would be especially life affirming.

Of the many deaths that occur every year on the New York subway, no one knows for sure how many are suicides, except — on some occasions — the driver of the oncoming train, who is often the last person to see the suicide before death. Those who hide behind pillars and leap in front of trains at the last second are obviously suicidal, as are those who walk as far as they can down subway tunnels, or lie down on the tracks and wait, or deliberately touch the third rail. Some people have been known to wink at the train driver, or tip their hat just before being hit. In other cases, unless a note is discovered it's difficult to tell whether the death is a suicide or an accident. Many subway deaths are filed away as 'undetermined', which is one of the reasons why suicide rates for many subway systems are never made public.

Most subway suicides are successful, and the trauma can extend to those who happen to witness such incidents. Simply being present during an event of this kind can lead people to need counseling or therapy; they may suffer from nightmares, anxiety, and a dread of using the subway in the future. More often, however, the worst sufferers in such situations are neither fellow passengers nor innocent bystanders, but the train drivers, who are often haunted not by what

> But what company, I wonder, would choose to promote its merchandise on a suicide barrier? Prozac, perhaps?

they see — the victim disappears from view some distance before impact — but by the sound that comes a second later. Subway drivers report that this sound is completely distinctive and impossible to get out of their heads. A certain station, platform, or suicide hot spot may carry horrifying memories for a long time afterward. With such frightening repercussions for those uninvolved in the case, there is a compelling argument to be made for releasing information about suicide statistics.

On the other hand, since statistics are now out of reach, is it possible that stories about subway suicides have come to function as urban legends — incidents which, while not unheard of, are far more common in rumour and anecdote than in real life? Brooklyn based author Ryn Gargulinski, who has made a study of the occupational folklore of New York subway workers, discovered that the same tales of suicides, severed heads, and smouldering corpses were circulated among different groups over many years, with certain recurrent themes and variations.

They include the story of the passenger who becomes trapped between the platform and the train, sometimes by accident, sometimes as a result of a suicide attempt gone horribly wrong. In most versions of the story, the victim's body gets twisted around like taffy by the moving train, while the head protrudes above the platform and the person remains quite conscious, sometimes unaware of the gravity of the situation. As soon as the weight of the train is removed, however, the victim's body will immediately unwind, leading to certain death. In most versions of this story, emergency workers offer the victim a final beer or cigarette, sometimes even going so far as to bring a priest or members of the victim's family to the scene so they can share a few last words. This story has become quite common since it appeared in the media; a version was told by an emergency worker to a cab driver on HBO's *Taxicab Confessions,* and it later formed the substance of perhaps the best known episode of the television series *Homicide: Life on the Street.*

Gory, dramatic events like this may indeed be witnessed from time to time, but according to Gargulinski, not as often as the cautionary stories that are told about them. The function of such tales is partly to encourage safety by reinforcing the importance of remaining alert and careful on the subway, and partly to warn people of the general dangers of urban life, with its sinister stalkers and slayers. Horror stories like these are shaped, told, reshaped, and passed along from subway worker to passenger, from friend to friend, sometimes with slight variations, but always with certain internal patterns and motifs intact, like the threat of anonymous lurkers on the platform, or the horrible retribution in store for those who come too close to the third rail.

For people who spend a lot of time on the subway, suicide hot spots are familiar, and sometimes even haunted by stains on the tracks — sites of bloody tragedies, the very spot where someone's life has come to an untimely end. These places, like the stories that are told about them, have become part of the traditional folklore of an urban community, evoking powers that are almost supernatural. Like depression, alcoholism, and mental illness, subway trains can be brutal and fatal, no matter how carefully we regulate their comings and goings. And in the same way, these stories tell us, the human bodies we so carefully discipline are liable to betray us at any moment — to slip, to fall, to push, to get trapped — or to experience perverse compulsions completely beyond our control. ■

HEADPRESS 27
The Darker Side of Serial Killing

In the inimitable HEADPRESS way, this will be an informed but informal look at homicidal nuts, along with the atypical assortment of HEADPRESS fayre. If you would like to contribute send your proposal to Headpress/Critical Vision, PO Box 26, Manchester, M26 1PQ, UK

Contents so far include

- Fred & Rose & snuff films

- An interview with Richard Metzger, the man behind the Disinformation Company

- Brian Kellman, director of the 1971 drug awareness short *Weed*

- The art of Jörg Vogeltanz

Publication Date: SEPT 2006

www.headpress.com

---

l'abecedaire chimerique
by Progeas Didier

VOULE DE VUÏRE : érrotique égérie des vents elle s'adonne, par ellipses, à la contemplation.

WOOGLOTIN : surnommé le lutin de wock, il distribue ses éclats de rires aux quatres vents

XYNOQUOBROCK : instable et incomprehensible il perpetue la mysterieuse et complexe tradition de l'x

To be concluded...

More Fun Than An Open Casket Funeral

**TanExpo 2004
Modena, Italy,
March 26-28**

Carlo Strappa goes to the exhibition of funeral and cemetery articles.

I WAS NOT QUITE SURE OF WHAT TO EXPECT FROM THE TanExpo 2004 show. During the trip to Modena I was trying to figure what the booths would look like, what sort of gadgets would be on display, and so on… I felt a bit like I was smuggling myself into a world where common mortals, unless they're dead, are not usually admitted.

On our arrival we were welcomed by a traditional hearse from the fifties and a very long line of professionals of this sector from all over Europe, patiently waiting to enter the exhibition to meet business partners and gather the latest information and learn of technical developments.

Once inside, the first glimpse was impressive — surrounded by shining new hearses, caskets and all sorts of funeral paraphernalia was like my most morbid fantasy come to life. The general atmosphere was professional rather than gloomy, as befitting any trade show. Still, it was somewhat striking hearing your typical salesman, dressed in a typical business suit, describing the technical qualities of a crematorium or a dissecting table. Not to mention your typical pretty hostess wearing a violet tailleur.

I felt much more relaxed when I overheard a group of gravediggers cracking jokes about misadventures in the routine of their daily work.

The exhibitors could be placed into one of the following categories: marble engraving equipment, marble and granite items, burial cells, urns and caskets, handles and fittings for caskets, funeral and cemetery items, hearses, sanitary products, cosmetic products, printed materials, trade press, trade shows, cemetery handling, and cremation equipment.

Among all the products and services on display there were highlights that particularly caught my attention and which I found representative of something more personal.

In the first place I would put producers of 'photoceramics', authentic full colour headstones, complete with the picture of the deceased. An exhibitor explained that through the wonders of digital photo retouching he was able to dress an image of the beloved in a proper ceremonial dress, even if in the original picture the beloved was wearing shorts; not to mention that he could insert a fresh background, from evocative sunsets to Caribbean landscapes. The problem for me was that the final result more resembled a television screen than the memory of a loved one. I imagined the horror of entering the local cemetery and being surrounded by hundreds of burial chambers offering a view similar to the stacks of TV sets normally seen in shopping malls.

Another interesting application was the fully aerographed caskets. Among the samples on display was an impressive black design featuring countless skulls painted on the surface. Ideal for a biker's eternal rest!

One absolute oddity was the vending machine that could be placed in cemeteries and churches to distribute lighters and candles.

A French company had a huge display of products covering all sorts of post mortem equipment, from biodegradable chin rests to funeral cosmetics that guaranteed high level drying properties that help delay decomposition, to all sorts of aspirating pumps and mouth sealing devices (resembling syringes from the early days of medical discovery).

Refrigerated containers, mortuary linings, chemical compounds, adhesives, body bags, and plastic devices to give a proper expression to the mouth of the deceased… The strongest memory I have of this particular booth is that of a mannequin — which I think they used for demos of cosmetic treatments — with half of its face destroyed.

The most luxurious booths undoubtedly were those of the foundries and producers of cemetery accessories such as crucifixes, vases, lamps, statues and urns, which suggest that there is big money to be made in this business.

In closing I would like to say that Padre Pio (1887–1968), the religious man from Pietralcina (Foggia) in the deep south of Italy, confirmed his status as one of the most holy icons in Italy. His face was the most widely reproduced in the statues, engravings and images on display at TanExpo 2004. ∎

PREVIOUS PAGE
Wax finished casket — does not pollute during cremation.

THIS PAGE
Padre Pio by Italian artist Daniele Cudin (above), and mouth sealing tool (below).

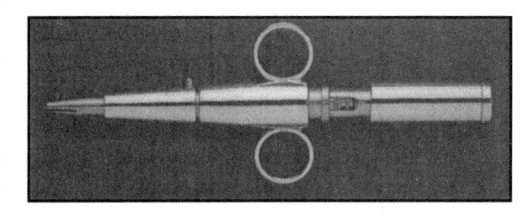

For the aspiring necro-aesthete, death related trade shows:

FunerMostra
8th Edition international Funeral Products & Services Fair in Valencia (Spain), June 2-4 2005
[w] www.feriavelencia.com

Devota 2005
6th Edition in Ried (Austria)
Nov 18-20 2005
[w] www.devota.at

Tanexpo 2006
3rd Edition in Modena (Italy), Mar 24-26 2006 [w] www.tanexpo.com

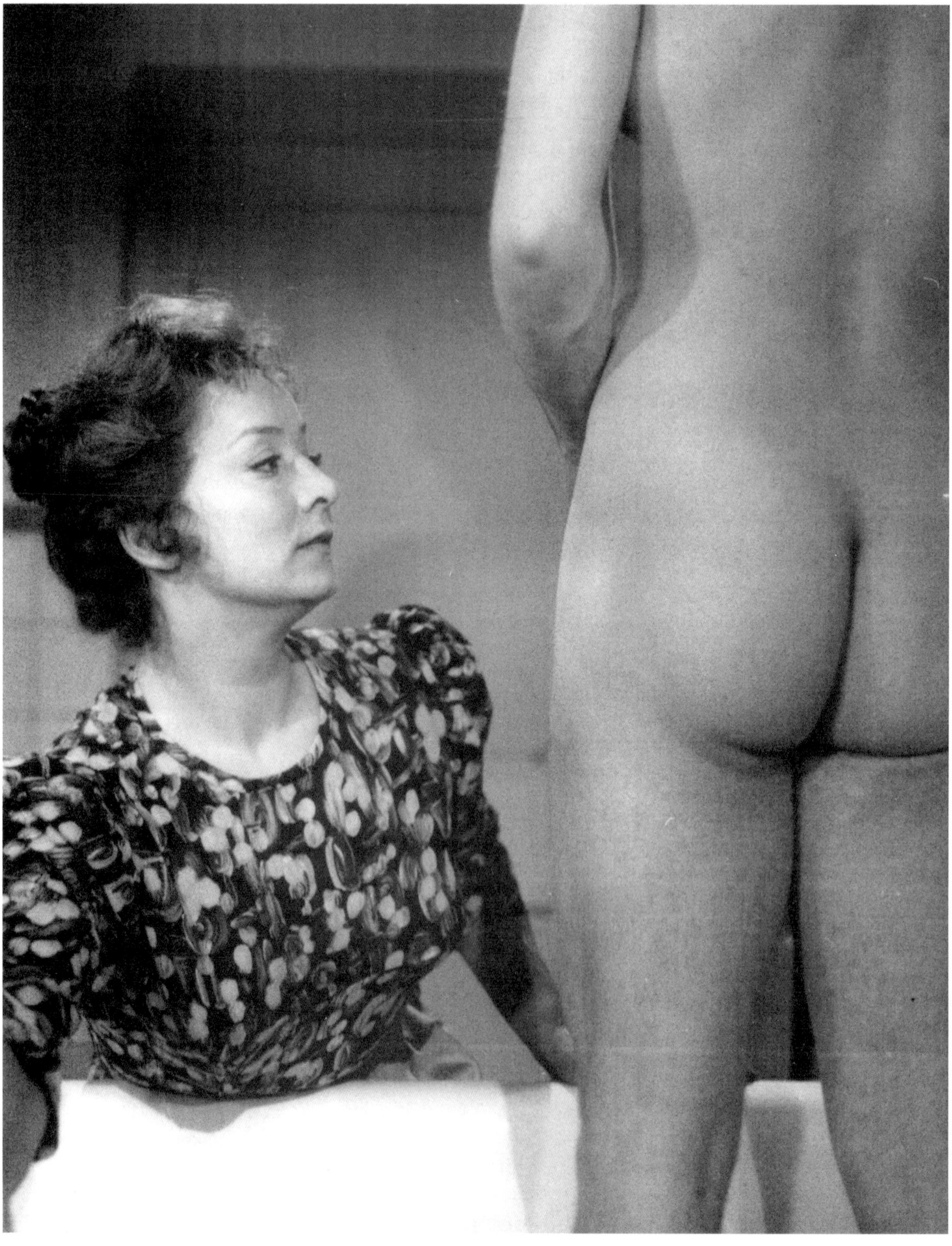

Carry On Denmark!

JACK LEMON AND WALTER MATTHAU NEVER ACTED IN pornographic films in America, but they did in Denmark, or at least their Danish counterparts — Ove Sprogøe and Dirk Passer — did, goofing their way through a sea of naked gals in a string of comedies that go all the way back to 1962. In America no agent would have permitted stars of like status to act in such pictures. First off, films containing full blown nudity would have been confined to the financially marginal grindhouse or arthouse circuits, and secondly they would have aroused the moral wrath of half the country!

The way in which pornography, both softcore and hardcore, came to be accepted in mainstream films by a wide general public in Denmark would have been inconceivable in America (or most if not *all* other countries), and illustrates in a nutshell the pronounced differences in mentality between two cultures that on the surface can seem so similar.

Nudity on the silver screen was not something that happened overnight in the liberated sixties. The nudist lifestyle first became popular in the thirties, giving rise to a string of movies that extolled in somber pseudo scientific fashion the virtues of stripping down. Yet for all the focus on nudity, these films were curiously asexual; producers bent over backwards to present the subject in an objective, scholarly light and to hide the actors' genitalia behind potted plants, counter tops, bushes and so forth, rendering the films more palatable to censors. Nudism was presented as a philosophy or ideology, and to ban these films would raise free speech issues. In America a series of court rulings in the late fifties and early sixties afforded them protection from hostile local censorship boards which had attempted with mixed success to prevent them from screening.

The 1938 American nudist film by Allen Stuart, *The Unashamed* — the only one with a full blown narrative — illustrates how differently Danes and Americans perceived issues of nudity and sexuality. The title itself infers that shame was synonymous with the state of being naked. Here were the bold ones, the free ones, the 'unashamed'. This reflected the time honoured American tradi-

PREVIOUS PAGE
A maid stares enraptured at Ole Søltoft's tackle in *Eric Soya's '17'*.

Jack Stevenson takes a look at Denmark's most popular sex comedy double act

Sexual hallucination scene from I Jungfruns Tecken.

Danish Porno

tion of equating sex with sin and guilt. Conversely shame never sold tickets in Scandinavia; when *The Unashamed* was imported into Denmark, the literal translation of its title *Vend Tilbage Til Naturen* was the less guilt ridden *Turn Back To Nature*.

The first American to introduce nudity in a narrative feature film context was Russ Meyer. His 1959 film *The Immoral Mr Teas* depicted the farcical adventures of a delivery man who has the power to undress women mentally. It had humour, a plot (of sorts), and broke with traditions long adhered to in sexploitation cinema: peddling the sex under flimsy cover of an educational lecture or via the promise of spiritual enlightenment (e.g. nudism), or couched in old school dramatic shorthand which permitted 'bad' (loose) women to have their fun before going straight to hell. In its unrepentant voyeurism, at least *The Immoral Mr Teas* was more honest. It launched the 'nudie-cutie' genre and spawned 150 imitations.

It was innocent cotton candy, hardly the stuff of dire controversy, particularly in light of what was to follow, but nonetheless Meyer had to go through hell to get it played. He was vilified in the press, attacked by moralist vigilante groups and sued and insulted as well as cheated by hypocritical theater owners who profited on the picture but disdained its creator.

The Danish counterpart to *The Immoral Mr Teas* was *Once Upon An Island* (aka *Crazy Paradise*) from 1962 which in turn introduced nudity in Danish commercial cinema, but the two films were as different as possible in every other way. *Once Upon An Island* was an ambitious comedy about the mythical Danish island of Trangø (famous for its potency enhancing egg production) that declares its independence from Denmark. It starred Dirk Passer and Ove Sprogøe, who were perhaps *the* most popular actors in Denmark, and lots of beautiful, willing and often naked women. It was a major production from a major studio, Palladium, and figured as the directorial debut of a stage actor named Gabriel Axel who would go on to become one of the country's most esteemed directors, helming the Oscar winning *Babette's Feast* in 1987.

There were no big stars in Meyer's film; his own well endowed wife of the time, Eve Meyer, played the female lead and the male lead was played by an old army buddy, Bill Teas. The rest of the cast consisted of pretty gal walk-ons hired through ads for their good looks and willingness to shed clothes. Meyer shot the film himself in four days without synch sound equipment and pretty much figured out the 'plot' on the fly. It played in the most marginal theaters, restricted to an adult audience. Nudity was its sole reason to exist. *Once Upon An Island*, for its part, was criticized for being too ambitious, for containing an element of political satire that made it unwieldy. But if the critics dismissed it, at least they were judging it as art. Meyer's film wasn't even on that radar screen back in the US

Once Upon An Island was also, like *The Immoral Mr Teas*, a new type of film, the first in a series of 'folk-sex-comedies', a kind of marriage of convenience of the popular light comedies that had dominated through the fifties and this new genre, the sex film, which for the time being consisted solely of decorative female nudity.

While sex films in America (and most western countries) through the sixties and seventies conformed to very primitive low budget formulas and were banished — at least until *Deep Throat* in 1972 — to the outer most margins of exhibition, Denmark was following its own curious path with more of these folk-sex-comedies which introduced the concept, as one Danish critic put it, of 'family-friendly porn.' It was a creature born of neces-

Filmography

Original Danish title followed by literal translation and English release title where applicable

Bedside Series

1970 MAZURKA PÅ SENGEKANTEN Bedside Mazurka

1971 TANDLÆGE PÅ SENGEKANTEN Danish Dentist on the Job

1972 REKTOR PÅ SENGEKANTEN Danish Bed And Board

MOTORVEJ PÅ SENGEKANTEN trans. Highway Through the Bedroom | Bedside Highway

1973 ROMANTIK PÅ SENGEKANTEN trans. Bedside Romance | Danish Pillow Talk

1974 DER MÅ VÆRE EN SENGEKANT Come To My Bedside

1976 HOPLA PÅ SENGEKANTEN trans. Jumpin' at the Bedside | Danish Escort Girls

SØMÆND PÅ SENGEKANTEN Bedside Sailors

In The Sign of... Series

1973 I JOMFRUENS TEGN trans. In The Sign Of The Virgo | Danish Pastries

1974 I TYRENS TEGN trans. In The Sign Of Torus

1975 I TVILLINGERNES TEGN trans. In The Sign Of Gemini

1976 I LØVENS TEGN trans. In The Sign Of Leo | In the Sign of the Lion

1977 I SKORPIONENS TEGN aka Agent 69 Jensen: I Skorpionens Tegn | In The Sign Of The Scorpion

1978 I SKYTTENS TEGN aka Agent 69 Jensen: I Skyttens Tegn | In The Sign Of Sagittarius

Miscellaneous

1962 DET TOSSEDE PARADIS trans. The Crazy Paradise | Once Upon An Island

1972 BORDELLET The Bordello

THIS PAGE
Ole Søltoft gazes at Susanne Heinrich after losing his innocence in *Eric Soya's 17*.

NEXT PAGE
Ghita Nørby and Paul Hagen in *The Crazy Paradise* — a rare example of promotion being more tame than the actual film.

sity since the Danish film industry was too small to support the multiple tiers of niche production and exhibition that characterised the American milieu — so why not just combine genres? — but it also owed to the fact that Danes had a much more relaxed attitude to nudity and sex, and that in Denmark producers of pornographic films were not stigmatised.

Eric Soya's '17', from 1965, was adapted from a novel and represented the next — and perhaps highest — stage of evolution of the folk-sex-comedy. It was a serious yet light hearted coming of age drama with the humour largely provided by the (relatively) tame mugging of Ole Søltoft who was cast as the shy seventeen year old lad on the receiving end of some sexual guidance from a servant girl. It figured as the directorial debut of Ms. Annelise Meineche, and Søltoft, along with Susanne Heinrich, who displays a natural sweetness and sensuality as the willing servant girl, submit stand out performances. Although at times obvious and over played, it was by and large a successful mix of humour, realism and sexual pathos that came complete with scenes of nudity and (non-explicit) intercourse. It was far ahead of what was happening at this point in America where the only movies dealing with sex in any direct way were cheap exploitation pictures. The tryst between Søltoft and the black haired Heinrich, who was no beauty in the classic sense and quite the opposite of the stereotypical blonde Danish bimbo — qualifies as a classic moment of erotic cinema.

Eric Soya's '17' was a huge success and served as the predecessor of Palladium's popular seventies softcore *Bedside* series, and for its hardcore *In the Sign of...* series which together took the mixture of pornography and comedy to new heights, or depths, depending on one's viewpoint.

Bedside Mazurka kicked off the Bedside series in 1970 with Søltoft playing the part he would soon be terminally typecast for, that of the nerdy futz who is pursued by beautiful over sexed women. Scorned by the critics but popular with the public, the eight films in this series, which lasted until 1976, contained lots of innocent erotic tomfoolery but occasionally attempted to comment on topical happenings, like the flower power movement for example.

The six *In The Sign Of...* films, produced from 1973 to 1978, were all hardcore and starred the omnipresent Soltølt in the (usually) non-fornicating lead.

They were actually pre-dated by Ole Ege's *The Bordello* from 1972, which was set in a bordello around 1900 and was praised by *Variety* on its US run. It was one of the first films to show hardcore action outside a documentary context and marked the marriage of the folk-comedy and hardcore porn. It was shot by Morten Arnfred who today works closely with Lars von Trier (he was assistant director on several of his films including *The Kingdom* and *Breaking The Waves*) and who is today one of the most respected directors in the country — a fact that indicates how crew as well as cast and directors could work in pornography without being finished in the industry.

The first installment of the *In the Sign of...* series was *Danish Pastries* from 1973, a tale of mass sexual arousal sparked by cosmic high jinks when Venus passes the sun. Despite a foolish plot and a lot of stupid slapstick humour, it is widely considered the best of the bunch. 'The only attempt by a serious Danish director — the Film School educated Finn Karlsson — to make a purely pornographic feature film', as a Danish critic noted. Although the same critic admitted it suffered from over acted ham performances, he thought that at its best it called to mind Walerian Borowczyk's period erotic films. It includes one of the most bizarre erotic dream sequences ever committed to film, lots of energy, plenty of pretty Danish babes and a closing underwater sequence where the cast swim about to an easy listening version of *What The World Needs Now*.

The two concluding films in the series, *In the Sign of the Scorpion* (1977) and *In the Sign of Sagittarius* (1978) unspool as lame parodies on a James Bond theme with Søltoft playing the role of 'secret agent 69 Jensen', indicating the level of humour on display and tempting one to conclude that the approaching end of the series could only be described as timely. People had gotten enough of this idiotic slapstick.

All *In the Sign of...* films had their premieres in the summer when a large segment of the audience consisted of porno curious tourists, although at the same time the participation of popular folk-comedy actors — albeit not on the level of Passer and Sprogøe — attracted the Danish public as they also did with the *Bedside* films.

It all came to an end as the happy naked glow of the late sixties/early seventies faded further into the past. Danish films no longer aroused excitement in the wider world, and in general the mood at home was turning somber as the oil crisis caused massive unemployment and near economic collapse. The film industry was changing too. Exploitation cinema was fading out as companies like Merry Film and Palladium went out of business and porn theaters and grindhouses closed down — as they did everywhere.

This period of Danish cinema that started with *Once Upon An Island* and ended with *In the Sign of Sagittarius* (1962–1978) constitutes a distinct self contained era, one that is so out of step with today's artistic aesthetic and politically correct tone that to some it is an embarrassment. Much of it is still despised by reigning critical opinion and unlikely to ever screen at the stuffy Danish Film Museum, but it is beloved by nostalgics and cult freaks alike, and offers much needed relief from the current wave of joyless Dogme inspired social realism when it does surface on TV or in revival screenings.

And occasionally it even gets some respect.

Like on a hot summer's night in 1996 when a huge crowd camped out in Queen's Park in front of a giant screen to watch a selection of quintessential Danish films selected to commemorate 100 years of cinema. How disconcerting — and wonderful — to see Lars von Trier's icy and severely mannered *The Element Of Crime* followed up by *Danish Dentist On The Job*. ■

THIS PAGE
Strangehaven landscape by
Gary Spencer Millidge and (left)
its inhabitants' favourite tipple.

NEXT PAGE
Curiouser and curiouser... Alex in
Strangehaven 7.

Village Life

THE TRAIN STATION AT LEIGH-ON-SEA IS SMALL AND situated away from the town itself, like an airport of a large city, but the view is gorgeous and rolls down into the sea.

Having made my connection at Fenchurch Street Station in London without any delay or trouble, the forty five minutes journey speeds by and so I arrive earlier than anticipated. Now I sit with a mug of coffee in the Leigh-On-Sea train station café, waiting for Gary Spencer Millidge, creator, writer, illustrator and publisher of the long running comic book series *Strangehaven*.

Strangehaven is a convoluting soap opera with magical elements set in the eponymous fictional village, which is inhabited by colourful, well rounded, curious and sometimes sinister characters. It isn't difficult to see how the people of Leigh-On-Sea may have provided Gary with his inspiration… if not, then I shall point him to this café and several potential new Strangehaven characters.

There is a TV set and a few other people in the café — not people travelling through but apparently regulars, killing time in idle chat. The old man with a white beard has bought a boat, though he also claims not to have been sailing for some thirty odd years. "It's something you never forget," he retorts in justification following the questioning glances. But then he forgets his basic nautical names and terms. "Doctors," the old man proudly informs the room, "have told me that I would eventually lose my memory. And it's true!"

A young man asks to see the boat. The old man thinks the re-

Strangehaven is a village from which there is no escape. David Kerekes takes a one way ticket to interview Gary Spencer Millidge, the creator, artist and publisher of this independent comics phenomenon.

quest terribly impertinent, but gives him directions to where the boat is moored nonetheless. He declines to accompany the younger man on the grounds that he has been walking all day, and besides, he has been down to see the boat no less than three times already this morning.

Indeed he lives on the boat.

The old man talks incessantly.

"Nobody ever wins any of these auctions." The guy in the apron working the counter responds to *Bargain Hunt*, the daytime television game show that has just started on the TV. He turns up the volume.

"Shaddap!" yells the old man at the sight of David Dickinson, the bronzed, well attired host of *Bargain Hunt*.

Two contestants make a profit of £25 on a top hat.

The old man complains of a job he applied for recently but failed to get. That of a lock keeper. "I could do that job with one hand tied behind my back," he announces. "But they said I was too old."

The owner of the café, wiping his hands on his apron, laughs. "You should have told them you were forty but have had a hard life!"

"I'd never lie about anything," responds the old man coldly, before joking: "I told them I was thirty seven before I told them I was seventy three."

Somebody else walks into the café, a skateboard dude who carries no skateboard. The café owner gets up out of his chair in front of the TV and walks behind the counter, muttering a complaint under his breath: *"...every time I sit down..."*

This he does whenever anyone walks in for service. And this he does when a business suited man with a mobile phone to his ear, engaged in conversation, walks in. The man with the phone goes to the counter and says, "Sorry mate, I didn't want to come in here," and leaves.

"Oh! Don't tell me!" chimes the old

man. "Don't tell me it's going to rain!" A cloud has covered the sun in the otherwise clear blue sky, but personally I don't think it signifies rain. No one else thinks it signifies rain, either. It's a glorious day. The smell of the sea hangs in the air.

I recall that on the train journey here this morning I caught the fleeting sight of a church and a cemetery that looked to have fallen into disrepair, and a fisherman on his back in a field taking a nap — maybe he wasn't really a fisherman, but that's how the woman in the seat next to mine referred to him. I wonder if she knew him?

With each passing mile, the industrial and urban landscape of London had fallen away to reveal green countryside and with it a certain isolation. I recall all of this as I sit in the café sipping my coffee. The old man doesn't shut up. The young man looking for the boat has given up and returned. The guy in the apron mutters something under his breath. Gary should be here any minute.

PREVIOUS PAGE
The cover to *Strangehaven 1* and (bottom) Gary at work.
Photo: David Kerekes

THIS PAGE
Alex as he appears on the cover of *Strangehaven* book one. All art this chapter © Gary Spencer Millidge

HEADPRESS Was there any one spark that inspired *Strangehaven*?
GARY SPENCER MILLIDGE It wasn't one particular thing, but more of a combination of things. *Strangehaven* would have been my last big attempt at doing a comic book, and I wanted to do something that would enable me to do anything that I wanted to do. I think I was watching *Twin Peaks* at the time, and it struck me that the soap opera format had a lot of potential. I wanted to do something that incorporated all the different elements of why I enjoyed that fiction in general, so I drew in all my own influences. Such as *The Prisoner*.

How far ahead do you plot the series and how closely do you adhere to that plan?
When I did the first issue it was certainly the longest comics project I had attempted at the time, and I had probably only scripted about thirty or so pages of the comic itself up to that point. (The first issue came in at around thirty two pages.) Although it was a soap opera, I was playing with the future leading into something and I couldn't actually go any further than that. To a certain degree I was making it up as I went along. But by the time I came to the decision about collecting the issues into a trade paperback I was already planning ahead, so that the next trade paperback ended on some sort of climax, because the first one ended pretty much mid strip. When I'd actually finished the second trade, which was the first twelve issues, I was thinking in terms of the general story overall.

Below Alice.

Strangehaven character sketches (L–R):

THIS PAGE
Alex, Adam and Ronnie, and the doctor.

NEXT PAGE
Elsie, the police sergeant, and Janey.

At that time I actually got asked to do a movie treatment, which was a good discipline for me because it forced me to sit down and work everything out. Part of the attraction of *Strangehaven* isn't that it's got a traditional plot — it has a certain amount of ambiguity — but I sat down and worked everything out as *though* it had a traditional plot. Now I've actually written out to the end of book four (that's scripted up to No 24).

The artwork changes quite dramatically as the issues progress.
When I did the first few issues I went back and re-read them, so before starting each new issue I re-read the preceding ones. Since I sat down and plotted all the issues I didn't go back and re-read them until very recently. They do make me cringe now and you do learn a lot. I do make a huge effort because I knew it would be around for a long time. I did everything to make them as good as I possibly could. There's no substitute for experience.

The early issues are more clinical looking, while now you are using more shade and shadow. It's interesting because it seems to be bringing the characters more to life.
A certain amount of that is just down to skill. I'd never used a dip pen before the first issue, I used to use felt pen. And with No 7 — which turned out to be the start of book two, although I didn't know that at the time — I bought a computer system to scan the artwork, purely because it was costing me so much money to send the original art over to America to the printers and back again. I thought there must be an easier way to do this, and so I bought a scanner. Then I discovered that I could probably do more than just scan the artwork, in fact the whole of the second book was just done in pencil and I worked on the pencils with the computer and also the lettering. At the time I

thought that this would speed up production a lot, but as it turned out, with the speed of computers back then, and spending time on elaborate toning, it worked out about the same. By the end of No 12 I was fed up with sitting in front of the computer monitor. I wanted to go back and do as much by hand as possible.

Eventually I went back to traditional inking. It's more fun to do although it really does take hours longer. No matter what technique you tend to use though, you can spend twelve, maybe sixteen hours on it.

When I first started to read *Strangehaven* I didn't like the elements pertaining to the secret society. I thought that this aspect was too brutal in a way; too much of a break from the quirky but otherwise good natured feel of the story.
Yeah, that was softened pretty early on along with the actual leaders of the secret society, who have got more power than they deserve.

There was a letter from a reader in *Strangehaven* 13 who said he was fascinated by your portrayal of the English village (and the portrayal of English villages in the media in general). I like that.
I did research on small villages and I've got a couple of quotes on the back of early issues... I think one of the quotes I pulled out was 'Behind an idyllic side of a West country village there lurks something darker'. This was just like a survey, and I did research for that and tried to incorporate things about Essex, and Essex villages and my own experiences of the West Country. And people regurgitate the prison of *Twin Peaks*, which helped to sell *Strangehaven* initially. I would also say *The Darling Buds of May* was a big influence. I always liked the fact that people draw this idyllic village — and the tax inspector went into Larkin's house and ended up staying and marrying his daughter. It was that sort of draw that I wanted to give to *Strangehaven*, and also the film aspect.

You mention *The Prisoner* aspect of *Strangehaven*, an influence that you plainly reference in the story.
Yes. *The Prisoner* and *The Avengers*. Also, what really inspired me to write the introduction, that cliché where Alex is driving down a dark road and crashes, is the *Holding the Baby* TV series. The whole show was always crap, but there's always that really eerie beginning. I always saw *Strangehaven* as constantly coming back to that point. It's that sort of thing I wanted to capture.

Have you ever been tempted to publish a map of Strangehaven?
I've got a roughly drawn map. It isn't in reference to any real place map. It's probably impossible to be where it is, to drive to the coast without coming across any major roads. But for a map of the village itself, that's under construction.

Strangehaven — it's not all magickal orders and murder, you know. Dr Houseman and his wife Maureen have another 'domestic' in *Strangehaven 15*.

Village life

I didn't anticipate your answer to that one. I thought you would probably have been against the whole map thing.
From a purely logistical point of view, when I draw a character walking up a road and he's going from the pub to the post office, I want him facing the right direction. So I do work hard at those details. It's not perfect. There are flaws.

You are basically a one man operation. Can you tell us a bit about that?
I've always been interested in self-publishing. When I got back into the comics industry I was thinking about getting together with a sympathetic publisher, but eventually I realised that was pretty much a non starter. A guy called Paul Gravett — journalist, comics scene spokesperson and co-editor of *Escape* — said, "Why don't you self-publish?" I just jumped in and started self-publishing. I needed a name and Abiogenesis was the first word I came across in the dictionary that hadn't already been used — which was handy because it literally means 'organic life from inorganic substances'.

What is your fan base like?
It seems very loyal and very resilient considering I've had scheduling problems over the last couple of years. My audience is very strong, and for a comic book has a strong female audience — twenty or thirty per cent. I would say it attracts people in their twenties to thirties, and a lot of people who publish as well, maybe supporting the whole idea of self-publishing.

You used to play in local rock bands. Does music inspire the way you draw?
No, not creatively. I still write songs and one day I'd like to do a project with art, comics and music — all of my interests together — but I haven't found enough common ground to justify it. I've probably been more ambitious in a marketing sense, because even in a band I started up my own record company, and now my own publishing company. I suppose I did both really in order to maintain control of what I create. In terms of marketing, the music business is much harder to succeed in and that was proved to me by years of trying, whereas my first issue of *Strangehaven* got a write up in the media.

Can you tell me a little bit about the characters in *Strangehaven*? Do you model them on real people?
They're not specific people. I think they're more aspects of my own personality. What I'm really interested in doing in *Strangehaven* is looking at individuals' perceptions of the world about them.

You've got these otherwise ordinary characters that generally seem to have this underlying sinister side to their personality or some weird trait...
One of the things I've taken from early episodes of *The Avengers* and *Twin Peaks* is the ambiguity. If it's done in the right way you don't really want to know what's behind these traits; part of the attraction is the mystery. But of course you've got to be careful not to be just strange, and whether I explain everything fully in the book or not there's an underlying thought behind it and whatever is portrayed as the truth in *Strangehaven* is only someone's perception.

Do you use pro models?
No, they are friends and family. When *Strangehaven*'s finished — which will be a tremendous relief — I will probably change my methods. Maybe I will use professional models.

You've got Basil Fawlty in a dialogue with one of the characters in one issue. I've got to admit, I thought that the character of Meg at first was supposed to be David Hockney, the artist, and I said to myself, "Ah, I know where this is going!" I was wrong of course.
Interesting. Meg wasn't consciously modelled on David Hockney.

How do you go about shaping the characters?
Although I use photographic models to actually draw them, I'm always very careful to write the character first. I suppose they are partly facets of my own personality. I'm very careful to write characters, some are just function characters, while others are more 'way out' characters that are crucial to the plot. I think that using photographic models probably adds another dimension

in terms of body language, which helps round out these characters.

How do you see *Strangehaven* ending?
I see an end at least in a temporary sense. I've written it to a climax. The length of time it has taken me to write, there are other things I want to do, and even though I said I wanted to do something that would allow me to do anything within a certain format, it turned out that there are certain things that I want to do that I can't fit in. So you are probably looking at starting a new magazine. I'll continue with *Strangehaven* in some way, but there are a number of prospects I can't fit in at the moment.

What makes the early issues different is that they're fairly chaotic — they go off on tangents. A number of readers are intimidated by the tangents because it is getting away from the plot, although I tried to introduce other stories — Alex and his relationship with Jane, for instance — but I also think it's the tangents that make *Strangehaven* unique.

Do you ever get to a point where you think 'I wish I hadn't done that because now I can't do this?'
No. I think every creator can go back and revise their work but I don't necessarily think it would be any the better for it. I could certainly brush up the early issues, and I did to a very minimal extent for the trade paperback; I just fixed one or two things. I actually sat down and looked at a calendar because there were too many full moons in one issue for the length of time it covered. Things like that I tried to fix. It could have been even better if I'd sat down and worked every letter out, but it would have lost some of the spontaneity. But out of that has grown this massive single plot where everything's connected, and it can be quite a headache to try and get all the events happening in the right order and still produce a balanced twenty four page comic.

You've got so many different things going on in Strangehaven and everything seems to be driven by its own agenda, but also by what seems to be some kind of supernatural thing.
There is an underlying supernatural theme there, but with all my research I try to be very accurate and with anything supernatural I try to base it on peoples' genuine supernatural beliefs, so I'm not just pulling it out of thin air. I'm trying to give alternative explanations for events; maybe it's supernatural, maybe it's not, it all depends whether you believe in that. But the more I research into things like that, the more difficult it is to make anything convincing out of it. When I was eighteen I was into astrology — I've probably got a dozen books on the subject. As you get older your appreciation for the unexplained wanes a bit, and I've probably become more interested in telling the story of relationships.

So Alex being unable to leave the village may be down to something mundane like the fact that he's hopeless with geography?
I think this is an example where the end has to be left ambiguous. That concept was not so much based on *The Prisoner*, but more of a magical thing where all roads lead there. It's a sort of gateway. One of my earliest memories is of going to Hampton Court with my parents and walking around a maze. I remember seeing the entrance to it, and I knew the entrance was there and I could see the way out, but there was a door that was made into a part of the bush wall, so you'd go into the maze and they'd shut the door. *Strangehaven* is a bit like that: there's a sort of trick going on there. It's got to be a mystical, magical place — that is central to the idea. It's somewhere where people go to meet their destiny. ■

Cover art, from pencil to inking stage through to finished item.

Village life

CZECH REPUBLIC | FINLAND | UK | NETHERLANDS | JAPAN | USA | FRANCE | SPAIN | UNDERGROUND | REVIEWS

Culture Guide

Mad artists

- y Book
- ☺ Comics & Art
- 📺 DVD & Film
- 📼 Audio

Against The Grain
Mad Artist Wally Wood
Edited by Bhob Stewart

BACK IN 1991 the comics-lit zine *Blab!* ran a feature titled 'Alcoholic Cartoonists'. It listed Wally Wood as case study #4.*

The shy and troubled Wallace Wood — or 'Woody' — stands as one of the greatest exponents of the comic book art form. His work is beautiful to behold and his composition and attention to detail truly mind blowing.

Born in Menahga, Minnesota on June 17, 1927, Wood honed his skills by working arduously long hours at the drawing board, often doing twenty four hour shifts. It paid off — if you ignore the constant headaches, heavy drinking and marital problems that followed.

Wood's strips for the legendary EC stable of sci fi, crime and horror comics are nothing short of amazing. And with the anti-comics campaign of the 1950s, Wood extended his talents into the realms of *Mad* magazine, sci fi book covers, advertisements and cartoons for men's magazines.

As the 1960s rolled on, Wood was becoming increasingly disgruntled with the industry of comics. His brief respite came with a company called Tower Books who, for the two years before they folded in 1967, gave Wood the creative control that he had always wanted.

Now working freelance, drinking even more heavily, Wood turned to self publishing.

Fittingly, the title that he gave to his new venture — a 'no policy' outlet for like minded artists that ran from 1966 to 1985 — was *witzend*.

Wood suffered a stroke in 1978, which resulted in kidney failure and partial loss of his sight. On November 2, 1981, he put a gun to his head and shot himself.

The piece in *Blab!* states that 'in the field of comic book publishing very few cartoonists can hold a candle to Wally Wood'. Given that he is such an important figure in the history of comics illustration, being a true innovator in the early days and working for such landmark publishing houses as EC, Marvel and Warren, Wood remains a tragic figure who appears as something of a shadow on the comics landscape.

Perhaps fans that champion the likes of Jack 'King' Kirby,

* The other studies are Bob Wood, Bill Everett, Graham Ingels, Roger Brand.

Against The Grain
y US $39.95 | 328pp | ISBN 1893905233 | Twomorrows 2003 | www.twomorrows.com

Will Elder
y US $49.95 UK £35 | 392pp | ISBN 1560975601 Fantagraphics Books 2003 | www.fantagraphics.com

B. Krigstein Vol 1
y US $49.95 UK £28.50 | 250pp | hb | ISBN 1560974664 | Fantagraphics Books 2002 | www.fantagraphics.com

B. Krigsten Comics
☺ US $49.95 UK £28.50 | 232pp | h | ISBN 1560975733 | Fantagraphics Boo 2004 | www.fantagraphics.com

and even hold Wood's contemporaries at EC in esteem, simply find the troubled artist's fall from grace too much to deal with. He essentially turned his back on the comics industry — and while this in itself is not unusual, given the fact so many artists became bitter over the poor pay, long hours and contractual obligations forced upon them, Wood perhaps overstepped the mark when in later years he started to lampoon his much loved and revered EC work (and even himself), ultimately squandering his talent when turning to crude and pornographic comics that were meant as much to shock as they were to titillate.

You will find only praise for the great 'Woody' in *Against the Grain: Mad Artist Wallace Wood*, the hefty tribute published by TwoMorrows. Anyone expecting this to be an extension of the TwoMorrows Wood tribute in *Alter Ego* No 8 will be in for a surprise. Edited by Wood collaborator Bhob Stewart, the 328 page *Against the Grain* was compiled almost twenty years ago, its existence becoming the stuff of debate and speculation in comics circles.

A comics authority, associate or friend of Wood contributes the material featured in the book. Included in their number are such luminaries as Al Williamson, John Severin, Russ Jones and Tom Sutton. The chapters follow a natural timeline and cover most of the major bases, from Wood's comparatively crude early forties drawings through to his defining work at EC and *Galaxy Science Fiction*, with plenty of little known detours along the way — such as unused spot illustrations for Roald Dahl's classic children's book *Charlie and the Chocolate Factory*; unseen preliminary sketches for various Topps' Chewing Gum trading cards, including the controversial *Mars Attacks!* and the story behind 'The Disneyland Memorial Orgy' poster which Wood drew for Paul Krassner's satire magazine *The Realist* following Walt Disney's death, and which, legend has it, has become the most pirated drawing in history. The original artwork was stolen from the printer, doctored with some bawdy language and reproduced many times over. Krassner didn't sue the pirates but Disney did.

The book indeed features a breathtaking wealth of Wood work — rough drafts and final copies, unused material and rejected art, and some great archive photographs.

Viewing Wood's art is always a pleasure and more often than not a genuinely uplifting experience. The same cannot be said of photographs of the artist himself however, who always looks a little awkward, tired and fragile. (Take a peek at Fantagraphics Books' *The Compleat Cannon* for a photo in which Wood looks just plain nuts.) *Against the Grain* doesn't dwell too long or hard on the later, heavily jaded aspects of Wood's character and career, and while no one wants his or her idols dragged through the gutter, for me the lack of material in this area is the only downside to an otherwise luscious volume.

It doesn't matter if you care for comic books or not, Wally Wood remains a master and this book is a lasting tribute.

Like the notice pinned on Wally's studio wall says: 'There is only one Wally Wood and I'M HIM!'

**Will Elder
The Mad Playboy of Art**
By Will Elder

B. Krigstein Vol 1
By Greg Sadowski

B. Krigsten Comics
Ed. Greg Sadowski

The caption to one of the photos on page ten of *The Mad Playboy of Art* reads: 'Elder playing the fool for the camera c.1938.'

In actuality, Elder plays the

fool for the camera in many of the photos in this book. Even in Boot Camp: 'Will trying to add levity to the not very business of war.'

Daniel Clowes — admittedly not having met the guy — comments in his introduction that Will Elder, comic artist and practical joker, was funny down to the bones, 'a Mozart of zaniness' not just in his art but also in real life.

The term zany often strikes a dissenting chord, conjuring images of annoying people trying desperately to be endearing. But at least Elder had a talent and was able to channel his 'zaniness'.

Paradoxically Elder's early work as a comic artist was in a serious vein, inking pencils for Prize Western Comics and *Justice Traps The Guilty*, EC's war, horror and sci fi books, and later the likes of *Trump*, *Help!*, *Pageant* and for *Playboy* 'Little Annie Fanny'.

But it is for EC's *Mad* magazine that Elder is best remembered. When *Mad* first appeared in the Summer of 1952, the crackpot artist's gift for satire and parody was let loose and Elder ran with the ball.

Elder's *Mad* strips are characterised by panels crammed with scenes of hyperactivity, the peripheral details of which threaten to spill through the very borders. Comics legend Harvey Kurtzman edited and wrote the first twenty eight issues. According to *The Mad Playboy of Art*, Elder 'was the truest conduit of Kurtzman's vision', contributing greatly to the twentieth century's most influential humour magazine. That's a fair enough comment and likely very true, but it's also a loaded one given that it — and indeed this book — are penned by Elder himself!

Yes, Elder does a pretty good PR job writing about Elder in the manner of a fond observer. Consequently the book covers all the bases you expect it would given this conceit.

Most chapters are devoted to specific periodicals on which Elder worked, incorporating key strips in their entirety with lots of spot illustrations both published and unpublished. In the case of EC's *Panic* — the mag that created friction between publisher Bill Gaines and Kurtzman, who considered it competition to his own baby *Mad* — its debut number was banned in Hartford, Connecticut, when Elder's strip 'The Night Before Christmas' was considered obscene and possibly sacrilege.

Also from Fantagraphics, the life and work of another EC artist is celebrated in an outstanding two volume hardback set: Bernie Krigstein is the dark to Will Elder's light, full of menacing angles and sharp lines. A talented painter in oils and other mediums, Krigstein was bothered enormously by the disdain with which the public and critics viewed comics. To the audience of the 1978 Boston NewCon, his sole comic book convention appearance, Krigstein lamented:

I belong to low culture. This is my thing. Not only do I belong to low culture, I don't think low culture *is* low culture. It's *all* culture.

His output for EC formed just a small part of his work in comics, but with EC Krigstein adopted a unique look with strips appearing almost abstract in their crushing oppressiveness, abundance of panels and emotive use of colour. Everyone in Krigstein's stories bore faces that reflected the dark misdeed unfolding, with sullen complexions, sunken cheeks and hollow eyes.

Landmark EC strips include 'You Murderer', 'Key Chain', 'The Catacombs' and, from *Impact*, 'The Master Race', probably the worthiest thing to emerge from the interesting experiment that constituted EC's post Comics Code line of titles.

Volume 1 of Greg Sadowski's *B. Krigstein* offers a general overview of the great artist's work, including plenty of samples of comic art as well as paintings and sketches.

Volume 2, titled *B. Krigstein Comics*, disperses with the text and offers thirty four definitive stories in their entirety. The reproduction is first rate, but the new recolouring by EC colourist Marie Severin makes for an uneasy alliance in some instances, given the digital veneer this grants to strips with a strong 1950s identity. A small gripe. Kudos to Fantagraphics for celebrating these two fine exponents of the comic book craft in such a wonderful and respectable way. [David Kerekes] ∎

The 100 Greatest
Disasters of All Time
y   UK £20.99 | 348pp | HB | ISBN
0806523417 | Citadel Press 2002
| contact: Kensington Publishing
Corporation, 850 Third Avenue, New York,
NY 10022, USA

A Serious Life
y   UK £20 | 416pp | hb | ISBN
0861301145 | Savoy Books 2004 |
www.savoy.abel.co.uk

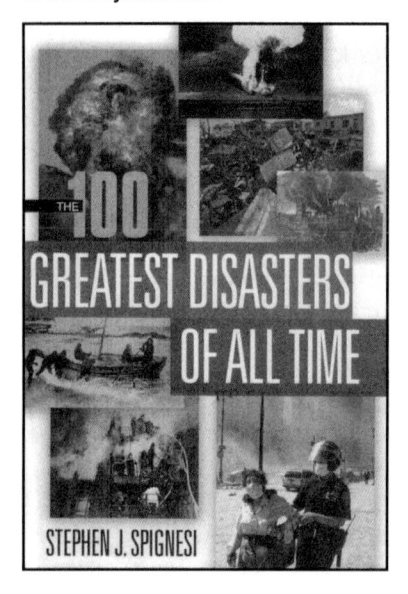

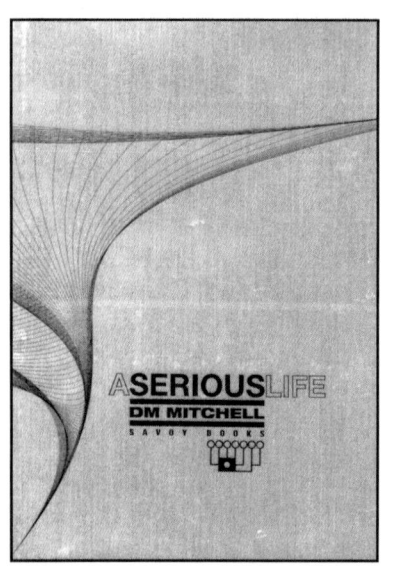

The 100 Greatest Disasters of All Time
Stephen J Spignesi

What is a disaster? I suspect a common definition would run something along the lines of 'a sudden cataclysmic event involving much damage to property and loss of human life'. But what's *not* a disaster? Is a war, for instance, a disaster? Or a pogrom, or a terrorist bombing? Or are disasters only accidental events? Does a disaster have to happen quickly, or can it extend over years, even decades?

These are relevant questions when considering *The 100 Greatest Disasters of All Time*, a hefty hardback compendium of the doings of the Four Horsemen of the Apocalypse throughout the ages. The disastrous events described get one short chapter each, and are ranked in descending order of body count, with the Black Death of the fourteenth century (seventy five million deaths) still firmly ensconced in top position after nearly 700 years. It remains to be seen whether it'll eventually be dislodged by the AIDS pandemic, currently at number three with around twenty two million deaths. Working through the book, it's clear that natural events — plagues, famines, fires, droughts, floods, storms and earthquakes — are the big guns of the disaster world, causing thousands of times more death and destruction than the relatively petty fuck ups caused by human incompetence (though some famines, like the Irish Potato Famine or the 1932 famine in the Ukraine, were greatly exacerbated by governmental policies).

It's not clear to me why terrorist outrages like the September 11 hijackings, the Lockerbie and Oklahoma City bombings are included in this book. These were premeditated human actions, not accidents or so called acts of God, and whilst they looked like disasters to most people, they were triumphs for their perpetrators. If these count as disasters, why not the Holocaust or the Rwandan genocide?

The latter two thirds of the book are largely taken up with events in which human failures have a part to play — industrial accidents, plane and rail crashes, ships sinking, buildings on fire. Some of these events have become household names: the *Hindenburg*, the *Titanic*, Bhopal, Chernobyl, Three Mile Island, the *Exxon Valdez*. Others are much less well known. The chapters are filled with facts and figures, but I'm not sure who, apart from an actuary, a meteorologist or a seismologist, really wants or needs to know whether the earthquake in Lisbon in 1755 was more or less destructive than the earthquake in Erzincan, Turkey, in 1939, or whether the tristate tornadoes of 1925 were worse than the Midwestern tornadoes of 1974.

Given that this is an American book, too, I guess I shouldn't be surprised to find that a very large proportion of the *Greatest Disasters of All Time* have occurred in America in the relatively recent past. At a rough count, around thirty five of the featured events happened exclusively within American borders (others, of course, like tornadoes and epidemics, crossed international borders), and whilst I can see that events like the *Challenger* space shuttle explosion or the 1851 fire in the Library of Congress are very upsetting and all, I do question whether they're really amongst the hundred worst things to ever happen in the entire history of the world. Seven people died in the *Challenger* explosion — motorway pile ups as bad as that happen reasonably often. Other countries which feature in this book with depressing regularity include India, China and Russia, though I'm quite prepared to believe that this is an accurate reflection of both their vastness and their disaster proneness.

Oh, and if you're wondering who Stephen J Spignesi is and what his qualifications to write about disasters are, allow me to quote the press release:

Stephen J Spignesi is the author of more than twenty books on entertainment, popular culture and historical biography, including *The Lost Work of Stephen King*, *The Robin Williams Scrapbook*, *The ER Companion* and *The Beatles Book of Lists*.

So that's clear then. Without doubt, it was compiling *The Robin Williams Scrapbook* which gave Mr Spignesi the *sang froid* and guts of steel necessary to contemplate endless scenes of devastation and piles of mangled corpses.

One thing I was interested to learn from this book was that the phrase 'Oh, the humanity!' was first uttered by radio reporter Herb Morrison, watching horrified as the giant German airship *Hindenberg* burst into flames whilst landing in Lakehurst, New Jersey in 1937. Surprisingly, only thirty six people died. A photograph of this disaster was later to grace the cover of Led Zeppelin's first album. Oh, the humanity! [Simon Collins]

A Serious Life
DM Mitchell

Latest in a line of increasingly lavish productions from the former scourge of the Greater Manchester Constabulary is this history of Savoy Books from their inception to the present day. Savoy have too often been considered solely in the light of their censorship battles, and *A Serious Life* goes some way towards redressing the balance, covering the publishers' inspirations and *New Worlds* related origins, detailed analyses of each of their titles (up to but not including their recent reprints of marginal speculative classics), and their brief but fiery foray into the record industry.

Boasting the usual resolutely non-commercial production values (heavily illustrated, glossy paper) and an exceptional design job from John Coulthart, this book really comes into its own in the interviews with Savoy mainstays Butterworth, Britton and Coulthart, which allow them to tell the Savoy story in their own words.

But the main voice in the book belongs to Dave Mitchell, who dots his full pelt breathless prose with repeated attacks on the poor reader for his purported inability to recognise the 'genuine' article when he sees it, or for misunderstanding Savoy's intentions. On the subject of political correctness, for instance:

> Why must we keep harping on about this issue? Look out of your fucking window! If you cannot see the reason there, as bold as day, then you are one of the millions dead before they are dead. Merely waiting, killing time until they bury you.

Mitchell's roll call of Savoy inspirations — de Sade, Blake, Nietszche — holds few surprises, but some surprising omissions: surely Swift is a more relevant precursor to Lord Horror than French symbolist writers? And the publishers' dedication to the primacy of the imagination and the British visionary tradition is glossed over, with no mention of David Lindsay, and only passing references to William Hope Hodgson; although to be fair Mitchell acknowledges that he has neglected certain aspects of Savoy which he

Anything But Straight
US $19.95 | 312pp | ISBN 1560234466 | Harrington Park Press 2003 / 10 Alice Street, Binghampton, NY 13904-1580, USA | www.haworthpressinc.com

feels 'do not have a broader relevance outside of purely personal taste'.

On Savoy's books themselves, Mitchell tends to write about the content without taking much of a critical tone, and often makes claims that, to this reader at least, are unsupportable. Is Lord Horror really comparable to the creations of Blake, or even Lautreamont and Rimbaud? The boasts about the importance of Lord Horror, and the Savoy project in general, also mean that scathing comments are made on related areas — erotic fiction, for instance, although some books by Aran Ashe or Aishling Morgan beat Charles Platt's smut hands down for imaginative richness. And for all of Savoy's championing of a marriage of High and Low culture, some of this book takes a sniffy tone to contemporary pulp that sits uneasily with the publishers' celebration of older neglected pulp writers.

This isn't to downplay Savoy's importance. Of British publishers, only Creation, Tartarus and FAB Press have anything like its independence of spirit, and all of these work in far more specific areas than Savoy's scattergun approach, a weird gestalt of Henry Treece and PJ Proby that works against all the odds. None, moreover, have been anything like as relentlessly difficult and dangerous as Manchester's finest irritant.

And Mitchell's occasional bursts of invective (which accurately reflect Savoy's vitriolic streak in any case — one photo caption here describes Salman Rushdie and Martin Amis as 'a pair of cunts') are tempered by a free associating wildness that is, ultimately, far more concerned with the author's own beliefs than Savoy:

> The iron in blood is formed from cosmic traces of first generation stars, so in our blood is the history of the universe etched into the cellular structure of our DNA. Our own neural network and cellular structure is an Akashic grimoire, a *Necronomicon* of buried lore replete with latent demons and gods.

Finally, another mention should be made of the design job. Savoy's books just look better and better, with John Coulthart's designs giving them an edge that's hard to match, and *A Serious Life* is their most exquisite presentation yet, full of book jacket repros, artwork (including an incredible spread of a Jim Leon painting involving a toad man and a woman's corpse), rare photos and the kind of wireframe swirls that wouldn't look out of place on an Autechre record cover.

Savoy have no illusions about *A Serious Life*'s commercial prospects, describing it as 'assuredly our least commercial book', but anyone interested in the company, in maverick publishing or British speculative fiction in general will find it a fascinating read. While deluxe editions of *The Exploits*

of *Engelbrecht* and *A Voyage to Arcturus* show a friendlier side to the company, Savoy's contemporary correspondence with Nicholas van Hoogstraten (also exerting a gravitational pull on Iain Sinclair) and Ian Brady show that they intend to carry on digging their peculiarly barbed thorn in the establishment's side; what better reason to lend them your support? [James Marriott]
NOTE There is another book about Savoy currently in production, Jon Farmer's *Seig Heil! Iconographers*.

Anything But Straight
Unmasking the Scandals and Lies Behind the Ex-Gay Myth
Wayne R Besen

Many of you may already be puzzling over that subtitle. '*Ex*-gay'? Doesn't that make less sense than 'ex-parrot'? Well, you know that and I know that, but the sad fact is that for large swathes of the American population, being gay or lesbian is simply not an acceptable lifestyle choice, and a large industry has grown up devoted to the proposition that it's possible to turn homosexuals into good, God fearing heteros through the power of prayer and quackery.

Anxious parents are sold subliminal message tapes which promise to return their bent teens to the straight and narrow, although the fact that one company marketing these tapes also boasts the fantastic-sounding *Stop Loss of Hair Music* in its catalogue should sound a warning bell about the level of psychological acumen being brought to bear here. Maverick therapists claim that 'homosexuality is like cannibalism', write pamphlets with titles like *Medical Consequences of What Homosexuals Do (It's More Than Merely Disgusting)*, and offer classes in gender appropriate behaviour, such as how to cross your legs in a non-queer manner:

> Real men cross ankle over ankle or on the opposite knee. But only the effeminate cross knee over knee.

I'm writing this review with my legs firmly crossed at the knee, but I have to say I'm not feeling especially effeminate!

Some of these counsellors, inevitably, turn out not to be quite the paragons of straightness they present themselves as. Colin Cook, the founder of Homosexuals Anonymous, lost a lot of credibility for offering phone counselling along the following lines:

> Get by your bedside naked, maybe with a hard-on. And say, Jesus, I would like to suck a penis right now.

Of course, in the mainstream American psychiatric community, homosexuality hasn't even been recognised as a disorder since 1974 — talking about 'curing' it makes about as much sense as a cure for left handedness or for ginger pubes.

The left handed analogy is an apt one, in fact. I'm not gay, but I am left handed. Was I born that way? Yes. Does it make me a visible member of a minority? Sometimes. Is it awkward and inconvenient? Sometimes. Do I want to be cured of left-handedness? Hell, no! The big difference between left handedness and homosexuality is that, as far as I'm aware, left handedness isn't condemned in the Bible, people don't go round looking for left handers to beat up, and there are no countries where left handers get beheaded.

To me, it seems obvious that homosexuality is an innate trait in a minority of people, which occurs in all populations and has done so throughout the ages. It's not surprising that graduates of these ex-gay treatment programmes show a very pronounced tendency to go back to their former ways. Many never claim to be 'cured' in the first place. The most disarmingly honest comment I found in *Anything But Straight* comes from a disenchanted woman who flunked out of her behaviour modification programme:

> I prayed endlessly. I even fasted for days at a time. But this did not make me straight. It just made me a hungry lesbian.

Testify, sister!

For all the palaver about homosexuality being 'unnatural', attempts to turn gay people straight are actually attempts

Choosing Death
  UK £13.99 US $19.95 | 285pp |
ISBN 193259504X | Feral House 2004 |
www.feralhouse.com

Creatures of Clay
  UK £7.99 US $12.99 | 127pp |
ISBN 1900486253 | Diagonal 2003 |
www.headpress.com

Gigs From Hell
  UK £14.99 US $19.95 | 189pp |
ISBN 1900486342 | Critical Vision 2003 |
www.headpress.com

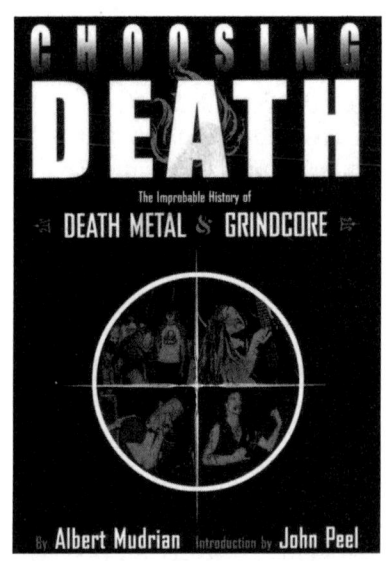

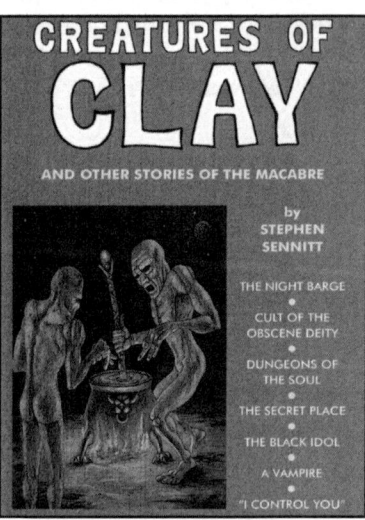

to go against nature. Anyway, who wants all the gay men becoming straight and then charming all the women away with their superior dress sense and gourmet cooking skills? Not me, for one!

Wayne Besen has written a sober, comprehensive, thoroughly researched and exhaustively referenced rebuttal of the ex-gay movement, from its roots in the Jesus freaks of the early seventies through major watersheds like the advent of AIDS in the seventies and the appalling homophobic murder of Matthew Shepard in Wyoming in 1998. Unfortunately, *Anything But Straight* is a ponderous and dry read, but perhaps this is necessary given the importance of the issues at stake. The temptation to resort to savage mockery of these bigoted pundits must have been considerable.

There are two things that really stick in my craw about this ex-gay nonsense. Firstly, the people involved in promoting it seem to be largely motivated either by greed or by religious ideology — they're not in the least concerned with actually trying to help people. And secondly, the argument that homosexuals can be helped to change their wicked ways is used as a justification for supporting discriminatory legislation.

Finally (and because I suspect that many *Headpress* readers stand in dire need of this kind of healing ministry), I offer this anti-masturbation prayer:

In the name of Jesus Christ I say that this creative energy from now on shall flow in its normal channel, and it shall not overflow anymore to the right hand or to the left hand, I build high dikes on the right hand and the left hand and in Jesus' name I command that it shall not overflow to the left hand or the right hand, but it shall flow quietly in its normal channel.

Hallelujah, brother! Let Jesus be your right hand man! [Simon Collins]

**Choosing Death
The Improbable History of Death Metal & Grindcore**
Albert Mudrian

Emerging from an unholy mix that combined the rigorous anarchism of Crass, the riffing speed of metal, and the brute aesthetic power of first wave industrial music, death metal and grindcore tore through eighties Britain (and the world) like an atomic blast. Bands such as Napalm Death, Carcass, Doom, Bolt Thrower, Extreme Noise Terror and The Electro Hippies toured endlessly, sang songs with lyrics about nuclear war, death and power, released records with titles like *From Enslavement to Obliteration, Scum, Holocaust In Your Head* and (my personal favourite) *Necrotism: Descanting The Insalubrious*. Performances were loud, fast and violent in a theatrical slam dancing stage diving and largely male bonding kind of way. Carcass released a record with a collage of surgical and corpse photos on the cover. John Zorn joined in, adding saxophones (and so much more) and scaring his more nervous jazz fans. I lived in a shared house where several of these bands stayed, and over the years I even promoted gigs by Godflesh, God and Axegrinder, I once DJ-ed at a Napalm Death gig. There was always something funny about watching a band on stage and then having tea with them and discussing vegetarian cooking tips.

The story in *Choosing Death* is wider than just the UK scene, and follows these bands and many others through the numerous sub genres until the present day, with the appearance of the inexplicably acceptable and poppy Slipknot, darlings of suburban maggots everywhere. Major players in the scene tell stories with wit and self awareness, and this volume makes a good compliment to Feral House's *American Hardcore*, and is an entertaining read. It also includes an intro by John Peel — an early and enthusiastic supporter of the scene — who died recently, making me wonder who in this ring tone charts, Bush voting world will encourage and disseminate such gleefully absurd subcultural mayhem now…
[Jack Sargeant]

Creatures Of Clay
And Other Stories of the Macabre
Stephen Sennitt

Like some dark liqueur a good horror story is well entertained before sleep. A great horror story, however, should capture one's full attention in the light hours too. I read most of *Creatures of Clay* under a burnishing sun and still felt chilled. A cheap line, but I do owe this collection of stories some regard for their compactness and immediacy, although for the dark depths of the depravities they depict and allude to, I am less convinced, never having fallen that far for the Lovecraftian arts of eldritch syntax and cosmically chunky mythos, all putrefying bogeymen, nameless horrors from nightmare dimensions. Short and to the point they are, rotating themes of exploration and confinement, transformation and regret. There are stylistic fixations — we are told — with Robert Aickman and Thomas Ligotti, writers I am not familiar with. The closest ancedetal bearings I can name are Lord Dunsany and, in certain cases, Vincent O'Sullivan, a friend of Wilde's whose wickedly humorous tales are well worth the effort it takes to find them. And there are echoes of Daphne DuMaurier — must be all that fog. This book is a debut from Diagonal, the Headpress answer to chilling fiction of which we hope and expect to see future titles. With these thirty odd stories, Sennitt shows his command of a deceptively simple form inside whose demon geometry lie super saturated snapshots from the rankest corners of Hell. [Jerry Glover]

Gigs From Hell
True Stories from Rock & Roll's Frontline
Sleazegrinder, ed.

Forget everything you've ever learned from rock and roll biographies and documentaries — the drugs, the fans, the groupies — *Gigs From Hell* vomits up some disturbing and hilarious home truths about what it's *really* like to be in a less than mega successful rock band. These are true stories from real people in the ninety nine per cent of bands out there that don't necessarily have record contracts, or loyal followings, or transportation, even instruments that work. This book is about the passionate dedication of those musicians who'll do anything — *anything* — for the love of rock and roll, even when they've got no cash for petrol, no drum kit, no money for drugs and nobody who turns up to hear them play except a couple of shuffling tramps who've come in from the cold. These dark and vivid anecdotes — none longer than a couple of pages — describe a descent into the Dantean inferno of rock and roll horror; gigs from the seediest clubs in the bleakest backwaters on the planet. My favourites include the guitarist whose back gave out while he was vomiting in the toilet, and he had to be carried on stage to play the gig lying prostrate on the stage before being picked up like a piece of furniture and stored in the back of the van; the band who spent a long

The Doofus Omnibus
UK £11.99 | 112pp | ISBN 1 56097 494 X | Fantagraphics 2003 | www.fantagraphics.com

The Five Biggest Lies Bush Told Us About Iraq
UK £6.99 US $9.95 | 140pp | Seven Stories Press 2003 | www.sevenstories.com

Maybe Logic
US $24.95 | www.maybelogic.com

road trip pissing into bottles and emptying them out of the van windows, only to find their vehicle the next morning surrounded by a sordid yellow armour of 'piss icicles'; the guys who spent the night with some girls they'd just met only to wake up to discover one of the girls' boyfriends had attempted suicide in the night, covering the room in blood. There are tales of violence, arrests, bad trips, belligerent audiences, thieving bookers and deranged groupies — all experienced by band members whose gigs often left them out of pocket, but who'd do it all again in a heartbeat — all for the love of rock and roll. This is the real story of rock and roll, and it makes *Sid & Nancy* look like a fairy tale. [Mikita Brottman]

The Doofus Omnibus
The Definitive Collection of his Greatest Adventures in Flowertown, USA
Rick Altergott

Who is Doofus? Who is Altergott? Carrying prominent endorsements from the likes of Daniel Clowes (who provides a gushing introduction), Terry Zwigoff, Robert Crumb and the Hernandez Brothers, it was clear that this comic might turn out to be something a little different. What it turned out to be was a beguiling mixture of profanity and antiquated innocence, as we follow bohemian bozers Doofus and his best friend Henry Hotchkiss through a series of more or less plotless adventures in the retro land of 'Flowertown'. They bicker constantly, they drink too much and more than anything they love to sniff women's used knickers. However, this strip is closer in mood to the sweet humour of *National Lampoon's Animal House* than it is to rank, soul destroying shit like *Freddy Got Fingered*; these people may be disgusting, but there is a sense of jaunty romance to their adventures, like they were Steinbeckian hoboes or Tom Sawyer and Huckleberry Finn (though with admittedly filthier minds). Whilst Altergott has a good handle on smalltown USA surreality (one might describe this book as 'Lynchian' were it not a horribly lazy and overused reference point), the artwork harks back to the more innocent times of Al Capp or Wally Wood. It's unusual for something to be simultaneously so sleazy and yet so gently innocent. Fine work, and a welcome alternative to the superhero nonsense and impenetrable obscurantism that constitutes so much contemporary comic material. [Anton Black]

The Five Biggest Lies Bush Told Us About Iraq
Christopher Scheer, Robert Scheer & Lakshmi Chaudry

This book is a collaboration between three authors — Christopher Scheer and Lakshmi Chaudry, who are both writers at AlterNet, an independent news and commentary website, and Robert Scheer, who is a professor of communications at the University of Southern California. Between them, these writers have produced a very clearly written, intelligent refutation of Bush's claims that Al Quaeda has ties to Iraq, that Iraq is in possession of chemical, biological and nuclear weapons, that the Iraq war will be a "cakewalk," and that Iraq can be used as a democratic model for other countries in the east. For those who already assume that these claims are lies — and I don't think I've met anyone who doesn't — this book will provide them with facts and statistics to back up their arguments. But I don't think anyone will buy this provocatively titled book except those people who already agree with its premise; I can't see it converting any hard line conservatives out there. And this brings me to a wider point about 'alternative' publications in general, including AlterNet and Disinformation.com. Why is 'alternative' always allied with 'left wing'? The fact that Disinformation and the Independent Media Institute send their books to Headpress for review suggests an assumption that any 'alternative' media outlet is necessarily sympathetic to left wing politics. Personally, I am interested in 'alternative' culture because I have no interest in politics or current affairs whatsoever, and want to get away from any kind of political discussion, from any perspective. To be genuinely alternative, it strikes me, is not to take an extremely left or right wing stand, but to take no stand whatsoever — not even to embrace the terms of discussion. [Mikita Brottman]

Maybe Logic
The Lives and Ideas of Robert Anton Wilson
dir: Lance Bauscher

As Robert Anton Wilson (RAW) was seventy at the time of filming, it was about time someone came up with the idea of making a full length documentary on him. Many people know of RAW by way of the Illuminati trilogy, an unhinged, conspiratorial sci-fi novel written with Robert Shea, his co-editor back when RAW worked in *Playboy* in the early seventies.

But the main output of RAW are over thirty non-fiction books that are so unique and unpredictable that they should have a shelf of their own in the bookstore. He also wrote 1,500 magazine articles. His writing is a weird mix of philosophy, quantum mechanics, religion, conspiracy theory and autobiography, sprinkled with humour and riddles. Try reading his *Cosmic Trigger* trilogy, *Quantum Psychology* or *The New Inquisition*. RAW is very well read himself. He calls Joyce's *Finnegan's Wake* 'The Good Book'. He is also influenced by Ezra Pound, his close friend Timothy Leary, and the architect Buckminster Fuller, amongst many others.

RAW was brought up catholic and had religion beaten into him by nuns. He broke away from that when he was thirteen. He advocates a constant process of change where one never succumbs to any belief system. He tries to keep his 'reality tunnel' as wide open as possible at all times.

The footage here spans twenty five years, but most is fairly recent. RAW suffers from post polio syndrome, and we get to see him and other Californians fighting for their rights to medical marijuana to ease their pains. He discusses a wide range of topics, like magick, discordianism, quantum physics, conspiracies and 'E-Prime', which is abolishing the word 'is' from your writing and speech.

Although most of the film consists of just talking heads, it never gets dull if you pay attention to what's being said.

People could order this DVD before it was released, thus helping financing it. The ltd. first edition had an extra disc of various bonus material. Fuzzy, video sourced lectures and exercises by RAW, and longer interviews with Paul Krassner, R U Sirius, Douglas Rushkoff, Rev. Ivan Stang and others, trying to explain the greatness of RAW and rephrase his ideas. Several of the extras seems to be crammed in on the single disc edition as well, which clocks in at over three hours.

Check out the trailer and get the DVD exclusively from the maybelogic website. [Jan Bruun]

Natural Beauties
 ▸ UK £17.99 | 368pp | Goliath | ISBN 3936709084 | www.goliathclub.com

Photography For Perverts
 ▸ UK £19.99 US $27.95 | 198pp | ISBN 1890159530 | Greenery Press | www.greenerypress.com

R. Crumb Sketchbook
 ⊕ UK £13.99 US $19.95 | 128pp | ISBN 1560974907 | Fantagraphics Books 2002 | www.fantagraphics.com

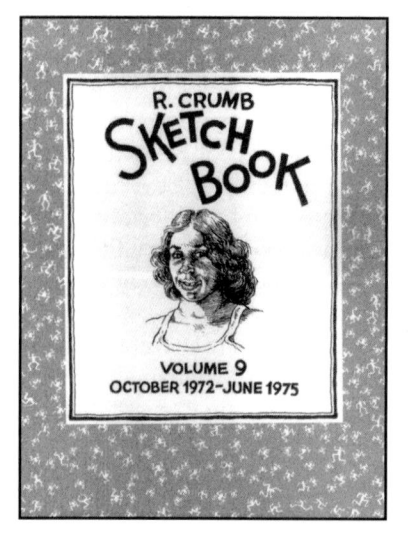

Natural Beauties
Eolake Stobblehouse

Goliath's bible sized tomes of erotic photographs are proving to be a pop sex success, and this is no different. Nearly 400 pages of naked women frolicking in fields, woodland and on beaches, in a style reminiscent of 1950s cutie movies and nudist magazines. There's some introduction that talks about DOMAI style photography — photos that celebrate nothing less than the beauty of the model, though I'm not sure that makes it different. If there's any big change it's in the lack of accoutrements, there's no bondage here, no penetration, piercings or fetishism. Further, all the models appear to come from Russia, Ukraine, Austria, Norway, etc, although why such a particular style should have emerged in this particular location is not explained. One thing that is certain is that these women look like they are having fun running around Eastern Europe in the nude. [Jack Sargeant]

Photography For Perverts
Charles Gatewood

I actually got to 'direct' photographers and even take some gonzo shots for various porno publications a few years back, and, while my brain is a crawling sewer of filth I never really was able to get said psychic quagmire onto celluloid. I have many pals who are photographers, and they all seem able to get cute girls to disrobe and perform various acts from inserting objects to smearing themselves with food. Not only that, but these photographers manage to take pictures that define the genre, whereas my efforts were defined by camera shake, sweaty finger prints on the lens, and so on (I jest — but not much).

Now, at last, one of the greats has revealed all. Charles Gatewood has documented sexual mores since 1966 (when he began by selling nude party pics to the *East Village Other*), he was there snapping away at Plato's Retreat when NYC was a 'moral sewer' (the good ol' days before gentrification), he was there in New Orleans for Mardi Gras to photo leather boys, he shot the first famous pics of Fakir's suspension rituals. Gatewood has shot blood fetishists, naked clowns, pierced pagans, techno primitives, and many nude folk. This fully illustrated book explains how he became a photographer and how he goes about his daily work. This isn't an academic book exploring subcultures, nor a pure autobiography, nor is it a how to book full of technically stupefying details of exposures, light meters, and so on, instead it is a book that touches on all of these elements, but truly comes into its own as a guide for the more pragmatic aspects of being a perverse photographer. The problems and issues are specific to the genre, and Gatewood takes the reader through various ideas, pitfalls, and scenarios. He explores how to approach models, how to get your work seen, model release ethics, shooting on location and so on. Many points are illustrated via candid examples from his own history. For those wanting to pursue a career there are also essential lists of contacts and resources. [Jack Sargeant]

R. Crumb Sketchbook Vol 9 (Oct 1972–Jun 1975)
Robert Crumb

My, it must be sweet being Robert Crumb these days, feted and adored from one end of the earth to the other, with your every grumpy, prejudiced outburst excused as the hallmark of an eccentric genius. But does he ever stop kvetching and whining? Of course not — it's how he's made his fortune. And now we have an endless series of his sketchbooks published in a sumptuous edition — we're up to volume nine (the *ninth* volume of *sketches*, for Christ's sake!!), and it's still only 1975. Crumb's work must be about as exhaustively documented as Picasso's by now. But when you look at it, you can see why — for Mr Crumb is a talented fellow.

This being Robert Crumb, of course, all your favourite racial and sexual stereotypes are well represented — the doughnut lipped negroes, sensual Jews, fiery Latin tigresses, a 'typical Middle-European woman' and an 'Italian peasant woman showing her muff to a little boy', and image after image of the archetypal Crumb bottom heavy goddess women, strapping of thigh and huge of ass, towering above homunculus like men, like mountain ranges just begging to be conquered. Some of these women are anonymous fantasy doodles (and a disturbingly large number have no heads), but there are also a lot of drawings from life of various statuesque women, notably Aline Kominsky, Crumb's long suffering wife for the past several decades. There is an engaging intimacy to a lot of these images, of Aline sitting reading the paper or asleep in bed. But Crumb's ugly little libido is never far away — as he confesses on one page:

> What is this constant obsession with the female body?… this all-encompassing desire and lust which dominates my every waking hour… my mind is the slave of my lust… it is put to work devising ever new variations of my fantasies, such as the following pages…

The term 'politically incorrect' could have been coined specifically to describe the work of Robert Crumb, but it seems mean spirited to find such psychological and emotional honesty offensive. Apart from the omnipresent female totems, the parade of humanity that marches through these pages contains many other recurring themes. These drawings were made between 1972 and 1975, and it shows — there are many depictions of the sort of coke spoon toting, Eagles listening, moustache cultivating men and Stevie Nicks-alike women so typical of the period, of the buzz cut, granite jawed alpha male types Crumb has never ceased to despise, and even a few cheeky Mr Snoids, hitching a ride on gigantic female feet. No Mr Natural though — aww!

Sometimes Crumb's relentless self revelation gets a bit too much, as in this account of a dream he had on Christmas Eve, 1974:

> …the man hauled the huge flopping fish in… I could see that the big creature had female breasts… like a woman's but blue-green in colour… inside its mouth was a large pink pulsating tongue…

Stop, stop, we don't want to hear any more!

As these are sketchbook pages, there aren't many developed narratives — a train of thought might be followed for a couple of pages, but that's about it. The drawing is mostly of high quality though, with a lot of images finished to the same degree as anything in his published comics. Crumb is endlessly self critical — one of the last images in the book, a gorgeous study of Aline drawing the back of their house is captioned, 'June 2nd, 1975 (too windy to draw good outside)'. Occasionally, a drawing by Aline or someone else appears alongside Crumb's work — these tend to be unflattering portraits of Robert himself. But no-one else's work is any-

True Vampires
ɣ UK £13.99 US $16.95 | 364pp | Feral House 2004 | ISBN 0922915938 | www.feralhouse.com

Smut Fest
📺 PAL VHS | USA | 2000 | not certificated | no further details

Time's Up
📺 DVD (region 0) | contact: Music Video Distributors, Inc., PO Box 280, Oaks, CA 19456, USA | www.musicvideodistributors.com

thing like as good as Crumb's. [Simon Collins]

True Vampires
Blood-Sucking Killers Past and Present
by Sondra London

This is actually not quite as bad as I thought it would be, though I find it a difficult task to make any effort to review it in detail. This is because there is something, well, not quite right about it, which I find difficult to pin down. Maybe because the writing is not consistently poor or consistently good, though there are some howlers, like describing the lurid atrocities of blood drinking murderers such as Daniel Ruda and Rod Ferrell and then asking whether such activities can be seen as 'harmless eccentricities'! (p.3) What?!

In addition, the author also describes Manuela Ruda's court appearance, wearing nail varnish London describes as being 'ghoul green' and 'midnight black'... not that she is trying to build up any goth glamour mystique here, folks, of course not. Then there is London's slightly pathetic email correspondence with the book's illustrator, Nicholas Claux, parts of which are printed twice, just in case some dozy teenager missed it the first time around, presumably.

Yet in other instances, there are some fascinating titbits of obscure information and some truly repulsive, detailed accounts of vampiric crimes certain to shock even the most jaded reader. But in the final analysis, *True Vampires* is strangely lacking any compelling qualities, other than Claux's disturbing portraits of the usual roster of serial killers, Manson, Ed Gein etc. These speak more eloquently of a disturbed and dangerously naïve mind than anything Sondra London has written about here.

Colin Wilson, Harold Schecter and other big names quoted in the book disagree with me. [Stephen Sennitt]

Smut Fest
dir: Jennifer Blowdryer

My first thought on pulling this video out of the envelope from Headpress — woo hoo, a lovely video of naked ladies doing rude things! My second thought — oh *fantastic*, now I own a video with SMUT FEST written on the spine in giant block letters — yet another item to add to the already huge pile of stuff I need to hide when my mother comes to visit. Actually, *Smut Fest* isn't really as smutty as all that (though I doubt my mother would see it that way). *Smut Fest* is a 'subversive politicised sex-art cabaret' which has been happening every year since 1988. This one hour documentary, filmed in NY and Hamburg, is a record of some of its highlights. There's loads of different acts on here, so I'll just describe some of my favourites:

Spiky booted Marissa Carr getting down'n'dirty with a cabbage — no, really!... Dominatrix Yvonne performing a dramatic and complex suspension bondage set piece... Billy Madley, a Veronica Lake-alike, performing traditional burlesque — opera gloves and feather boas a go go... Allison, a fit looking brunette, cruelly violating female and male blow-up dolls with a strap-on... Dillon, a willowy blonde, headbanging to what I think is Metallica with a hula hoop spinning around her neck. Sadly, she kept her clothes on... Spider Webb, cult NYC tattooist, indulging in a little vampirism to the strains of Amazing Grace on bagpipes... Thrust, an all woman shock rock band featuring the best flaming codpiece since Blackie Lawless. Shame about the music... Minx Grille (aka Jane Stamp), proving her Northern lass credentials by serving chip butties with ketchup to the bemused American audience, before proceeding to get just a bit smuttier than anybody else.

And of course, no event of this kind is complete without dear old Annie Sprinkle getting her cervix out for the lads.

As you might imagine, there's all sorts of gender bending shenanigans too — drag queens, drag kings, transvestites, transsexuals and what have you. *Smut Fest* is let down by its low sound and picture quality, and the lack of camera angle variety makes it less dynamic and exciting than it otherwise might be, but the low budget glam and brio of the festival shines through the technical limitations. [Simon Collins]

Genesis film & book

Time's Up
Psychic TV — Live at the Royal Festival Hall 1999
dir: Josh Carter

ON MAY DAY 1999, the Royal Festival Hall in London underwent a strange mutation. Haughty uniformed ushers more used to showing wealthy dowagers to their private boxes for symphony concerts had to contend with hordes of body pierced and dreadlocked youth, as a major gathering of the tribes took place. The occasion? The first British (dis)concert in a decade of Genesis P-Orridge's notorious occult multimedia experiment Psychic TV.

Indeed, this was P-Orridge's first appearance in Britain since 1992, when he went into self imposed exile following wild allegations of Satanic ritual abuse made by the Channel Four programme *Dispatches* against both the magical order he'd founded, Thee Temple ov Psychick Youth, and himself personally. P-Orridge had made a career out of baiting the British establishment, and finally, the establishment retaliated. Tabloid newspapers (and, to their shame, broadsheets which should have known better), joined in the vilification of P-Orridge, dubbing him 'the sickest man in Britain', and trumpeting the existence, at last, of evidence that 'Satanic abuse really happens'.

By 1999, however, all this rancour had died down. No evidence was ever found to substantiate the abuse claims, a spate of revisionist articles and interviews with P-Orridge appeared in the quality press, and, as if by way of an official apology for the way he had been hounded, the Royal Festival Hall was handed over to P-Orridge to 'curate' (oh, lovely middle class word!) an evening of entertainment: the Time's Up gig. This event neatly coincided with the publication of *Wreckers of Civilisation*, Simon Ford's definitive biography of P-Orridge's pioneering performance art and industrial music projects, COUM Transmissions and Throbbing Gristle. (My interview with Simon Ford can be found in *Headpress 19*.)

Time's Up was really a mini festival, not a gig. It lasted about six hours, and acts appearing in addition to Psychic TV included P-Orridge's new band Thee Majesty (he sang two sets that night), the Master Musicians of Jajouka featuring Bachir Attar, Robin Rimbaud alias DJ Scanner, Billy Childish and Thee Headcoats, and ? and The Mysterians. Fellow exiled 'Englishman in New York' Quentin Crisp acted as Master of Ceremonies, via videolink:

> Good evening. I am only Quentin Crisp, and I have no idea what I am doing here. I have always said, music is the most amount of noise conveying the least amount of information.

Quentin Crisp's drawling introductions are reused on this DVD, and one of the disc's many extras is a cosy chat between Gen and Quentin, discussing their outsider status. The evening as a whole had a celebratory, revivalist feel about it, with many references to sixties psychedelia and counterculture.

Following the revved up hot rod punk of Billy Childish, the Hammond organ driven Tex Mex garage sound of ? and The Mysterians (and yes, they played 96 Tears — twice!), and the covert surveillance cut up beat constructions of DJ Scanner — each represented

The Royal Festival Hall concert, 1999

THIS PAGE
Gen in PTV.

NEXT PAGE
The Master Musicians of Jajouka.
Photos: Simon Collins

by a single song on the DVD — it was time to proceed to the main business of the evening.

As Gen took the stage in sharply tailored evening dress and immaculate silver bob haircut for his set with Thee Majesty, he couldn't resist having a little gloat over his cultural rehabilitation:

> Well, I'm back [cheers]... And so I say, people of control, fuck you. [To audience] You're very nice! We are... we are... we *are* nice. That's what they don't understand yet, isn't it?

The Thee Majesty set itself consisted of loosely structured spoken word pieces from Gen, backed by Larry Thrasher on drums and Bryinn Dall playing a modified guitar. This worked better live than on CD — the Thee Majesty *Time's Up* CD is one of my least favourite pieces of work featuring Genesis P-Orridge. The two Thee Majesty tracks on the DVD are Eshu (At Last) and Flowering Pain Gave Space. A line from the latter, 'I'm sickly in a strange way,' could stand as a neat summation of Gen's entire career.

Next up were The Master Musicians of Jajouka, who livened up proceedings considerably on a carpet strewn stage with a storming set of sinuous, ecstatic traditional Moroccan trance music. The Jajouka musicians are the inheritors of an ancient musical tradition, and there is reason to believe that the spring festival over which they preside, celebrating the return of a goatskin clad fertility spirit called Baba Jeloud, is directly descended from the worship of Pan — their music has exercised a fascination on many countercultural westerners, including Brion Gysin, William Burroughs and Brian Jones of the Rolling Stones, who released a record of field recordings from Jajouka before his untimely demise.

Gen took the stage again for the Psychic TV set, clad in a long trenchcoat and colourful shirt designed, I believe, by Vivienne Westwood. The band included Larry Thrasher (in a kimono and wig!), Alex Ferguson, Barry Stillwater and Malcolm Best. They played in front of a giant screen projecting an endless stream of symbols, texts and images, and for the record, the full track listing of the PTV set was She Touched Me, Riot In The Eye Of The Sky, Seduce Me, Jigsaw, I Like You, Feet Of Broken Glass, and of course Godstar, P-Orridge's elegy to Brian Jones, with a cover of The Rolling Stones' Play With Fire for an encore (the audience included Anita Pallenberg, Rolling Stones muse and seminal sixties chick). It's notable that the PTV set concentrated on their mid eighties work, presumably out of a desire to use to the fullest the guitar talents of Alex Ferguson, who appeared as part of the band for the first time in many years. As comparison of this set with much of the extensive PTV live documentation produced over the years will prove, by PTV standards the *Time's Up* gig was orderly, tight and musically orthodox.

Aside from the live performances, the DVD features plenty of extras. There are interviews with Quentin Crisp, Gen, Bachir Attar and DJ Scanner, various trailers, a twenty two minute 'Cut Up Concert' documentary about how the Time's Up event was put together, and a couple of Psychic TV videos, Scared To Live, which features William Burroughs and Godstar (Hyperdelic) — both these

Painful But Fabulous
y UK £13.99 US $20 | 200pp | ISBN 1887128883 | Soft Skull Press 2003 | contact: Soft Skull Press Inc., 71 Bond Street, Brooklyn, NY 11217, USA | www.softskull.com | www.genesisp-orridge.com

Romance Without Tears
UK £15.99 | US $22.95 | 160pp | ISBN 156097558X | Fantagraphics 2003 | www.fantagraphics.com

videos are full of the kind of primitive eighties 16-bit computer generated psychedelic effects which PTV became so associated with. There are probably some other extras I haven't seen yet too — this disc has a lot of nooks and crannies! A nice extra feature of the PTV footage from my point of view is that there are occasional glimpses of, erm, myself, as I was right at the front of the crowd — I can see this isn't likely to be a big attraction to most punters though! The DVD runs for three hours in total, and is a more or less essential purchase if you were there on the night. If you weren't, but you're a Psychic TV fan anyway, then it's still well worthwhile. This is a high quality release, and a worthy memorial of a classic gig. [Simon Collins]

Painful But Fabulous
The Lives & Art of Genesis P-Orridge
Genesis P-Orridge, Richard Metzger, Douglas Rushkoff et al

In the history of rock music, quite a few people have claimed shamanic or priestly status over the years — some have even deserved it. But surely no performer has fitted the title of 'shaman' more neatly than Genesis P-Orridge, who has been a cultural pioneer and establishment irritant for over thirty years now, from the early days of performance art troupe COUM Transmissions through the porn on the rates scandal of the *Prostitution* exhibition at the ICA in 1976 and the innovative industrial music and graphics of Throbbing Gristle from 1976–1980 to his DIY chaos magickal order, Thee Temple ov Psychick Youth (TOPY) and his work with Psychic TV, Download and Thee Majesty during the 1980s and 1990s. In a world in which Argos sells body jewellery and every Sharon or Tracy down the local Wetherspoons has a face full of piercings and a pseudo tribal tattoo on her pimply butt, it's hard to remember just how revolutionary and influential the long interview with Genesis and Paula P-Orridge which appeared in RE/Search Books' *Modern Primitives* in 1989 really was. In a world in which fascist chic has been flirted with by acts from Depeche Mode to Marilyn Manson, and 'industrial' has become just another flavour in the incessant barrage of dance music, it's hard to remember just how challenging the sound and look of Throbbing Gristle was — and still is. *Painful But Fabulous* serves as a timely reminder.

Structurally, the large format book takes the form of a *Festschrift* — a collection of essays, interviews and testimonials by cultural fellow travellers (Carl Abrahamsson, Douglas Rushkoff, Richard Metzger and Julie Wilson are among the contributors), as well as writings from Gen himself. E am glad that thee book does not adhere to P-Orridge's eccentric conventions ov SPELLing throughout — E think E understand P-Orridge's reasons, butter it does beCOUM very annoying to read after a short while! There is also copious visual material — photographs documenting the multifarious looks of P-Orridge as knock kneed schoolboy Neil Megson, loon panted bearded freak, shaven headed boot boy, dreadlocked crusty and (his latest incarnation) steel toothed hermaphrodite, interspersed with album cover art, occult sigils, scandalised newspaper reports ('THIS VILE MAN CORRUPTS KIDS', 'SICKLY P-ORRIDGE'), pictures of P-Orridge's bizarre conceptual artworks and exuberantly pornographic collages. There is a list of selected exhibitions and performances, a bibliography and discography. *Painful But Fabulous* is a valuable research tool as well as an appropriately extravagant tribute to an extraordinary life.

Maybe the final comment should go to Douglas Rushkoff, from his essay 'Good Trip Or Bad Trip? The Art And Heart Of Genesis P-Orridge':

> ...as I listened to him recount his saga, I realised that Genesis was not a musician, a writer or even a collagist any more than he was a performance artist. Gen's life was his art project...

Most of all, I realised that Genesis P-Orridge is not scary. He's a sweetie. A trickster, for sure, but not a demon from hell. Just a guy on the edge — living there to show the rest of us where that edge is. [Simon Collins] ∎

Romance Without Tears
50s Love Comics — With A Twist!
John Benson

Well endowed young girls in tight sweaters, short skirts, or negligees. Pre-marital sex, adultery, good girl art by Matt Baker. When you look at it that way, romance comics — which could boast all of those characteristics — would seem to be a neglected field. Of course they also contain sappy boyfriends, prissy heroines and endless variations on a plot where the good young girl is tempted by a handsome lothario who is only interested in one thing. Some of the most ridiculous examples of this neglected genre, which to modern eyes often look like surreal comedy stories, were reprinted some time ago in New England Comics' *My Terrible Romance*. *Romance Without Tears*, however, is a collection which reproduces stories written by Dana Dutch for St John romance comics such as *Teen-age Romances* and *Diary Secrets* in the early fifties.(A note to budding cultural historians: the title *Teen-age Romances* started in 1949 and the 'teen-ager' was a phenomenon in the United States at least by 1947, not just in the fifties as most people seem to think). Dutch, and his publisher Archer St John apparently decided that these comics could be a little more sophisticated — the central girl character could be strong, with a mind of her own, and that act, which no good girl should never indulge in before marriage, could actually happen! In the story

Tortures and Torments of the Christian Martyrs
 ̌ UK £10.99 US $16.95 | 280pp | Feral House 2004 | ISBN 1932595015 | www.feralhouse.com

TYR Vol 2
 ̌ US $22 430pp | + 17 Track CD | ISBN 0972029214 | Ultra, PO Box 11736, Atlanta, GA 30355, USA

'Masquerade Marriage', for example, two teenage girls, Pat and Jetta, meet Bob and Harry at a waterfront tavern. Soon Pat and Bob are 'lying on the ground, our feverish emotions straining for fulfilment'. Bob and Harry, who turn out to be untrustworthy petty crooks, arrange a fake double wedding. Later that night Pat muses, 'It wasn't anything like the wedding nights I've read about… Bob wasn't sweet and gentle… h… he was rough… almost brutal!' The girls find out about the hoax, however, and of course retribution follows. The boys end up in jail, and back in Hendersville, the girls find that, 'None of the nice fellows ask us for a date now.' Some of the other titles in this collection, 'They called me boy crazy', 'Loneliness made me a pickup', 'I tried to buy love for kisses', and 'Thrill seekers weekend' indicate the territory they tend to cover. The book is nicely produced with all but one of the twenty complete stories reproduced very effectively in full colour from the original comics and includes thirty one covers by Matt Baker as an added bonus. It would have been nice if the introduction was a little longer — it is only eight pages — but it does set the stories nicely in context. It also indicates the amount of research that has still to be done in so many comparatively neglected areas of comic production. The book's title is somewhat misleading though, as most stories feature the main character bursting into tears at some point. This often takes place on the heroine's bed whilst she is in a state of undress. As most of the stories in the book are illustrated by Matt Baker, and despite the fact they were clearly aimed at educating young girls in how to behave, it also seems possible that teenage brothers may have wanted to peek at these titles for entirely different reasons. [Dave Huxley]

Tortures and Torments of the Christian Martyrs
Rev. Father Antonio Gallonio

Mel Gibson's *Passion of the Christ* is a feature length sadistic gore fest in which one man is arrested, beaten, tried, tortured, given the death penalty, carries a heavy wooden cross up a hill, gets nailed to the cross and left in the desert sun to die. Sure, the film is meant to be about Jesus, but there's no love here, no Sermon on the Mount, no miracles, and certainly no exploration of theology. If you want to learn anything about the Christian religion then this isn't the place to look. If filmmakers such as Passolini and Scorsese brought their theological vision to the story of Jesus, then Gibson seems to have brought a mix of splatter movie mayhem and medieval art. Gibson's is a bloody Catholic Christ whose wounds and suffering serve as a visceral testament to Gibson's own fundamentalist Biblical interpretation. This is a movie that cops its chops from just shy of two thousand years of religious mayhem, of which *Tortures and Torments of the Christian Martyrs* is a fine example.

This is a welcome reprinting of a barely available and long out of print early pre-Feral House Parfrey publication (I first picked up a copy in Compendium in 1989). *Tortures and Torments* is a snuff hagiography written by Rev Father Antonio Gallonio and first published in 1591. A book that describes in meticulous detail the numerous methods by which early Christians and saints were dispatched to meet their maker by the Romans two millennia ago. Divided into chapters according to the mode of torture the reader can find out exactly who was crucified, who was stuck in a brazen bull, who was beaten, etc. Of course anybody with even the vaguest notion of history will be aware that some of the most zealous applications of these tortures were at the hands of the Inquisition. History is a bloody business and many people of many faiths have been both victims and torturers.

Also included in this volume is an essay exploring the medical evidence for Christ's demise on the cross and by implication the authenticity of His resurrection. With its medical details that note during scourging 'the lacerations would tear into the underlying skeletal muscles and produce quivering ribbons of bleeding flesh', this essay clearly informed the splatter *mise en scène* of Gibson's project, and is a fascinating analysis, not just into medicine and death but also into the beliefs that still retain their power over a sizable number of people.

Tortures and Torments also benefits from illustrations from the original volume and modern interpretations by hip/underground/outsider artists and criminals. [Jack Sargeant]

TYR Vol 2
Joshua Buckley & Michael Moynihan, eds.

It is a sad fact that few publications dedicated to 'pagan' or 'occult' themes produced these days offer any real challenge to their readers, coming across at best as 'preaching to the converted' (to coin a phrase) or at their worst as pandering to a terminally deluded readership. The fact that *TYR* is whole different proposition was more than hinted at in my review of Vol One (see *Headpress 25*). Volume Two builds on the inaugural issue and delivers a product higher in standard — both in presentation and content — than could ever have been anticipated, even by the exceptional standards of Vol One.

TYR Vol Two is a third bigger than the previous volume, is even more diverse and incisive in its carefully selected collection of essays, interviews and reviews, and takes even fewer prisoners in its trenchant criticisms of post modern culture and society's eroded values. But not only that, as mentioned above, *TYR Two* hits home; particularly in the writings of French radical philosopher, Alain de Benoist, who provides a telling critique of current popular paganism and its propensity to churn out homogenous and relatively valueless 'new age' beliefs, which Benoist sees as a symptom of spiritual decay rather than a legitimate 'new' path to enlightenment. No doubt this will make many a neo pagan squirm with outrage (I wasn't exactly comfortable myself, what with my years of involvement in chaos magic, Thelema and Lovecraftian sorcery!) but this is balanced by Benoist's cogent attack on Christianity, likely to cause even more of a shock to any casual Christian readers picking up *TYR*. The fact that his scholarship and powers of expression are of the first water will no doubt be the issue causing the most offence to both groups, who traditionally — like their equivalents in 'secular' society — tend to find fault with any body or any thing which requires them to think beyond their preconceived, secondhand paradigms. But if any such readers are particularly lazy, they might breathe a sigh of relief in realising that Benoist is 'Right Wing', thereby invalidating his opinions with the PC seal of approval. If he's 'Right Wing' he can't be a real 'intellectual', eh? The irony of this is that I would say there are very few self stereotyped fascist 'bovverboys' who could get past the first few sentences of any

We Got The Neutron Bomb
US $13.00 | 286pp | Three Rivers Press 2001 | ISBN 0609807749 | www.randomhouse.com

Panic DHH
CD | DHR CD 39 | Digital Hardcore Recordings | www.digitalhardcore.com

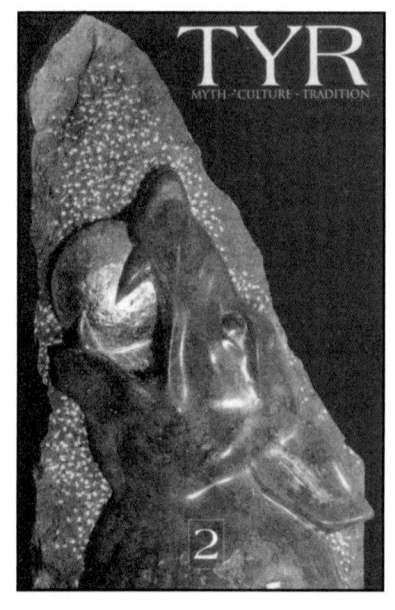

of the remarkably thorough and well researched articles which appear in *TYR*, drawing, as they do, on the works of Heidegger, Nietzsche and the like (that's if the recent BBC documentary on the BNP is anything to go on.) In fact the editors have gone out of their way to make a similar point in dissociating themselves from the Nazi worshipers inherent in some quarters of the 'Pagan Right'. This is completely fair in considering that Buckley and Moynihan's sympathies lay with Radical Traditionalism, a free 'movement' which rejects modernist materialistic political values of any type, in favour of a folk/traditional culture — an outlook in complete variance with the regimented, rationalist industrialist Nazi state envisaged by Hitler.

It is not so surprising, then, that the majority of these 'controversial' articles — written by the likes of Collin Cleary, Stephen Flowers, Marcus Wolff, Peter Bahn and the legendary Julius Evola (who writes a classic piece on 'The Doctrine of Battle and Victory') are heartfelt, but exceptionally careful to define their terms, resulting in a heavy, taxing, contemplative but ultimately *rewarding* read, contrasting tellingly in an age characterised by academic apologetic, woolly, circumlocutions on one hand and vapid journalistic soundbites on the other. Not that there are no shorter, more easily assimilated articles: Nigel Pennick, Steve Pollington and John Matthews provide lively discussions of various folkloric themes; heathen holy places, Germanic 'war bands' and the giants of Albion, respectively. And particularly fascinating is Michael Moynihan's essay on divine sacrifice, contrasting the spiritually empowering self sacrifice of Odin with the seemingly pointless, passive crucifixion of Christ. All are well illustrated with judiciously selected images.

There are also over 100 pages of book and record reviews, all equally as exacting and considered as the articles (especially in the case of Joshua Buckley's efforts) enhanced by short interviews with the likes of Allerseelen's Gerhard (aka Kadmos), Coil's John Balance and chaos magician-cum-traditionalist story teller P D Brown (anyone remember P D's & Rodney Orpheus' *Chaosphere* tape?!)

Finally, in an almost 'embarrassment of riches' situation, TYR Two comes with a seventeen track CD featuring some of my favourite esoteric 'bands', such as Blood Axis and Coil — as well as good quality material from Apoptose, Changes, Steve von Till and others, representing a broad spectrum of heathen influenced sounds.

It only remains to be said that *TYR* now categorically sets the standard for all other pagan/esoteric/'occult' journals, not just in terms of its impeccable production values, but also in terms of its dedication to clear sightedness and commitment to absolute honesty — however unpopular such notions might be to a large portion of its prospective audience in the pagan community. [Stephen Sennitt]

We Got The Neutron Bomb
The Untold Story of LA Punk
Mark Spitz & Brendan Mullen

The authors Mark Spitz and Brendan Mullen describe themselves as 'two record-collecting music geeks', and they have assembled an absorbing and easy to read oral history of the early days of punk in Los Angeles. In the introduction they state that their aim is 'to get people talking again. To show others what they've been missing', which is especially pertinent in the contemporary era of manufactured pop music. Their book destroys the naive misconception that punk was a manufactured fad which began and ended with the Sex Pistols. Punk was an expression of wild youth that could be traced back into the sixties, full of energy and ideas, with a DIY ethic which dominated in the bands and the zines.

In a similar vein to what Legs McNeil and Gillian McCain accomplished in *Please Kill Me: The Uncensored Oral History of Punk* (2002), Spitz and Mullen shift the focus to Los Angeles. Their survey starts in the late sixties with The Doors and ends in the early seventies with the appearance of MTV and the mainstream success of The Go-Gos. In doing so they provide a useful precursor to existing works such as Henry Rollins' *Get In The Van* (1994), based on the journals he kept while touring with Black Flag, Michael Azerrad's *Our Band Could Be Your Life* (2001) which gave a more detailed account of a number of the influential bands of the 1980s, and Steven Blush's *American Hardcore: A Tribal History* (2001), which gives a national overview of the hardcore punk scene in America.

The birth of LA punk took place in a climate of national unrest, the aftermath of Watergate and the resignation of Nixon in disgrace, the Vietnam War, the Oil Crisis and recession. The music appealed to bored teenagers from dysfunctional families, who were frustrated and disillusioned with their lives. Bands like The Descendants, Redd Kross, The Adolescents and Black Flag were teenagers when they began, with some members as young as twelve years old. Their music was a reaction against 1970s progressive rock which filled huge stadiums, and effete disco. The punk bands played anywhere they could, anytime, for anyone. One of the most entertaining anecdotes in *We Got The Neutron Bomb* involves an incident when an early incarnation of Black Flag played at Polliwog Park in Manhattan Beach in the Summer of 1979. Somehow Greg Ginn convinced the organisers that Black Flag were a Fleetwood Mac covers band to get on the bill. When they played Keith Morris, the singer, was drunk and swearing at the people in the park who were already disturbed by Black Flag's loud obnoxious songs and responded by throwing food from their Sunday afternoon picnics at the band. The promoter stopped them after ten minutes, but in such a situation it is a wonder that he waited that long.

Spitz and Mullen have chosen to write about music about which they obviously feel strongly, but their work is not simply romanticised nostalgia. They point out the highs and lows of the punk scene, acknowledging the local gang rivalries, increasing levels of violence at shows, the devastation caused by drugs, and the unfortunate death of Darby Crash. They discuss not only the bands (The Germs, The Runaways, X, The Go-Gos and many more) and the scenesters, but also the radio DJs, the fanzines (*Flipside*, *Slash*, *Bomp*, *Lobotomy* amongst others) and the venues that promoted the music.

In the introduction Spitz and Mullen not only open up the possibility of a second volume of LA oral history, but the publication of their book, as a companion of sorts to *Please Kill Me*, also invites authors in other regional centres to do the same. Their book is an entertaining popular work which helps develop a broader picture of one of the most imaginative and exciting periods in American popular music. [Dr Spike]

Panic DHH
Panic Drives Human Herds

As one of DHR's latest signings, Panic DHH place their own distinctive mark on the label. More metal than noise — aside from the blistering opening track, Leader — *Panic Drives Human Herds* moves DHR into more accessible territory. The first two tracks, pure noise then straight into the much more poppy Sterile are a great introduction to DHR's first new release in way too long. It's these that really mark the band as one to watch along with seventh track, No More, a full on industrial screamfest. My only real criticism here is that at certain points we can hear loud and clear exactly who their major influences are. The more atmospheric moments on this album don't really work for me but the band cover the heavier side so well that it doesn't really matter. This is a debut that proves the band more than worthy of joining DHR's formidable lineup. [Miss Nailer] ∎

Send materials for review to

Headpress/Critical Vision
PO Box 26
Manchester
M26 1JD, UK

Be sure to include order & contact info, price, p&p, etc.

Rather, A fishy end in the tank of the crocodiles Some recent books by Kenneth Grant

THE NINTH ARCH is Kenneth Grant's final book in a series of nine works examining the Typhonian current of Magick, a dark and primal gnosis leading back to the most archaic examples of religious, psychological and creative modes of human consciousness, and beyond, into realms of far flung extraterrestrial dimensions and nightmarish inner planes where the nexus of conscious states combine and recombine in nirvanic ecstasy.

In a nutshell, that is. In practice, reading *The Ninth Arch* is a far stranger and more patience stretching experience than even this description would suggest. In some ways, this final volume of the final Trilogy of the 'Typhonian Trilogies', is the *Finnegan's Wake* of occult books, in which personal reminiscence, subjective states of mind, and allusions to both fictional and ostensibly non fictional narratives converge to create a dense hodgepodge of bizarre speculation, morbid introspection, and, at times, amazingly impressive revelation.

The main body of text concerns itself with a long commentary and extrapolation of an 'inspired', somewhat sinister communication, which, simplistically stated, Grant claims to have clairvoyantly received in the 1950s, entitled *The Book of the Spider*. This weird and obscure document, takes the form of a kind of prose poem and draws on traditional occult doctrines, personal memories, transient states of altered consciousness, and the novels of Richard Marsh (*The Beetle*) and Sax Rohmer (!), as well as other writers, such as HP Lovecraft, Aleister Crowley, AO Spare, to create a distinctly idiosyncratic result which only Kenneth Grant could pull off with any degree of aplomb. Mixed in with the esoteric visions and qabbalistic exegeses are, however, phrases which even the Master Occultist Grant finds hard to interpret, such as the line 'Rather, a fishy end in the tank of the crocodiles', something worthy of the surrealists… or even Vic Reeves and Bob Mortimer.

Amidst all this strangeness are references to many of Grant's own works; the previous eight volumes of Typhonian Trilogies are referenced (as would be expected), from the sober, historically focussed *The Magical Revival* — where Grant's 'public' odyssey into these realms began in 1972 — to the aggressively esoteric *Beyond the Mauve Zone* (2000), along an increasingly subjective (or as some critics have insisted, demented) trajectory in the intervening years, whose most quoted 'landmark' would seem to be *Nightside of Eden* (1977), a postmodernist grimoire which allows for traffic with the demonic denizens of the infernal zones 'beyond the abyss'. More unusual even than this, is the self referencing of several fictional works by Grant which have recently been issued by his current publisher, Starfire, in beautifully produced hardcover editions. These are as follows:

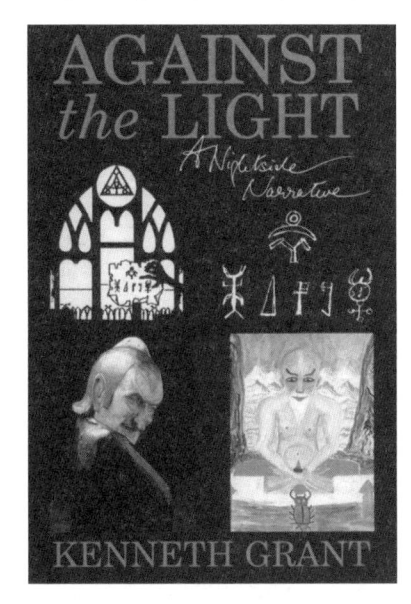

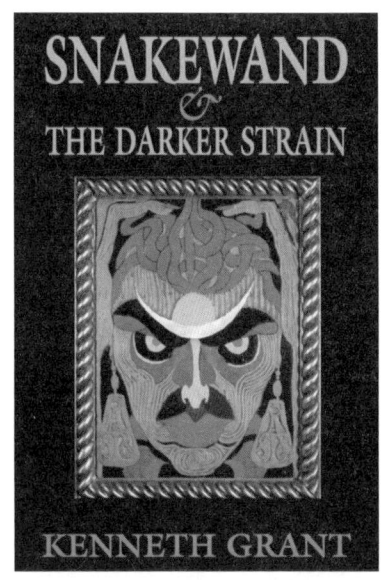

> Against The Light
> ISBN 0952782413 | £15.99
>
> Snakewand & The Darker Strain
> ISBN 0952782472 | £25
>
> Gamaliel, The Diary of a Vampire & Dance, Doll, Dance
> ISBN 0954388720 | £25
>
> The Other Child and Other Tales
> ISBN 0954388747 | £25

It is in the less rigid discipline of *fictional expression* where Kenneth Grant seems to really excel in creating disturbing and impressive narratives, whether their content is based on 'real' events, as Grant sometimes claims, or not. *Against The Light* is a short novel which features Grant and members of his 'clan' (eg, his family, in laws, and ancestors) as characters, along with old friends of his from the 1940s and fifties, and Grant's old mentor, Aleister Crowley. But don't expect a simplistic Tim Powers, or Alan Moore, type read. The author is not trying to be clever, or demonstrate his 'education', by using the '*real people in fictional situations*' ploy, as so many of today's moribund writers do, desperate as they are to foist their reading tastes on their audience in lieu of any talent of their own. No, Grant's novel instead demonstrates a strange melding of realities and altered states of consciousness which undermines the reader's trust in commonplace reality in a way which is difficult to put into words. Perhaps it is only the sheer strangeness of his concepts and his artistically committed mode of expressing them which creates the illusion of stark originality... whatever the reasons, one leaves off reading *Against The Light* as one does having had a dream where it is felt some integral information had been imparted, but which has now drifted beyond one's grasp.

All the above KENNETH GRANT titles, including *The Ninth Arch* (ISBN 0954388704) £30, and reprints of some of the older volumes, are available from Starfire Publishing Limited, London, WC1N 3XX. For current prices and p&p [e] starfire.publishing@virgin.net

The second and third volumes comprise of two novellas each. *Snakewand* is an effective tale of voodoo and *The Darker Strain* transports the 'cult of the spectral hyena' to fifties/sixties London, and is one of Grant's more conventionally constructed and carefully developed narratives. *Gamaliel* is probably the most frightening of these tales, effectively creating a sordid, dissipated atmosphere centred on drug addiction and psychic vampirism which makes for queasy reading. *Dance, Doll, Dance* has a livelier pace which contrasts well, including some provocative scenes of sex and violence linked to a malevolent tantric idol. The final volume has an odd and somewhat more amusing than usual title story, and several effective short pieces. It also includes the colourful and splendidly decadent novella *The Stellar Lode*, whose Egyptian background seems more authentic, than, say, Stoker's *The Jewel of Seven Stars*.

It is important to realise that whilst Grant's fictional works are on a par with the very best in the annals of weird fiction, they are by no means an 'easy read', such as even the most profound tales by the likes of Arthur Machen, Algernon Blackwood, HP Lovecraft, and more recently, Thomas Ligotti, prove to be. In this respect, but in this only, they are closest to the 'strange' stories of Robert Aickman, in that they conjure up a tangible atmosphere of vague but discernable 'otherness', capturing a facet of that elusive sphinx all weird fictioneers attempt to portray, but of which so few succeed as well as Aickman or Grant.

Aickman, however, is a very unlikely candidate to have written anything as remotely 'unhinged' as someone coming to 'a fishy end in the tank of the crocodiles'. As Lovecraft wrote in reference to Clark Ashton Smith, 'In sheer daemonic strangeness he is unexcelled' — this applies to Kenneth Grant in spades.

Kenneth Grant was born in 1924. He became associated with Aleister Crowley in the Beast's final years, serving as his secretary and 'apprentice' for several months, and undergoing occult training which led to his initiation into the Ordo Templi Orientis (O.T.O). After Crowley's death, Grant determined to carry on the Beast's work by forming a new lodge of the Order and claiming directorship as its 'Outer Head'. This organisation, Nu-Isis Lodge (1955–62), was not recognised as legitimate by some members of the O.T.O, and Grant's claims have been heatedly disputed in some quarters ever since. This is a subject of some complexity which appeals to 'occult anoraks' the world over. Much more to the point to aficionados are Grant's credentials as the undisputed first rank occultist of the post WWII era, demonstrated by his friendship and innovative work with AO Spare, his many books on abstruse areas of occult doctrine (elucidating material which no other writer had previously covered), and his collaborations with artist wife, Steffi, whose distinguished drawings and paintings appear in all of his books. [Stephen Sennitt] ∎

M is for Moore Alan Moore in 2004

I FIRST SAW THE NAME Alan Moore in the little credit card for one of Tharg's Future Shocks he penned for *2000AD* around 1982. His humour and, although less consciously in that juvenile time, his sense of tone and timing were what struck me then. By the time 'The Return of the Two-Storey Brain' had appeared (after the 'Last Rumble of the Platinum Hoard', a tale that made me brood, and the uproarious 'The English/Phlondrutian Phrasebook') I was getting the feeling that the Alan Moore touch was what I wanted from *all* my Tharg's Future Shocks. Even in those b&w three page weekly strips (before 'sequential art' was coined) he had a singularly unforced ability to weave himself into the worlds he'd imagined. That and his knack for ballooned speech that made you forget the balloon was there. I knew nothing then of V for Vendetta, Marvelman or The Bojeffries Sagas — they were aimed at slightly older kids via the pages of *Warrior* and when I got back into comics after a lapse Moore had done *Watchmen*, which got me through a spell of being a lab rat, and the *Swamp Thing*, with its growing reputation as a primer or suggestion to explore the boggy fiefdoms of ecological politics and hallucinogenics. You never know what you're missing with Moore. Beneath the enchanting, rip roaring tales are masquerading questions of public relevance, of war and increasingly through his fourth decade, a very personal journey to reconcile science with magic.

The latest batch of books celebrating the life and works of the snake worshipping Northamptonshire Nightingale represent a very Victorianesque amassing of Mooreania, so much and so ranging has been the quest that not so much as a doodle on a beer mat has been left unscanned, unadapted, unoptioned as a movie I should imagine. Does Alan Moore still have anything in his bottom drawer? Does he own a shredder? His refuse collection day must be the best kept secret in publishing. Really, though, how are we to approach the stack of titles that have been issued variously to coincide with Moore's fiftieth birthday on November 18, 2003? Thankfully they are easily divided into those by him and those about him, the latter works being both hagiographic and eclectic. Highest in both qualities is *Portrait of An Extraordinary Gentleman*, published in honour of Moore's fiftieth birthday with all proceeds to charity. The illustrations from a whole school of European and American artists from Sam Keith to Brian Bolland, Kevin O'Neil, David Lloyd and Stephen Bissette, to name a few, flows freely. Written contributions play like speeches, from the anecdotal to the scholarly. It would be like The Comics Industries Lifetime Achievement Dinner and Award Show. If this book was about me and my works, and no matter how famous and successful they'd been, I'd be cringing a tad at how over the top the tributising had gone. An exception is the dialogue with Cerebus' creator Dave Sim, *Correspondence From Hell*. Reprinted here for the first time it is worth half the price in itself. This birthday present is entirely engrossing and as bright to examine as a box of sketchpads. My pick of the dozen or so story strips here is *Hungry is the Heart* by Moore and 'Dame Darcy' (Melinda Gebbie his long time girl), a chapbookish tale of a girl called Wellington, named by a button prospector after a spaniel that was killed by a meteorite when he finds her abandoned on a marsh. After various single frame adventures (e.g. 'She ends up in a neighbourhood so poor even the pets have been forced into prostitution') she is remerged with the meteorite. Glorious Goreyesque surrealist gothica in twenty-three panels.

The *Extraordinary Works of Alan Moore* is by contrast to the award show of *Portrait of…* more a talkshow or single camera doc. The subject is a more than unusually loquacious speaker when called upon to give verbal copy, which makes this a very well conceived project. Known for the length of his scripts, his speech is as good to read as I'm sure it must be to listen to. The format is nothing fancy, a straight chronological recollective haul through the work, from first feeble stipplings to the wrangles with giants and great plans in collapse. All phases of his work (at least all we know of) are touched upon. Sumptuous colour pages make up the centre, and the treasure is rounded out with rare posters, strips, and an unpublished Judge Dredd script (the weakest writing of Moore's I've seen — he *can* be mediocre!), a full reproduction of the collaboration with Harvey Pekar, original work from Dave Gibbons and Brian Bolland, Maxwell the Magic Cat, and numerous other full page repros from classic stories. The final bibliography is an exhaustive map to the most ranging and prolific storehouse of fantastic tales in English since those built by Wells and Tolkien. A case for the similarities between these three is not for here, yet their shared anxieties for the natural world and the politics of technology stand out as well as the more surrealistic spectacles so cherished by the movies. Where the book fails to dig deep is into Moore's magical experiments; *Portrait* is much more illuminating on that score.

Heroes & Monsters: The Unofficial Companion to The League of Extraordinary Gentlemen has an introduction by Moore. His qualitative stamp proves to be a valuable one indeed. What Jess Nevins has done in this incredible glossary-concordance is to sweep out every corner of just about every panel of the *League* and cross reference it with a contemporary first hand source from Victorian literature. Moore says in the introduction, 'The patient work contained within this volume has played an important part in the construction of this vast, imaginary global edifice that we're constructing and will certainly be of an invaluable guide to any reader, no matter how knowledgeable they may like to think themselves.' What, does he mean *himself* by any chance? When presented with any books that may have been cross referenced in connection with the work, the author merely has to nod and that reference has become added to the total of the story of his creation of it… Nevins has scrambled up the farthest shelves of Victoriana and fished out the nuggets that makes the enjoyable neo-chapbook that is *The League* even more engrossing — which is a spectacular thing to have happened considering how overrated the *League* has been. So not everything's going to be a *Halo Jones* or *From Hell* masterpiece but can't Moore and O'Neil turn their collaborative attentions to the *future* more often (have they ever?). How much more enthralling that would be than the under the covers romps and fights of *League* (taken to excruciatingly witless depths in that movie starring Shur Shorn). *Heroes & Monsters* remains an astonishing piece of scholarly work though and doubly useful as a catalogue to a treasure of rare stories, fruits from Moore's deep bibliomaniacal roamings.

The League of Extraordinary Gentlemen Volume II is the six collected issues comprising the further developments of the secret history of Victorian fictionalia: you know, interplanetary war, sex, mutations and munitions. Characters from out of copyright literature all over the world must be pestering their agents to get themselves into this ever expanding new universe of the genre. Kevin O'Neil does a fine job as always, even if it doesn't quite match the Nemesis heights he once scaled. Moore's blend of marauding monsters and taboo sex, all fortified with lashings of violence and steampunkery, should be requisite reading for burgeoning lads and lasses all over the Empire!

For those who need a deeper view, *A Blazing World*, Jess Nevin's unofficial companion to the second volume of *The League of Extraordinary Gentlemen*, is the standard guide. As well as the comprehensive frame by frame notes there are interviews with O'Neil and Moore, who outlines the genius of his League masterplan: to embrace around every fictional character in existence (and copyright). It is a scheme worthy of Moriarty. His rapture upon the 'discovery' that there was no limit to the universe of the League, is matched only by the lack of reflection on the reputative effects of his work on characters not originated by him. Tribute to his confidence, and Nevins' softly soft questioning this subject is sadly not explored. How for instance would Moore feel about a future writer providing further instalments in the life of Halo Jones? What if a future Moore like genius decided to put V into a story where he hangs out at the beach for the rest of his days until one day an old friend puts upon him to resurrect his bomb making skills to get himself elected. Would Moore care? We cannot say whether the creators of Rupert Bear would enjoy the League's depiction of their trousered bear. All artists must have a stance on the question of expropriating the ideas of those now dead. That's why the work of Jess Nevins is worthwhile — highlighting the depth of research gone into for the League while reminding future generations of readers that Moore did not create Mr Hyde, M, Doctor Moreau, The Invisible Man and the rest: he is merely an interloper in their fictional lives, however smartly he does it.

In *Promethea Book 4* Sophie Bangs, the girl from New York in a science orientated reality, continues her journey as the goddess Promethea up through the ten sephiros of the Kabbalah, an odyssey that allows Moore to comment with great lucidity on the various realms of grace and knowledge that constitute the Tree of Life. A more refreshing primer for this arcane wisdom you will never stumble upon again, despite some dialogue that, in the deepest mystical sequences, creaks worse than Crowley's bathroom door. The main characters voice their emotions to such an extent they could be talking to doctors. Visually it is on a par with *Ulysses* for its dexterity of technique. Each of the tree's spheres embraces a brand new template of framing and colouring techniques devised by J H Williams (assisted by Mick Gray and Jeromy Cox), from the uplit skies of Chesed to the violet black lit Miltonic tundra of Daath, the geometric understanding of Binah, monochromatic orgasmic Chokmah, and finally Kether where the flow of frames dissolves into the eternal moment or peak experience depending on your chemistry at the time. Moore keeps the learning from turning into too much of a lecture. The story remains one of women, sex, gods, and the ancient ethos of 'as above so below'. And if all that sounds a bit deep, there is one heck of a fight near the end, and one of the writer's finest revelations. *Promethea 4* burns with joy in the work of everyone concerned.

Conceived as a piece for *AARGH!* (Artists Against Rampant Government Homophobia) in 1988 the Top Shelf reprint of *The Mirror of Love* falls slightly short, not as an edition which is sumptuous, but as a song to same sex love. Swathed in reproductions of shots by Jose Villarrubia, three thousand years of gay culture is conveyed in just two thousand words, fully annotated by Moore, who was in the full flourish of his politicized breakthroughs in the eighties. Not a great poem but of its time, summoned more out of books than experience. The photographs are atmospheric, if hotel corridor-ish. With just one poem between its covers this is very much a gift book for an out and Out friend.

Top Shelf continue their revivalist concerns with *Voice of the Fire*, a novel of discrete chapters (which also work as individual short stories), each one set in Northampton roughly two hundred years apart. The conceit manifests itself most closely in the dialogue, which undergoes mutations as the years pass. Always aurally highly nuanced, Moore takes his strip experiments in alien language onto the prose canvas, summoning great powers of elocution that doesn't lapse into Pythonesque historical subnormals. The book strives to entertain. Much of it appears to have been written very rapidly, so that Moore literally talks himself into a glossalia in the notoriously 'difficult' opening chapters, as even Moore himself acknowledges, that while not provably accurate is sufficiently inventive as to create a scrim of authenticity.

'Persevere and you get the goods, no real fear or dread we want from our history,' we learn. In *Angel Language AD 1618*, the dread that has been lurking since the kindling of the fire in 4000 BC, manifests in the form of a witchhouse, a snare for the unwary traveller, and in which Moore finds full flight:

> Their words are from a glossary of light , lips moving silently as if beyond the scrying glass and in my ears the singing has achieved a perfect clarity, the rounds and phrases of it now resolved. Above the roaring of the altitudes each foreign syllable is bright and resonant, is

Titles discussed in A IS FOR MOORE

Portrait of An Extraordinary Gentleman
smoky man & Gary Spencer Millidge, eds. UK £10.99 | Abiogenesis press, PO Box 2065, Leigh-On-Sea, SS9 2WH, UK | www.millidge.com

The Extraordinary Works of Alan Moore
George Khoury & friends | US $25.95 | TwoMorrows Publishing, 1812 Park Drive, Raleigh, NC 27605 USA | www.twomorrows.com

Heroes & Monsters by Jess Nevins ($18.95) and **A Blazing World** by Jess Nevins ($15.95) | MonkeyBrain Inc., PO Box 200126, Austin, TX 78720, USA | www.monkeybrainbooks.com

League of Extraordinary Gentlemen Volume II ($14.95) & **Promethea Book 4** ($24.95) America's Best Comics, LLC., 888 Prospect St. 240, La Jolla, CA 92037, USA

The Mirror of Love ($24.95) and **Voice of the Fire** ($26.95) by Alan Moore | Top Shelf Publications, PO Box 1282, Mariette, GA 30061-1282, USA | www.topshelfcomics.com

Alan Moore's Another Suburban Romance ($7.95), Alan Moore's **Writing For Comics** ($5.95), **Yuggoth Cultures and other growths**, issues 1–3 ($3.95), **The Courtyard** ($6.95), **Hypothetical Lizard preview** ($1.99) | Avatar Press, 9 Triumph Drive, Urbana, IL 61803, USA | www.avatarpress.com

achingly familiar in its alien profundity, a layered murmur echoing in everything. I know this song. I know it.

Since 1997 Avatar Press has carved a niche for itself as a company 'that pushes the boundaries between mainstream and independent'. Their latest Moore issues are a genius publishing *coup* in the foolscap ratio. Alan Moore's *Another Suburban Romance* is the creation of Moore and Jan Jose Ryp, the superstar Spanish artist, known also for his work on the *Shi: Pandora's Box* series. First of the three stories in this volume is 'Judy Switched Off The TV'. It follows the nameless boyfriend (or friend or brother) of Judy, a woman given to leaving her bathroom backwards while zipping up her face, takes us on a trip of the crawling chaos that is the neighbourhood, an urban everywhere with cannibal children in the subways, police wolfhounds, and bombs on plague buses. The lines accompanying each frame are a stanza on a Moorian ballad. For example, and my favourite of the lot is, 'By that time the flamethrower girls had just reached the suburbs' as the girls rain fire from the roofs of cars, their fire snowlike and slushy in Ryp's black lines, his borderline graphomania exuding motion and texture. 'Old Gangsters Never Die' is a sentimental, silver screen cooked, yet as fractally visual, tale of gangsters and romance in 1930s Chicago as the others in this collection. Finally, in *Another Suburban Romance* Moore himself wanders a city of anarchists, junkies, and raging drivers. This hell of depravity has no comforting captions to orientate us but the setting looks more American than anything and hint at degeneration and fascism — one of the lightning conductors for Moore's deep sense of moral disgust with the modern condition. The collection is Ryp's great achievement. He is the missing master between Goya and Bellardini, no instance of form too infinitesimal for him to express and relate to the whole composition, no sight too painful to render. By eliminating shadows entirely he opens our eyes to a world of pure light, and therefore of perfect visibility of every direction at whatever depth. Only graphic art can achieve this, the camera can only approximate it.

Alan Moore's Writing For Comics (as if we didn't know that already) is the writer sharing his wisdom of how he goes about creating stories, characters, pacing and scripting. There are no examples of his own scripts to illustrate what he means so the whole project is a stately exercise in… well, in lecturing the audience, which I mean in the best possible way since Moore is usually compelling, yet how much this can benefit anyone thinking of having a go at writing comics is, like all books explaining the methods of writing, debatable. He is so far ahead of the game that his advice is all too often related to rules he broke which are now clichés. As he acknowledges at the end of the book, you might as well ignore most of what he discusses since — really, when it's just you and that blank document window — you're on your own. The least equivocal advice is Moore's five rules for those thinking of writing for a living from another book, four of which are don't do it. If you need *Writing For Comics* because you want to read Moore for the sake of wanting to hear him talk shop then this is one to have. If you think you need it because you want to write comics and don't know how, desist until you have completed work you feel secure with lest you be dazzled to a blindness by the Master's lofted proclamations.

Yuggoth Cultures and Other Growths is a series feast of rare short strips going back to the days of Curt Vile, Moore's *Sounds* pseudonym back around 1979. The series kicks off with 'Zaman's Hill', a lyric given mind bending geological dimension by Juan Jose Ryp. Then 'Nightjar', a semi-legendary lost story from the *Warrior* days, commentated by artist Bryan Talbot with wistfulness about what may have been had the series been completed. In issue two, 'Cold Snap' and 'Itchy Peterson', and 'Nativity on Ice' are playful and delirious pieces from Moore's Future Shocks phase. In issue three, 'Leviticus' is an ultra-violent Hunt Emerson collaboration spotlighting Biblical inconsistency. The Oscar Zarante collaboration 'I Just Keep Coming Back' is the psychogeographic near epilogue to *From Hell*. And 'Me and Dorothy Parker' and other adaptations from Moore's lyrical collaborations with musician Tim Perkins — all visually literal in interpretation — fill out the series. And there's cthulic capers galore with hardboiled tales, the beauty of their telling lifted by Antony Johnson's adapting skills. *Cultures* is an anthology of fine writing, given spine by works from Moore's Lovecraft period. The artistic standards are not as high as say those afforded to Clive Barker's graphic horrors — notwithstanding Jan Jose Ryp's cthonically creepy covers, all fractal fronds and oozing tentacles. I laughed and gaped at this remarkable series.

The Courtyard comes out of Moore's further urban cthulic roamings and tells a hardboiled tale of an investigator in some inner America seeking a semi-mythical drug called Aklo. The twist and conclusion are psychedelically satisfying and truly surprising as Aklo turns out to be an angel of a twist (and I don't mean it's a goddess or anything like that). 'Sequential adaptation' is by Anthony Johnstone who does a credible job of pacing the ambience and surprises, while Jacen Burrows monochrome artwork is both strong and subtle. This is an incredible idea told in that funky *NYPD*-ish style that Moore didn't get out of his system until the curiously undemanding Top Ten.

Less of a slam dunk in terms of execution is *Hypothetical Lizard*. It contains script, character designs and a few frames to preview Moore's proto novel of physical and relationship schisms in another 'sequential adaptation' by Antony Johnson. Time will tell if this exercise in retrofitting plays out, the story will have to be good since Lorenzo Lorente's artwork is merely competent, and the frames have little or none of the wealth of detail we come to expect from a 'real' graphic Moore. Might bring in a few Terry Pratchett fans.

Line by line, page by page, Moore's reputation as a creator of books swells like a mushroom cloud sketched by Dave Gibbons. His output — for once deserving the prefix 'prodigious' — has been matched by his imagination, a chameleon like phenomenon that has eschewed the fiscal gains to be had from furrowing a single track, churning out endless superhero variations, or remaining a writer known by his genre. The publishers have done that for him (the Mooreian imprint Vertigo). Hollywood has cherry picked and blended, poisoned and distorted his stories, and there are more to come — *Watchmen*, *Constantine*. At this rate, who knows, we may yet well see a big screen Maxwell The Magic Cat. Or a Return of the Two Storey Brain television show. Where will the Northamptonshire wizard head to next? Shelves and minds, that much we know. [Jerry Glover] ■

Fantastic new & recent books from Headpress

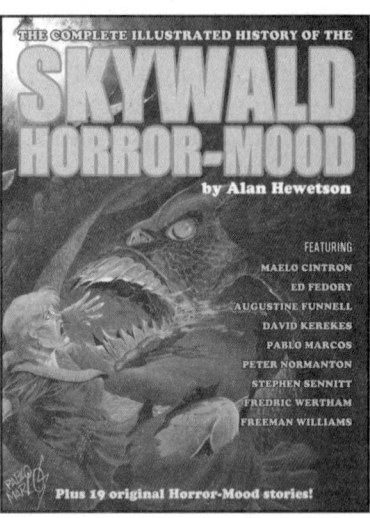

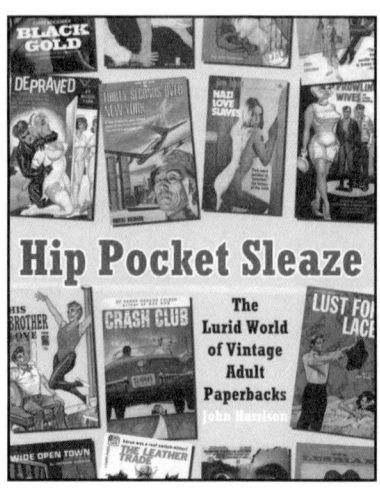

Info & secure online ordering: www.headpress.com

An SAE/2 x IRC gets a catalog: Headpress/Critical Vision, PO Box 26, Manchester, M26 1PQ, UK